# Your First Home

# Your First Home

## The Smart Way to
## Get It and Keep It

**Lynnette Khalfani-Cox**

ADVANTAGE WORLD PRESS

Published by Advantage World Press
P.O. Box 1307
Mountainside, NJ 07092
www.AdvantageWorldPress.com

Book and Cover Design: AMV Publishing Services (africarus1@comcast.net)
Layout/Formatting: 'Damola Ifaturoti
Cover Artwork: Dapo Ojo-Ade

Khalfani-Cox,Lynnette.
    Your first home:the smart way to get it and keep it / Lynnette
Khalfani-Cox -- 1sted.-- Mountainside, NJ : AdvantageWorld
Press, c2008.
    p. ; cm.
    ISBN 13: 978-1-932450-85-9
    ISBN 10: 1-932450-85-8
    Includes index.


        1.House buying--UnitedStates--Handbooks, manuals, etc.
    2.Mortgage loans--UnitedStates--Handbooks, manuals, etc.
    3.Consumer credit--UnitedStates--Handbooks, manuals, etc.
    4.Finance, Personal--UnitedStates--Handbooks, manuals, etc.
    5.Home ownership--UnitedStates--Handbooks, manuals, etc.
    I.Title.

HD259.K432008
643.12/0973--dc22                              0801

Printed in the United States of America.

SPECIAL SALES Advantage World Press books are available at special bulk purchase discounts to
use for sales promotions, premiums or educational purposes. Special editions, including personalized covers, excerpts of existing books, and corporate imprints, can be created in large quantities for
special needs. For more information, write to Advantage World Press, Special Markets, P.O. Box
1307, Mountainside, NJ 07092, Fax (866) 494-2461 or e-mail sales@advantageworldpress.com

# Table of Contents

## Part III: The Future Part: Determining Your Own Destiny

### Chapter 11: Manage and Preserve Your Biggest Asset

### Chapter 12: Follow the Path to Sustainable Homeownership

### Chapter 13: Avoid Foreclosure and Other Pitfalls

# Dedication

*To my husband, Earl: Your warm and loving presence always reminds me of the true definition of home.*

# Acknowledgments

I began writing *Your First Home* before the "mortgage meltdown" first hit the United States in August 2007. Soon after, the book took on a far greater sense of urgency. As the foreclosure crisis grew, homeowners nationwide began contacting me requesting help and advice to save their homes.

Therefore, I first want to acknowledge those who have written me and others seeking guidance about homeownership preservation. I know it's a hard thing to reach out and ask for help. There is so much shame, guilt, helplessness and fear involved when someone faces the loss of their home. That probably explains why, in 50% of all foreclosures, the homeowner never once speaks to his or her lender.

Above all, I hope *Your First Home* will put a dent in this country's foreclosure problem – by teaching people the smart way to acquire and keep their homes.

I also want to acknowledge all those who agreed to be interviewed for this book: from homeowners and real estate professionals to mortgage industry experts, lenders and brokers. Thank you sincerely for sharing your knowledge, expertise and experiences. Your wisdom will help countless others.

To all the non-profit agencies and community-based organizations that tirelessly promote financial literacy, teach credit education, provide counseling to homeowners, and support sustainable homeownership, thanks for all the wonderful work that you do. Your efforts have helped inspire this book – and changed many lives for the better.

My heartfelt appreciation also goes out to Damola Ifaturoti of AMV Publishing Services for his creativity and skill in producing the beautiful interior design, layout and index for *Your First Home*. As always, Damola, it is a pleasure to work with someone so thorough, responsive to every request, and cheerful throughout the whole process.

# Your First Home

# Your First Home

At age 27, I bought my first home, a beautiful, three-story Victorian that featured six bedrooms, two bathrooms, expansive bay windows – and a wacky next door neighbor we used to call "Janet from another planet."

Some days, it seemed as if Janet lived for no other purpose than to irritate my family and the rest of the people who lived on Cedar Avenue in the University City section of Philadelphia. One afternoon, we were enjoying the company of some good friends, when Janet suddenly came banging on our door. She told our friends, who had brought along their dog and left him chained on the front porch, that she was going to call animal control on them and report them for "abuse" because the dog was panting and was therefore obviously "dehydrated." My jaw dropped since I knew that dog was healthy as a horse and always very well-treated as a member of the family.

Then there were the times when we would hear Janet fumbling around in our backyard late at night, taking water from our sprinkler system and using it to fill up buckets for God knows what purpose. When we confronted Janet about the matter, she denied stealing our water – until we finally busted her in the act.

And I'll never forget the day, when I was nine months pregnant, that Janet came onto our property with a lawn mower and plowed away some tomato vines growing in our small garden. Her rationale: she "thought they were weeds." After we explained that they were budding tomatoes – and insisted that she get off of our property – Janet inexplicably fired up her lawn mower a second time and mowed down additional tomato plants. Needless to say, the cops got called out to Cedar Avenue that day.

## The Joy of Owning My First Home

Despite the occasional headaches and frustrations Janet caused, I nevertheless remember my first home with tremendous fondness. Not only was that 100-year-old Victorian the first house I ever bought, it was also the first home I'd ever lived in. I was born in Manhattan, and when I was two years old my parents moved to Los Angeles. Growing up in various parts of L.A., I lived in a series of apartments – none of which were terrible, to my recollection, but they certainly never represented a place of our own. There were always landlords to pay, rules about what you could or couldn't do in an apartment, and other tenants to deal with. As a result, my mother's dream was always to have her own home.

As fate would have it, I reached that goal before my mother did. And boy did I love my first home, especially its gorgeous formal dining room and magnificent country kitchen, which came complete with large terra cotta tile floors and exposed brick walls. Beyond aesthetics, the home held a world of emotional value to me as well. It was the place I celebrated the birth of my first-born child, and where I met my daughter's future Godmother too.

So I certainly wasn't going to let Janet's antics or anything else take away that special milestone. I viewed purchasing my first home as a huge personal and financial accomplishment. Going from renter to homeowner meant that I could do whatever I wanted in my house – from painting the walls or ripping out carpeting to nailing family photos on the wall and changing the bathroom fixtures. I also enjoyed knowing that Uncle Sam gave me a rebate, of sorts, for the roof over my head in the form of deductions for mortgage interest and property taxes.

## Sick and Tired of Renting?

My guess is that you're ready for your first home too – or at least you're seriously weighing making the leap to homeownership.

Some of you are fed up with dealing with wacky neighbors of your own. Most of you are undoubtedly sick and tired of throwing away your money by renting – while your landlord gets richer year after year.

Others of you simply long for a place of your own in order to have the satisfaction, pride, and personal freedoms that come with being a homeowner. No matter what your motivation, this book will help you to achieve something you've probably being craving for a long time: getting your first home. Once you do, think of how marvelous you'll feel the next time you fill out an application or a form that asks: Do you own or rent? The intangible, emotional benefits of being a homeowner are nearly as plentiful as the financial advantages. And to be sure, there are scores of economic reasons to make homeownership a priority in your life.

## The Financial Benefits of Homeownership

No matter what your age, gender, income, race, religious, professional, or marital status, being a homeowner affords you a range of financial perks, privileges, and options that simply are not available to renters. Do you realize that as a homeowner you are legally entitled to write off up to $100,000 a year in mortgage interest on your taxes? This is a huge economic benefit, especially in the first few years after you obtain a mortgage, because most of the mortgage payments you make early on go towards paying interest on your loan, not the principal. As a homeowner, the federal government also lets you take a tax deduction for property taxes, a tax break that doesn't exist for renters. Additionally, for those of you who will be fortunate enough to watch your home appreciate significantly in value, Uncle Sam provides the mother of all tax deductions: if you're single, and you sell your home, you get to keep up to $250,000 in profits completely tax free; for couples this tax benefit is a whopping $500,000. Lastly, being a homeowner entitles you upon your death to pass on your home to a spouse completely tax free. Alternatively, you could leave your home to your children, another family member, a friend, or a charity on a tax-advantaged basis if you do some smart financial planning.

I'm going to assume that you already know (or at least suspect in your heart) that you'd be better off owning in the long run instead of renting forever. That's why *Your First Home* focuses on the proactive steps you can take – starting today – to get yourself ready for homeownership, and learn how to keep that home without losing it to foreclosure. Once you cross the threshold into homeownership, you'll be positioned to enjoy your dream house for all its worth.

## How to Use This Book

This book contains three sections. The first section, called "The Hard Part," is pretty much what it sounds like. This is where I'll explain all the heavy lifting you'll have to do in order to get that house you've been fantasizing about. Getting your first home is very doable for most individuals, couples, and families. In fact, by following the steps I outline in this book, most readers will be able to buy a home in one year or less. I'm not promising you it will be easy. If it were, there would be lots more people as homeowners in this country. As it stands, 73% of whites own their own homes, compared with 53% of Asians, 50% of Latinos, and 49% of African Americans. Chapter 1 of "The Hard Part" is where you'll evaluate your mental readiness, and find out if you've got the right mindset to make the transition from renter to homeowner. As a Money Coach, I honestly believe that the overwhelming majority of people would be better off – financially and otherwise – as homeowners rather than renters. Nevertheless, the hard truth is that some people simply aren't ready for homeownership. You should know upfront if you fall into that latter category. Chapter 1 will tell you.

## The ABCs of Finding and Financing Your First Home

In the first section of *Your First Home*, you'll also learn all the critical steps you must take to make sure you can qualify for a mortgage with no problem. Chapters 2 and 3 address the topics of credit and cash – two essential areas lenders will take into consideration when you apply for a home loan. For many of you eager to buy a home but unsure whether you have enough savings to turn your dream into a reality, Chapter 4 might be the most exciting section of the book. It's here that I'll let you in on the many hundreds of first-time homebuyers programs available nationwide that can provide you with much-needed cash. These special programs offer everything from free grants and down payment assistance to financial help with your closing costs and tax credits just for becoming a homeowner. There are also many lenders and homebuyer assistance initiatives that offer you loans at great interest rates, even if you have less-than-perfect credit. Chapter 5 contains special insights into how you can put your best foot forward – making yourself irresistible to a lender when you're applying for a mortgage. Pay special attention to this chapter because it contains advice from mortgage industry pros who explain what you need to do so that nothing holds you back from getting a mortgage – not even bad credit, a lack of savings, big debts, or a small income. Chapter 6 walks you through the important process of getting pre-approved for your mortgage. After reading this section, you'll know how to avoid the most common mistakes that trip up many would-be homeowners.

Upon the conclusion of Chapter 6, you're ready to start "The Fun Part," which is the second section of *Your First Home*. I call this section "The Fun Part" because with that pre-approval letter in hand, you're now ready to actively go house-hunting, as opposed to merely window shopping for homes.

In Chapter 7, I'll give you the inside scoop on how to find your ideal home, using everything from drive-by techniques that don't waste your time, to the Internet and the Multiple Listing Service (MLS), referrals and For Sale By Owner networks. Chapter 7 also reveals how to build the right team to help you during the house-hunting process. After all, you'll need to know how to pick the right real estate agent, a competent home inspector, and possibly a real estate lawyer. You also need to know what questions you should ask these professionals. Chapter 8 offers you step-by-step advice for negotiating the best possible deal from the seller of the home you're buying. I'll highlight the best buying strategies to use, no matter what the conditions are in your local real estate market. Throughout Chapter 9, you'll learn why it's critically important that you select the right lender – and the right loan – in order to make your home-buying experience a positive one. Since your home purchase is likely to be the biggest financial transaction of your life, you need to get a great deal on your mortgage – and be aware of the pros and cons of all the new-fangled mortgage products available, like interest-only loans or hybrid adjustable-rate mortgages. I'll also point out what you should look for in a quality lender, and what pitfalls and even scams to avoid if you encounter unscrupulous individuals or predatory financial institutions. Chapter 10 will help you sail through the closing process. For many homebuyers, this can often be the most nerve-wracking time of all. Even if you've got nerves of steel, signing on the dotted line for a loan that could be hundreds of thousands of dollars is enough to give anyone pause, but don't worry. I'll tell you what to expect at the closing and how to make this phase of your home-ownership journey as stress-free as possible.

The third and final section of *Your First Home* is called "The Future Part." What happens at this stage is totally up to you. Once you've made it through "The Hard Part" and "The Fun Part," you now have a choice about how you will live as a homeowner. In many ways, the choices you make now will help determine your future financial destiny. Chapter 11 describes the ways in which I hope you'll ulti-mately leverage the benefits of being a homeowner. In this chapter, I'll tell you about savvy estate planning techniques and the prudent ways in which you can take advantage of tax breaks exclusively available to property owners. If you follow the advice in Chapter 11, you'll not only build your personal wealth, you'll also be able to turn your real estate holdings into part of the financial legacy that you pass on to your heirs. Chapter 12 highlights the "Seven Commandments of Successful Homeownership." These are the Golden Rules you must follow if you want to sustain your status as a homeowner. In many ways, Chapter 12 is a cautionary tale about the mistakes I want you to avoid making once you get into a house – every-thing from neglecting to maintain your property, to falling behind on tax payments, to squandering the equity in your home to fund frivolous purchases. The point of this chapter, and especially Chapter 13, is to help you avoid foreclosure. To that end, Chapter 13 offers you specific guidance about your options in the event you ever do face foreclosure. Unfortunately, experts predict that up to 5 million homeowners could lose their houses to foreclosure between 2007 and 2010. I don't want you to become part of those statistics. So here's where you can learn about homeownership preservation strategies, along with the efforts being initiated nationwide by govern-ments, non-profits, and even lenders to prevent foreclosure. After all, part of making a smart transition from renting to owning is being able to *keep* your home – and own it for as long as you'd like.

Contrary to popular opinion, being a homeowner won't completely insulate you from oddball people – like my old neighbor, "Janet from another planet." Hopefully, you'll never encounter such an individual. However, I promise you this: *Your First Home* is the secret weapon you need to help you achieve the American Dream. So if you follow my advice, you'll be so thrilled at getting your first home that even a pesky neighbor won't be able to steal your joy.

# Part I: The Hard Part: Preparing for Homeownership

# CHAPTER

$$\boxed{1}$$

## Determine if You are Really Ready to Own

So you're finally going to do it. You're going to save up money, whip your credit into shape, find a home that you love, and get a mortgage, right? You're absolutely, positively committed to becoming a homeowner. Well, mostly. You think. Maybe. Sort of.

If you have doubts about your readiness for becoming a homeowner, or your ability to qualify for a mortgage, take heart. It's natural to go through a period of wondering if you really have what it takes to make the leap from renter to owner. After all, you've been dreaming about it forever. You've been talking about it with your relatives and friends. And Lord knows you're fed up with renting. If any of this sounds familiar, rest assured knowing that before they bought their first property, millions of other current homeowners experienced the same worries and uncertainties that you now face.

### Your Eureka Moment

Some of you might have decided on becoming a homeowner when you got your latest notice of a rent increase from your landlord. Others might have opted to buy a home when you heard about a great bargain someone else got on a new house. Or perhaps your eureka moment came when you realized that if you'd bought a home years ago you'd be a lot better off financially because you'd have equity in a home, as opposed to nothing to show for all those rent payments you've made. Whatever the case, it's important to hang on to that critical moment when you made the decision to go for it – or to at least explore the possibility of homeownership. Whatever it was that spurred you to act, and to seek out information, let that be your initial motivation to carry you forward. Keep it in mind as you read this book, and learn what's involved in buying your first home.

But as you'll soon discover, your eureka moment was only a beginning. There's a reason people talk about getting on "the path" to homeownership. That's because there is a process, much like making a journey, to becoming a homeowner. And the only way you're going to make it to your final destination – when you have a set of keys in your hand and you walk into a beautiful house that you own, with a huge smile on your face – is to go beyond that first thought you had telling you "I should buy a home." Once you get beyond *thinking* about a home, you get into the active phase of *preparing* yourself for homeownership. No more talking about it. Now you need to take action, and sustained action at that. To succeed at buying your first home requires two ingredients: time and commitment. Notice that I didn't say it takes a big down payment, or a college degree, or the world's best credit. If you're willing to put in the time to make the necessary commitment, anything that you're lacking – whether it's money, good credit, or something else – will eventually fall into place. Nothing will prevent you from becoming a homeowner.

## A Necessary Reality Check

Right now, some of you might be asking: how much time is this going to take or how much of a commitment do I have to make to this process? The answer is: as much as it takes. I'm not trying to be glib. I'm merely trying to give you a much-needed reality check about what to expect. Please realize that buying a home isn't like other purchases you might make on a whim, even if they're fairly large purchases. Let's say you have a sudden urge to take a vacation. You can whip out your credit card, and charge a $3,000 week-long trip to Jamaica right on the spot. If you want, the very next day you can be lying on the beach, sipping an island drink, and enjoying the sun, surf, and sand. Or what if you feel the need to get a new car? Just trade in your current car, maybe pay a small down payment, and voila! Just like that, you can walk out of an auto dealership the same day with a brand new vehicle costing $30,000 or more. You've achieved instant gratification in both cases. But that won't fly when it comes to real estate. The preparation process takes time and commitment, as does the mortgage process. The specific time required will vary, based on your individual circumstances. In most cases, though, you should be able to get yourself ready to buy a home in a year – less time, if you've already been working toward this goal.

## Get Emotionally and Financially Committed

The commitment required to become a homeowner is two-fold: you have to make an emotional as well as a financial commitment to the process. The emotional part involves adopting the right mental attitude. It's about knowing in your heart and mind that you want, need, and deserve a house you can afford. It's about overcoming your fears of the unknown because you're able to replace them with knowledge and well-grounded financial decision making. Ultimately, it's about refusing to settle for being a renter because deep down you want the better, more financially stable lifestyle that homeownership can offer.

For a lot of people, getting emotionally committed is the easy part. It's the financial commitment that's tricky, because this likely will require some sacrifice. If you are earnestly committed to getting a home in the near future, you may have to give up various things or change certain financial behaviors so they're not roadblocks to your meeting your goal. It's easy to say "I want a house," and keep right on buying or doing all the other things you enjoy. But what if you had to give up this year's vacation, take fewer trips to the hair or nail salon, forego eating out for a while, and generally just cut back on your spending? Are you willing to make those commitments if necessary? Start thinking about this now; later, when you look at your budget, you might need to make short or long-term sacrifices in the name of getting – and keeping – your first home. If, on the other hand, you already know that you are not going to make the emotional and financial commitment required to become a homeowner, you might as well just throw in the towel right now.

However, I hope you won't quit and take the easy way out. Why would you want to give up before you really even get started? I know that each one of you reading this book can become a homeowner – if you make the choice to do so. Buying your first home isn't a cake walk. But it's not rocket science either. Unfortunately, many people stay stuck in the "dreaming" phase of becoming a homeowner. They experience their own eureka moment, but then they fail to move beyond it. Instead, they spend their whole lives wishing, wanting, and sometimes even praying for a home. But even God didn't reward dreamers who refused to take action. That is why you have to go beyond your eureka moment. It's great to come to the realization that you want and need a home, but how exactly do you go about it? Between the pages of this book I'll tell you everything you need to do, step by step, to bring your home-buying dreams to life.

## Some Words of Wisdom for Women

Right off the bat, I want to encourage all my female readers with this message: you can do it! Don't think that because you're a woman, and perhaps a single woman, that you can't get a home of your own. Where is it written that only men, or only married folks, are entitled to become homeowners? That's nonsense.

You might not have many positive, supportive people in your corner cheering you on and trying to help you keep focused on your dream of homeownership. In fact, you might have doubters, negative people, or individuals who are simply ignorant about the path to homeownership who try to splash cold water all over your plans to own a house. "Girl, what do you want with some big old house all by yourself?" they ask, looking at you like you're crazy. "The bank won't give you a loan because you don't make enough money," they say – as if they're the expert on all lending institutions in America. "Your credit is too bad to get a mortgage," they claim – as if they have special insights into your entire credit history and what is, and is not, acceptable to bankers. Or maybe they tell you: "It's too expensive to buy a house. You don't even have any savings or enough money for a down payment."

Well, you have to get those negative people – and those negative thoughts – out of your space immediately. If you truly want to be a homeowner, this goal is well within your reach, so don't let anyone convince you of anything to the contrary.

However, if you're not careful, you'll start to internalize what those doubters say because their negativity can be contagious. Think about how you respond when someone nearby you sneezes uncontrollably all over the place. As soon as that person lets loose with a big "Achoo!" you turn your head, cover your face, or take a step back. By the same token, you need to put some distance between yourself and people who are small-minded, negative, or just ignorant. You don't want to get infected by whatever comes spouting out of the mouths of unsupportive people in your life. It would be a shame if you were to let them poison your thoughts and rob you of your dreams. So even if you have poor credit, earn a modest salary, or have little or no savings, in *Your First Home* I'm going to teach you how to overcome these and any other obstacles that might be standing in your way of getting a house. And trust me: when you do, you'll have the last laugh, and even your most vocal naysayer will have to eat their words.

Having said all that, a word of caution is nevertheless in order for any of you who have just separated from a former spouse or are recently divorced. Many of you might be renting now as you recover from the financial impact of a separation. If you lived in a home before your breakup, it's certainly natural for you to want to own a home again, and maintain the standard of living to which you were accustomed. Particularly if you have children, I can understand why you'd want them to be raised in a home in a good neighborhood. Despite these very natural feelings, don't let your emotions cloud your common sense. That can lead to poor financial decisions. Take some time to adjust to the new financial realities of your situation. Figure out how tight – or maybe even how much better – things will be financially, now that you're on your own.

When I decided in late 2004 to separate from my ex-husband, I went through a transition period emotionally and financially. I rented an apartment for nearly one year, in 2005, to get my bearings and get used to the additional financial burdens of maintaining two households instead of one. You might receive child support or alimony – or, like me, you might be the one paying those expenses. Whatever the case: make sure you're emotionally and economically prepared for homeownership on your own in the wake of a separation or divorce. There's no shame in waiting for a while, if necessary, until you regain your financial footing. This advice applies to men just as much as to women. By the way, I've since remarried, and so has my ex. We both now live in and own homes that we love. So as you can see, even divorce doesn't have to be a long-term impediment to homeownership.

## Advice for Singles – and Couples

When you're single, you should know that it can sometimes be more difficult to get a mortgage than it is for married people to get a loan. The reason for this is that banks take into consideration the probability of repayment in determining whether to grant mortgages. If you are the only person on the mortgage and you lose your job, you might be at a higher risk of default than another borrower in a two-income household. Consider the 30-something couple in which both the husband and wife work outside the home. If the husband gets a pink slip, it will no doubt be tougher on the family financially, but at least the wife still has income. Banks factor this in when they weigh the risk of extending credit to singles and couples. On the other hand, it's not always the case that couples have the upper hand in getting mortgage financing. A couple might need both incomes to qualify for a home loan. But what happens when one party in the marriage has bad credit? Banks won't take an average of the two scores. Instead, many lenders will simply use the party with the lowest credit score to decide what interest rate the loan will carry. In that case, the single person with good credit will likely have an advantage over the couple with so-so credit. Also, if you're a single person with a decent income, lenders won't hesitate to loan you money as long as your earnings can support the mortgage.

If you are married and desire to buy your first home, please make sure you get your partner on the same page. It can be fruitless and counterproductive to put in the work necessary to achieve such a big goal, only to have it shot down by the person you love. Also, it's far easier to achieve your dream of home ownership if the two of you are pulling together as a couple. In fact, it can be downright fun as you make progress together, reinforce each other's positive financial behavior, and make joint sacrifices knowing that together you're getting closer and closer to becoming homeowners. By joining the proud ranks of homeowners nationwide, you also lay the groundwork for a solid financial future, creating a better life for your kids in ways large and small.

## Money Matters Minorities Must Know

As an African-American woman, I've heard from a lot of minorities who feel slighted by the banking system. They worry that their race or ethnic background will hurt their chances of getting a mortgage, or they complain that lenders unfairly saddle them with higher interest rates and bigger loan fees. Unfortunately, predatory lending and discrimination do exist. For instance, recent independent studies by the Federal Reserve Bank, the Center for Responsible Lending, and the Consumer Federation of America all revealed that African-Americans, especially black women, are two to three times more likely than whites to be steered into more costly sub-prime mortgages, regardless of credit history or income. But savvy buyers of all persuasions know how to sidestep these landmines. Later in this book, I'll share with you some tried and true tips for making sure that you're fairly treated when you apply for a home loan. I'll also tell you how to avoid unscrupulous lenders, and explain what to do if you suspect you are being taken advantage of because of your status as a minority. In the meantime, however, don't worry that your racial, religious, or ethnic heritage will prevent you from finding and financing the home of your dreams. It won't. In fact, when you become a homeowner, you'll be a positive role model and a good example to other family and community members. If you become a first-generation homeowner, you'll feel especially proud of your achievements – and with good reason.

## People Who Shouldn't Become Homeowners

Up until now, I've tried to get you in the right frame of mind to prepare for your homeownership journey. I'd be remiss, however, in my duties as your Money Coach if I didn't express one cold, hard reality about homeownership: it's not necessarily for everyone. As a matter of fact, there are some groups of people who probably shouldn't become homeowners – at least not anytime soon. That might sound odd coming from a proponent of homeownership and the author of a book designed to help you purchase your first home. However, as a Money Coach, I've also seen people get themselves into trouble unnecessarily by biting off more than they could chew and buying a home before they were truly ready. Read on to discover if you fall into any of the following groups of people. If so, you're probably better off renting, instead of buying a home prematurely.

### ■ You are Mr. or Ms. Entitlement

Do you think the world owes you something? Are you convinced that you could "get ahead in life" if only someone – the government, your boss, and yes, your local banker – just gave you a break? If you have that mentality, chances are you're not ready to become a homeowner. Owning a house is not an automatic right. It's a privilege that is chock full of benefits as well as responsibilities. But people with a sense of entitlement don't get that. They want the perks and rewards of homeownership, but only on their own terms. Translation: they seem to always want the easy way out. They don't want to sacrifice, get their hustle on, and work hard for the things for which everyone else has to work. So if you're one of these people, stay put where you are. Keep shelling out money to your landlord each month, and the next time your toilet gets backed up at 2 a.m., call your superintendent and tell him to come fix it – immediately. After all, I'm sure you figure he *owes* it to you, as much rent as you pay.

### ■ You are Living in the Dark Ages

Remember the 1950s TV show "Ozzie and Harriet"? The husband went to work each day, while the wife stayed home and tended to the house and the kids. I don't recall their talking about a mortgage too often. But if they did, the serious conversation would've come from Ozzie, because he was doing "man's" work and actually earning the family's paycheck. If you subscribe to the philosophy that a woman must be taken care of by a man – any man, including hubby, Daddy, or even a sugar daddy – you are still living in the dark ages. Consequently, your arcane views will probably hold you back from making a serious commitment to becoming a homeowner. Why should you become a homeowner anyway? Why would you want to would go through all the preparation and hard work needed to buy a house when you can get a man to buy one for you? Being financially independent and learning to manage your own money is over-rated anyway, right?

### ■ You Have FDD – Financial Deficit Disorder

We've all made our share of money mistakes: sending in late payments here or there, wasting money on frivolous purchases, or blowing opportunities to save cash – even when we knew better. It's one thing to have a few dings on your credit report, or to even feel like you're living paycheck to paycheck. But some of you really take fiscal mismanagement to the extreme. You are constantly broke. You couldn't save a dime if your life depended on it. You borrow money from anyone silly enough to lend it to you. Truth be told, your situation resembles something akin to financial spaghetti: it's a tangled mess. Now, mind you, this is a far cry from having messed up in the past, but trying to do better now. Some of you seem to make no effort whatsoever to get out of your dire financial straits. In fact, you make a habit of digging yourself deeper in the hole month after month after month. You know who you are, too. Or maybe you recognize the following behavior in a friend.

You're the person who never seems to make payments on time; not your rent, your car note, your utility bills – not even the $100 your mother loaned you, which you were supposed to repay last week, and didn't. Since you can't ever pay your debts on schedule, you're practically on a first-name basis with the clerks and cashiers at the gas company, electric company, and your local cellular phone company, where you can be constantly found trying to get your service reconnected. You frequent these places so often that you bring 300-page novels with you, so you can catch up on your reading because you know the process and you accept those long lines as a fact of life. You've gone to Western Union so often that you have a Western Union card. Needless to say, you're always waiting to receive money, rather than send it. You're more familiar with the inside of the payday loan shop at the corner than you are with the inside of the local bank. You live life on the edge financially and nothing is sacred. You've taken out credit in the name of your five-year-old daughter – and your six-month-old son. You regularly park your car away from your apartment, trying to dodge the repo man.

Unlike other people with run-of-the-mill financial problems, you're not just credit-challenged or economically impaired. Unfortunately, you have a serious, long-term money malady. I call it Financial Deficit Disorder because you pay no attention whatsoever to money – besides spending it, of course. Until you change your crazy ways, and eliminate much of the drama in your life, do yourself a favor and don't add to your woes by trying to get a home. It won't be pretty.

The good news is that you aren't banished from home ownership for life. Just mend your ways and then pick this book up again when you're ready to get serious – in words and deeds – about your finances. You'll know you've turned a corner when you can go at least three to six months without borrowing money from family or friends, missing a payment, or dealing with calls and letters from bill collectors.

Hopefully, you don't fit into any of these categories. I trust that you are far more serious and enlightened, or at least far more willing to learn about handling your finances. If so, read on to discover the steps you'll need to take to get your first home.

# CHAPTER

$$\boxed{2}$$

## Improve Your Credit

It's no secret that mortgage lenders want you to have good credit. But what's the secret to achieving a good credit rating, so that you're a shoe-in when you apply for a home loan? It doesn't matter wh
ether your credit is golden, or whether you have the worst credit in the world, upgrading your credit profile always starts with reviewing your credit files as reported by each of the "Big Three" credit reporting bureaus: TransUnion, Equifax, and Experian. It's amazing how many people have never taken the time to look at their credit files – even though the information contained in them can have so much impact on your financial life.

By law, you are entitled to receive one free copy annually of your credit report from each of the credit bureaus mentioned above. The easiest and fastest way to obtain copies of your credit files is to get them online at http://www.annualcreditreport.com. Alternatively, you can write directly to each of the major credit reporting agencies.

Your credit files will give you an in-depth look into all your financial obligations that are reported by various creditors. You'll see your credit card accounts, listings for any personal loans or lines of credit you might have, and records about auto loans, student loans, and more. Needless to say, your credit reports will also indicate how well – or how poorly – you've handled your bills in terms of making payments on time. If you had any bills that went 30 days or more past due, that will show up on your credit file. Any collection accounts, or public records related to your finances will also appear. Such public records might include judgments against you, auto repossessions, or bankruptcy filings. While it's important to know exactly what information is contained in your credit history, it's just as critical to know your three-digit credit score, commonly known as your FICO credit score.

**What is Your Current FICO Score?**

There are lots of different types of credit scores used in the United States. By far and away, FICO credit scores are the most popular credit scores relied upon by the financial community. More than 90% of the largest U.S. banks use FICO scores when making credit decisions. Therefore, FICO scores are the ones with which you need to be most familiar. FICO scores get their name from the Minneapolis-based company, Fair Isaac Corp., which does credit scoring for tens of millions of Americans. Officials from Fair Isaac have created a statistical way of analyzing all the information in your credit file and assigning a three digit number, or FICO score, to your credit file based on a variety of factors. FICO scores range from 300 to 850 points. The higher your score, the better a lending risk you are. This means you'll get the very best rates on all types of consumer loans – such as auto financing, student loans, credit cards, and yes, mortgages.

I've met many people who told me that they had "bad" credit, yet they've never pulled their FICO scores. These people usually indicated that they had late payments, outstanding bills, or some other financial transgression from the past. Nevertheless, they didn't know their actual FICO score. Often, their ignorance was rooted in fear. "I'm too scared to see my credit score," one woman once told me, as if seeing her credit history and FICO score in black-and-white was akin to viewing a horror movie. Well, even if you have been horrible about handling your financial affairs, you can never move forward and start to improve your FICO credit score if you don't at least know your starting point.

Think about it this way: if you said "I want to lose 20 pounds," you have to first step on the scale in order to know your current weight. That way you can track your progress, so you'll know when you finally reach your goal of being 20 pounds lighter. In many ways, getting your FICO score is like stepping on the scale. In this case, instead of getting a three-digit number that reflects your weight and physical health, you'll get a three-digit number that tells you a lot about your financial health. So even if you've never peeked at your FICO score, now is the time to go ahead and immediately get yours.

Your FICO credit score is available online at http://www.myfico.com. Fair Isaac Corp. offers three FICO scores, each one corresponding to the information that's available in your credit files from each of the three main credit bureaus: TransUnion, Equifax, and Experian. There is a charge for obtaining your scores. As of this writing, it cost $47.85 for the FICO deluxe product, which gives you all three credit reports and their three corresponding FICO scores.

## Why You Need All Three Credit Reports and FICO Scores

Don't cut corners by purchasing just one credit report and FICO score. You really should get all three for a few reasons. First, each report might contain different data. Two of your credit reports might have correct information about you and your credit accounts, while one credit bureau might be reporting inaccurate or outdated information. You need to know that in order to have the incorrect information fixed. Also, when you apply for a mortgage, lenders often pull what's called a "tri-merged" credit report – meaning they get information and credit scores from all three credit bureaus.

Let's assume your Experian score is 686, your TransUnion score is 702, and your Equifax score is 679. The good news is that your mortgage lender will throw out the 679, which is your lowest score (hooray!). The bad news, though, is that the lender will also disregard that 702, which is your highest score (darn!). Instead, your lender will use your middle score as the one upon which to base your application and interest rate. This is why it's vital that you know all three scores. In fact, there's no time like the present to get started. So why don't you stop reading for a moment, hop online, and go get your FICO scores right now? Don't say "I'll do it later," because you'll probably get busy with work, school, family, kids, or what- ever else is going on in your life. Before you know it, improving your credit and making progress toward becoming a homeowner will get put on the backburner. So instead of procrastinating, just do it. You do recall that I told you that you'd have to make time and commit yourself to this process, right? Well, here's your first chance to prove you are flat-out committed. Just go to www.myfico.com, get your credit information, and let's start strategizing about how you're going to boost your credit score to the best of your ability.

### How Your Credit Rating Stacks Up Against Others

Here is my own, completely subjective assessment of your credit, based solely on your FICO score and my personal and professional dealings with bankers and lenders of all kinds:

| If your FICO score is ... | Then your credit is: |
|---|---|
| 760 - 850 | Perfect |
| 759 - 700 | Good |
| 699 - 650 | Average |
| 649 - 620 | So-So |
| 619 and below | Poor |

For many financial institutions, 620 is somewhat of a magic cutoff number. For example, many banks will require you to have a FICO score of at least 620 in order to get a decent mortgage rate. If your score is less than 620 can you still get the loan? Yes, in most cases. However, depending on the severity of your credit problems, you might have to pay a lot higher interest rate, which translates into a bigger monthly payment and more finance charges over the life of the loan. That's true at every level of the credit spectrum. Those in the "perfect" credit range will generally pay less than those with "good" credit; those with "good" credit will get better terms than people with "average" credit, and so on.

The exception to this rule is that some loan programs, such as FHA loans, offer great rates even if you have terrible credit. Also, many government programs at the state, county, and city levels offer mortgage programs, particularly for first-time homebuyers, with competitive interest rates even if you don't have sterling credit. In fact, some of these first-time home buyer initiatives boast below-market interest rates. So imagine that: in certain instances, people with bad credit can actually wind up getting just as good, or even better, a deal on their mortgages than people with great credit!

## The Five Factors That Determine Your Credit Score

Alright, now that you've seen your credit files and know your credit scores, how are you feeling? Were you pleasantly surprised or did the numbers leave you depressed and thinking you're a financial basket case? No matter what your FICO scores, you can improve them. If you scored in the 700s, your goal should be to get into the 800s. If you had a score below 620, you obviously have some work to do to achieve a great credit rating. Still, don't let today's score upset you; it's just a snapshot in time of how things stand. You have the power and the ability to change that score over time, if you engage in healthy financial behavior. I'm going to give you the blueprint to do just that.

Actually, I'm going to do more than just tell you what I think works in terms of improving your credit rating. I'm going to give you some information that comes straight from the horse's mouth, in this case the horse being none other than the Fair Isaac Corporation itself. Fortunately, for the past few years Fair Isaac has made credit scores available to the public, along with specific tips directly from the company about what you can do to strengthen your credit profile.

Under Fair Isaac's credit scoring model, your FICO credit score is based on five primary factors:

- 35% of your score is based on your payment history
- 30% of your score is based on the amount of credit you have used
- 15% of your score is based on the length of your credit history
- 10% of your score is based on your mix of credit and
- 10% of your score is based on the new credit you've taken on

Knowing these facts, here are some guidelines to help you maximize your credit score.

### ■ Pay Your Bills on Time

Since the single-biggest component (35%) of your credit score is based on your payment track record, the best way to boost your credit score is to simply pay your bills on time. Not some of them; all of them. Even if you can only make minimum payments, that's better than being late with a bill because late payments of 30 days or more can drop your FICO score by 50 points or more.

### ■ Don't Max Out Your Credit Cards

Some people mistakenly think that simply paying their bills on time each month will give them a stellar credit rating, but that's not true. Your FICO score also considers how much credit you use on a regular basis. Having a lot of debt signals that you are a potential risk for getting into financial trouble and not paying bills on time. If your credit cards are at or near their limits, you can raise your credit score by knocking down your balances. In general, try to keep your balances to no more than 30% of your available credit limit. For instance, if you have a card with a $10,000 credit line, make sure you don't carry a balance of more than $3,000 on that card. If you can pay off your credit cards each month, that's even better. But if you can't, it's better to spread out debt over a few cards, to maintain lower balances, rather than max out any one card.

### ■ Keep Older, Established Accounts Open

It feels good to pay off a credit card and finally get that statement showing a zero balance. However, if you pay off a creditor, don't make the mistake of closing that account because 15% of your FICO score is based on the length of your credit history. The longer a credit history you have, the better it is for your score.

### ■ Avoid "Bad" Forms of Credit

I'm sure you've walked into a department store and been offered 10% off – or some other discount – just for opening up a credit card with that retailer, right? Did you take the bait? If so, realize that you might have hurt your credit score. Here's why. The FICO scoring model rates some forms of credit more favorably than others. For instance, the presence of a mortgage on your credit report will help your score, but too many consumer finance cards (i.e., the cards issued by department stores and retailers) can hurt it. For this reason, do yourself a favor and say "No" to those credit card offers from stores you patronize. Just use a major credit card – like a Visa, MasterCard, American Express, or Discover Card – if you need to use credit to make your purchases.

### ■ Only Apply for Credit When You Truly Need It

Just because you get a pre-approved offer in the mail, or some telemarketer calls you to solicit for a credit card, doesn't mean you should accept it. You should only seek out credit when you absolutely need it because taking on too much new credit – or even just applying for it – will lower your credit score. Each time you apply for a loan – whether a credit card, an auto loan, a mortgage, or a student loan – the lender pulls your credit report and generates an "inquiry" on your credit file. That inquiry remains there for two years.

### Why Great Credit is Better Than Money in the Bank

Have you ever heard the expression "cash is king?" Well, don't believe it – at least not all the time. If you want to obtain the best possible rates and terms on your mortgage, in many instances having an outstanding credit reputation is often just as good as, and sometimes better than, having cash in the bank. How so? You can often get access to cash, in the form of loans, grants, and other aid, based solely on the strength of your credit report. Let's say you have $10,000 available in cold, hard dollars. That's wonderful, but having perfect credit could give you access to 20 times that amount of money – or more. This is why having outstanding credit should be a goal you relentlessly pursue. It's not enough to have "average" or even "good" credit. Besides, why should you settle for just a "good" credit record, when you can have A-1, prime, "perfect credit?"

**How to Fix Credit Problems and Establish Perfect Credit**

If your FICO credit score falls between 760 and 850 points, you rate among the top tier of all consumers, and have what I call "perfect credit." This means you can use the strength of your good name alone, and sign on the dotted line to get direct access to a whole host of products and services – including mortgages, automobiles, credit cards, business lines of credit, and personal loans – all at the most favorable terms available in the marketplace.

I've developed a fool-proof system for you to get "perfect credit" in seven easy steps. This method for improving your credit works for anyone, regardless of your age, income, professional background, marital status, or level of financial sophistication. Are you interested in achieving "perfect credit?" Then read on to learn how you can implement this system – and use it to get a mortgage for that fabulous new home you want. By the way, once you get "perfect credit," you'll never want to settle for anything less. I speak from personal experience – having had really rotten credit when I graduated from college, to having excellent credit now.

| The PERFECT CREDIT 7-Step System: |
| :--- |
| **P – Pull Your Credit Reports and FICO Scores Regularly** |
| **E – Examine Your Credit File Thoroughly** |
| **R – Reduce Debt and Manage Bills Wisely** |
| **F – Fix Errors and Protect Your Credit** |
| **E – Enhance Your Credit File Constantly** |
| **C – Contact Creditors and Negotiate** |
| **T – Take Time to Frequently Re-evaluate Your Options** |

■ **Step 1: Pull Your Credit Reports and FICO Scores Regularly**

Thanks to a relatively new law, called the FACT Act, consumers nationwide have the right to get their credit reports free of charge once a year, at http://www.annualcreditreport.com. You can also get your credit reports directly from each of the "Big 3" credit bureaus: Equifax, Experian, and TransUnion. I've provided their addresses, phone numbers, and websites at the end of this book. But you should also log onto Fair Isaac's consumer web site, http://www.myfico.com, and get all three of your FICO scores. Although you must pay for your FICO scores, this is money well spent because Fair Isaac offers you a range of credit-related tools and information to help you boost your credit score. In my mind, it's always best to get information directly. Since the people at Fair Isaac are the ones doing the credit scoring, where better to get credit improvement and FICO score tips?

Pulling your credit reports and FICO scores is the first way that you can make an investment in yourself and start enhancing your credit reputation. Don't be afraid to see what's in your credit file. I realize that some of you might be reluctant to see what your creditors have reported about you. Perhaps you've been turned down for a credit card so you're imagining the worst. Well, no matter how bad things might be, ignoring a sickly credit file won't fix it, any more than ignoring a broken arm would fix that bone. If you're hurt; you've got to go to the doctor. If your credit report is ailing, you have to check things out and get on with healing it. You can't improve your credit if you don't know where you stand.

So if you haven't already pulled your credit reports and FICO scores, at least mark a date on your calendar when you will do so within the next 30 days. Then get into the habit of checking your credit files regularly – meaning at least once a year. Don't worry that pulling your credit reports will lower your credit score. It won't. When you review your own credit files, that's a "soft" inquiry, meaning it's one that doesn't count against you. Only "hard" inquiries – which are those made when you apply for credit – affect your FICO score. So don't wait until you're heading to the bank to apply for your mortgage to know your FICO scores and what's in your credit file. Get that information ahead of time so you'll know where your credit is strong and where it's weak.

### ■ Step 2: Examine Your Credit File Thoroughly

Once you get your credit report, it's up to you to interpret what's in there – which can sometimes be confusing. You might notice that there are differences among your three different credit reports. For instance, perhaps there's a charge account on one report that doesn't show up on the other two, or maybe the last car you bought is showing a balance when it should be reported as paid off.

At this point, you want to get a snapshot of how you are viewed by the rest of the lending and financial world. Are there any negative items listed, such as late payments? What about public documents such as liens or judgments against you? These are obviously big red flags that hurt your credit reputation considerably. Perhaps you have lots of accounts with small balances. In the eyes of some lenders, that might be a negative factor because having "too much" access to credit means you could go out and run up a boatload of bills. If you've gotten your credit reports and FICO scores from Fair Isaac, the most important thing for you to do at this point is to read the company's analysis of why your credit score is a certain number. Beyond late payments and other delinquencies, some other reasons that your FICO score might take a hit are if you have too much debt outstanding, if you have too many recently opened accounts, if you have a high number of credit inquiries, or if you have a very short credit history. Once you see the factors that are impacting your credit score, you know what areas you should tackle first in order to improve your credit rating.

### ■ Step 3: Reduce Debt and Manage Bills Wisely

As I've already told you, there is a very strong link between your debt and your credit standing. Since 30% of your FICO score is tied to the amount of debt you're carrying, you'd be wise to keep your revolving debts (i.e. your credit cards bills) to a minimum. Additionally, since your payment history – or how good you are at paying your bills on time – is the number one factor in determining your FICO score (35%), it is imperative that you take managing your debt very, very seriously. Start by doing whatever it takes to never, ever miss a payment – for any reason whatsoever. If you do that one single thing, you will start to increase your FICO score. If you've skipped or been late with payments in the past because money was tight, I suggest you adjust your budget to ensure that you can faithfully pay every single bill you owe on time. (See Chapter 3 for budgeting strategies). And when I say "every bill," I mean exactly that.

Don't neglect your electricity bill, in the mistaken belief that a local energy service won't report your delinquent account to the credit bureaus. They can – and they will. The same is true for cell phone providers and water companies, as well as public utilities. Don't believe for one minute that the only bills you have to keep up to date in order to protect your credit are your mortgage, car loan, and credit cards. These obligations should certainly take precedence over less urgent bills. Nevertheless, a 30-day late payment – even if it was just for a telephone bill – still looks bad on your credit report. Would you believe that in some parts of the country even parking tickets and overdue library fines are being reported to credit bureaus? It's true. Can you imagine being denied a bank loan, or having to get one at a higher rate, just because of a fine you got for failing to promptly return a library book?

As I said in the beginning, perfect credit is something for which you should constantly strive – and being diligent in managing your bills is the chief way to do that. In addition to being judicious about paying your current bills, you need to get serious about knocking out long-standing debt in order to boost your financial reputation and enhance your credit standing. If you haven't been able to get a handle on your debt, I suggest you pick up a copy of one of my previous books, called *Zero Debt: The Ultimate Guide to Financial Freedom*. In that book, I offer you a 30-day action plan to turn around your financial life and get rid of debt once and for all. You can also get regular debt reduction tips by signing up for my free personal finance newsletter, which is available online at: http://www.themoneycoach.net. I write from personal experience on this topic because I once had $100,000 in credit card debt alone. Fortunately, I paid it off in just three years. What's more, I never missed a single payment. So if I could become debt-free, so can you!

### ■ Step 4: Fix Errors and Protect Your Credit

Consumer groups estimate that 70% of all credit reports have mistakes in them. That's an awful lot of misinformation – and it could be costing you money. If you have errors in your credit file and you're in the market for a loan, you could wind up paying a lot more in interest than you rightfully should. Mistakes happen for a lot of reasons. Sometimes there's an input error by a clerk who erroneously types something, like the spelling of your name, and then you are confused with someone else. Or maybe one of the digits in your social security number is inadvertently transposed, and inaccurate information starts to be reported about you. In other cases, family members have found that their credit files somehow get mistakenly co-mingled. For instance, Fred Jones Jr. might find that his credit report lists some accounts that belong to his father, Fred Jones Sr.

Whatever the cause, mistakes in your credit should be dealt with as soon as you discover them. Also, because of the massive amounts of credit information flying around, it's no wonder that mistakes routinely occur. Roughly 100,000 organizations supply information to the credit reporting agencies. These organizations include banks, lenders, collection agencies, credit card companies, leasing firms, utility companies, and any other entity that extends credit or reports information about you. The average person's credit report is updated five times each day. Two billion pieces of information are added to credit files every month and two million credit reports are ordered on a daily basis from scores of credit bureaus. We all know about the dominant players in the credit bureau industry – Equifax, Experian, and TransUnion – but there are actually more than 1,000 consumer reporting agencies in the United States. Clearly, because of sheer volume alone, errors in credit files are bound to happen. However, if there's a mistake in your credit report, it's up to you to fix it. Each credit bureau has a dispute resolution process that requires you to write a letter to the credit agency and state what information is inaccurate or incomplete in your credit file. Any data that is erroneous, or that can't be verified, must be deleted. Under the Fair Credit Reporting Act, the credit bureau has 30 days to investigate your claims and notify you of the results.

### ■ Protect Your Credit From Identity Theft

To enhance your credit reputation, you can do more than fix mistakes that might be in your credit file. You should also guard yourself against identity theft, which is the fastest-growing white collar crime in this country. Identity theft occurs when someone steals your personal information, such as your social security card or driver's license, then uses that data to make purchases, open accounts, or obtain credit under your name. Unfortunately, identity theft affects up to 10 million Americans each year, as crooks get increasingly sophisticated and more determined in their efforts to target new victims. Some identity thieves use online "phishing" scams to get you to divulge private information; others use decidedly low-tech methods like stealing your wallet or "dumpster diving" to obtain credit card numbers and other information about you.

To prevent identity theft, shred sensitive documents before discarding them and never carry your social security card with you. You should also consider purchasing identity theft insurance. A handful of insurance companies nationwide offer this coverage. Since the average victim of identity theft spends about 200 hours and $1,000 cleaning up the mess brought on by this heinous crime, identity theft insurance reimburses you for a range of things like attorney's fees, phone bills, and time lost from your job. Coverage usually goes up to around $25,000. If you are the victim of identity theft, alert the credit bureaus so they can put a notice in your credit files; notify your local police department, contact the Federal Trade Commission (877-ID-THEFT or www.ftc.gov), and seek help from the Identity Theft Resource Center (858-693-7935 or http://www.idtheftresource.org) in San Diego.

### ■ Step 5: Enhance Your Credit File Constantly

The experts at Fair Isaac say that paying your bills promptly results in a positive payment record, which is the top factor in calculating your FICO score. When you keep those accounts open and in good status, over time you also create a lengthy credit history, another factor in your FICO score. But do you know that there are a number of other little-known ways to improve your credit standing? The first method is by adding positive information to your credit file. Up until now, you've learned how to pull your credit reports, examine them, and fix any errors. Now it's time to get proactive about what's contained in your credit file. The information that you and others currently see are based on what creditors have indicated about you. What about what you have to say? That can – and should – count for something. If you're smart, you'll augment your credit file to put yourself in the best possible light. For example, if you notice that a mortgage or student loan you paid off appears on one credit report, but not on others, you should write to those two credit agencies and ask them add that information to your credit file. It doesn't matter that the account is no longer open or has a zero balance. To lenders and others who view your credit file, it's a significant accomplishment and a positive sign if you've paid off a previous mortgage – even if it was from selling or refinancing the house. The idea is to show you had a track record of managing a bill or financial obligation. Another tip: make sure your creditors are reporting the credit limits on your credit cards. Without this information, your credit score may be lowered because Fair Isaac's credit scoring model can't accurately compute the percentage of credit you have available.

If you see that your home address is incorrectly listed or that your job of 10 years is omitted from your credit file, have that added to the report. Where you live and your job information aren't taken into consideration for the purposes of computing your FICO credit score. However, most creditors and lenders will look carefully at that information to determine how stable you are, and therefore how much of a risk you are financially.

Some experts also recommend having the credit bureaus delete all your old address and previous names as a way to boost your credit score. Carolyn Warren, the author of *Mortgage Rip-offs and Money Savers* and a mortgage industry insider, swears by this technique. Warren says her score was in the high 700s and she'd tried everything to crack the 800 mark. But it wasn't until she had the credit bureaus get rid of previous references to her past addresses and delete other forms of her name that her score jumped more than 20 points, putting her among the rare breed of consumers with 800-plus FICO scores. Warren runs two great websites (http://www.AskCarolynWarren.com and http://mortgage-helper.com). Each will give you a great education about credit issues and home loans – as well as help you save thousands of dollars on your mortgage or refinance.

### ■ Step 6: Contact Creditors and Negotiate

A crucial step in achieving perfect credit involves getting creditors and bill collectors to work with you when you've had past financial problems. You can greatly enhance your credit standing if you get late payments and other blemishes deleted from your credit file. The way to do this is to call up your creditors and negotiate. Ironically, when your account is past due, that's the time you're in the best position of all to negotiate. You have something the creditor or bill collector wants – cash. They also have something you want – the power to update your credit report. So your strategy, in a nutshell, should be to dangle the cash carrot before their eyes. Depending on the status of your account (open, closed, charged-off, etc.), and how far behind you are in your payments, your goal should be to make your account current, set up a payment plan, or agree on a reduced amount that the company will accept in lieu of full payment.

In all these cases, what you're really doing is settling your account and restoring it to good standing. In exchange for doing that, you must insist on getting the creditor or bill collector's agreement to delete negative information that was previously reported about you. At the very least, they should update their records to reflect a "paid" current status. Often creditors will do this, yet keep in your credit file such notations as "was 60 days late." Therefore, in most cases, it's best to firmly negotiate for the outright elimination of negative information in your credit report. When you reach an agreement, put it in writing and have both sides sign the pact before you pay a dime. This way you're protecting yourself if the person you're negotiating with reneges on your deal. Note: if you have old accounts that were charged off, be careful of making payments on those. Credit files maintain information on your payment history based on the "last date of activity." Ditto for your FICO credit score, which counts recent activity as more important than things that happened years ago. So if you start repaying a bill that was long since charged off, you may restart the clock, making that account appear to be a recent delinquency.

### ■ Step 7: Take Time to Frequently Re-evaluate Your Options

In your quest to achieve and maintain perfect credit, it's imperative that you reassess your credit life from time to time. This entails scrutinizing the terms of your current credit cards and loans, analyzing any new credit offers you get, and planning for the unexpected. For instance, have any of your interest rates changed while you were not paying attention? If they've been ratcheted up, because of no fault of your own, you'll want to call up your creditors and negotiate for a lower rate. In other cases, you might find that your credit card company is implementing some new change with which you don't agree. It could be a switch in the financial terms or the company notifying you about their plans to sell or rent customer names to their marketing affiliates. If you object, you should write to voice your displeasure. It might be that you have to pay the card off or switch cards to avoid being subjected to terms you find onerous.

Finally, just because you have a line of credit or credit card today, doesn't always mean that it will forever be the right product for you. Your needs may change, and maybe you no longer need a personal line of credit, for example. The idea is to make sure that your current credit picture adequately reflects your needs. In doing so, you don't want to think exclusively about life in the "here and now." Be forward-thinking, and make sure you have the appropriate credit you might need for the future. Part of proper credit management involves planning for the unexpected and giving yourself some wiggle room when necessary.

Let's say that your company starts firing workers, and you've been notified that in 60 days you'll be getting a pink slip and no compensation package. Let's also assume that your downsizing couldn't have come at a worse time – because your spouse also just got axed, or maybe took ill and can't work. Under normal circumstances, I tell people to decline those insurance offers from credit card companies. In this scenario, however, since you have some advance notice, it might well be worth your money to get that credit card insurance protection which allows you to forego or reduce your credit card payments in the event of a job loss. This way, even if your money gets especially tight, you protect your credit standing.

**Can You Piggyback off Another Person's Good Credit?**

Until recently, if you were close to someone who had excellent credit, you could use the "piggybacking" technique to boost your credit standing. Piggybacking is where you essentially share a credit history with someone who has a better credit rating than you do. For instance, a parent might add on a child as an authorized user on a credit card account that the parent has used and paid faithfully for years. Or a wife might add her husband on a credit account to improve his credit standing. In both these instances, the party being added to the credit account gets the benefit of the other person's great credit standing. This system worked when the creditor in question listed you as an authorized user and reported the information to the credit bureaus separately in your name, and not just in the name of the person with the good credit.

Due to the widespread – and some say illegal – use of piggybacking, Fair Isaac has now closed this loophole. Fair Isaac became concerned about piggybacking in the wake of the emergence of businesses such as Largo, Florida-based InstantCreditBuilders.com, or ICB, which charges a fee to people with bad credit and then matches them up with individuals with good credit. Critics say companies like ICB thwart the credit-scoring system and help would-be homeowners commit mortgage fraud, by allowing a person with bad credit to piggyback off of the good credit of a complete stranger. In many cases, people with bad credit – and FICO scores in the 500s – were able to boost their credit scores by 150 points or more just by "borrowing" someone else's credit history. Lenders complain that this practice helps people hide their true credit history. As of September 2007, Fair Isaac no longer considers an account where someone is listed as "authorized user" in its formula for computing a consumer's credit score. Therefore, despite what you might have been told, piggybacking off of someone's credit won't work anymore. The unfortunate thing is that students, married people, and others who were using piggybacking in more legitimate ways can no longer do so.

## Building Credit With Limited or No Credit History

For those of you who are just establishing credit, there is some good news. In the past, in order to get a credit rating going, you had to go into debt – by applying for and using a credit card, obtaining an auto loan, or getting a mortgage. Now there's a new way to establish credit and demonstrate fiscal responsibility without going into debt. A service called Payment Reporting Builds Credit (http://www.PRBC.com) lets students, the newly divorced, immigrants, women, minorities, and others prove their credit-worthiness by tracking their habits at making timely payments for rent, utilities, and other recurring bills. This is a huge market: an estimate 50 million people don't have a broad enough traditional payment history in order to have a standard credit file, according to Fair Isaac. If you're caught in a catch-22 where you can't get credit because you have no past credit, then build your credit history by logging onto www.prbc.com. It's a voluntary service and one that I believe could be worthwhile for many individuals.

Fair Isaac has even launched a new product called the FICO Expansion score, which calculates a FICO score based on non-traditional payments. You can learn more about it on the company's website at: http://www.myfico.com. Lastly, consider taking out a secured credit card as a way to start building your credit history. These cards require you to put money into an account, with your credit limit being determined by the amount of your deposit. Even if you have a card with just a $500 limit, if you charge a nominal amount on that card monthly, or on a regular basis, and then pay the bill off each time, that will go a long way toward proving that you can handle credit responsibly. After a while, you will no doubt start getting offers for traditional credit cards, with better interest rates, higher credit limits, and no requirement to pay upfront deposits for the cards.

**Correcting Errors in Your Credit Report – In Just 48 Hours**

Whenever you notice a mistake in your credit report, you should always dispute it. Sometimes it's best to go right to the credit bureaus but, in other instances, you're better off contacting the creditor reporting the erroneous information.

Writing the credit bureaus is typically most effective when there is identity confusion, personal information about you is listed incorrectly, or your file contains completely wrong data – such as listing an account that you never opened. Let's say that you find an error based on misinformation that was supplied by one of your creditors. This would be the case if you closed an account, yet the account still shows up as open in your files; if you have been reported as paying late, but you actually made your payment on time; or if you paid off an account, but your credit report still shows a balance remaining. In all of these instances, it's best to contact the source of the information and ask them to fix the mistake. If it's a legitimate error, without much to dispute, the company will readily address the problem. Even if they have to do their own investigation – perhaps because your claim is not so cut-and-dried – it's usually better to start with the creditor. The reason is that when you dispute something with the credit bureau they might change the information, but then the next month it's possible that it could reappear in your credit file. Errors that are disputed and resolved at the creditor level are far more likely to remain off of your credit report. Updates to your credit file usually take about 30 to 45 days to be registered in your file. However, if you're in the market for a mortgage, you can have mistakes in your credit report fixed in as little as 48 hours through a process called "Credit Re-Scoring."

Credit re-scoring allows bankers, mortgage brokers, and other lenders to submit proof of a mistake in your credit file directly to the credit agencies. The proof has to be something official, such as a letter from the IRS showing that a tax lien has been paid or a court document that indicates a previous bankruptcy was discharged on a certain date. With satisfactory proof and a request from a mortgage professional, the credit agencies give your file priority status, and quickly update your credit information electronically. This way, an error in your credit file doesn't cost you more money or jeopardize your chance of getting a mortgage.

One limit to this process, however, is that you can't initiate a request for credit re-scoring on your own. Only lenders and other mortgage professionals can do so. The good news is that some companies, such as Novi, Michigan-based Credit Technologies (http://www.credittechnologies.com), can help you connect with a lender that can request credit re-scoring on your behalf. Credit Technologies provides this information free of charge to consumers. They'll even email it to you, so you can get a list of lenders quickly. Alternatively, if you already have a lender, but they don't know about credit re-scoring, have the lender contact Credit Technologies directly at 800-445-4922 in order to do credit re-scoring. Credit Technologies doesn't guarantee that your score will increase as a result of credit-rescoring, but the company does report that the typical client experiences a 30-point jump in his or her FICO score.

If you can get your lender involved, your credit report will be updated much faster than you could have done on your own. Fixing erroneous information that is lowering your FICO score could mean the difference between your getting a so-so deal on your mortgage, or getting a home loan with a great rate and attractive terms.

# CHAPTER

## 3

## Save for a Down Payment and Closing Costs

One of the most worrisome aspects about Americans' financial behavior is that, over the generations, many of us have lost the ability to save money. In 2006, the savings rate in the U.S. was negative 1%, meaning Americans not only spent every dollar they earned, they also dipped into savings or used credit to pay for the things they wanted. This negative savings rate represented the lowest savings rate in the country since 1933, when the savings rate fell to negative 1.5% during the Great Depression. Back then, however, one out of four workers was out of a job so people needed to use their savings and borrow money to pay for basic necessities like food and shelter. What excuse does the average American have now?

In a lot of cases, people never learned how to save money in the first place. Therefore, I'm not surprised that such people find it difficult to save on a regular basis, or to save as much money as they would like month after month.

Learning how to save – and yes, the ability to save is a skill that you learn and acquire over time – is of utmost importance for anyone trying to buy a home. Moreover, if you can become a disciplined saver, this is a positive habit that will help you throughout the rest of your life, with homeownership and in other areas of financial planning.

Back in 1985, Americans saved an average of more than 10% of their net pay. Ironically, some experts blame the currently lack of savings in the U.S. on rising home prices. These observers say that when the real estate market experienced a huge run-up, many people mistakenly concluded that they no longer needed to save money. Instead, they would just tap the equity in their homes when they needed cash. As you prepare for homeownership, I want you to learn to manage your finances the right way. That means you must learn to sock away money on your own, based on your earnings and ability to properly budget. You shouldn't count on using your home as a piggy bank, squeezing every dollar out of it to pay for routine things that your savings account should handle. So now let's turn to why you need a cash cushion, and how you're going to get it.

## The Importance of Having a Cash Cushion

Having a nice nest egg can provide you with a profound sense of comfort, stability, and even financial independence. It's essentially the opposite scenario, however, if you have no cash cushion at all. In the latter instance, you feel stressed and uncomfortable about your financial situation. You experience unsteadiness and insecurity, rather than stability. Without money in the bank, you always feel like you're a slave to your mounting, never-ending bills; financial freedom seems like a distant pipedream. While it's nice to experience the emotional benefits and positive feelings that come with having a financial cushion, it's just as wonderful to experience the practical economic benefits that arise when you learn how to save money.

Unfortunately, too many of us claim that we "can't save." In truth, you may not be *committed* to saving. Everybody can save something. I don't care if it's $10 a week. Every little bit helps. Even small amounts of money build quickly over time, if you're consistent about adding to the pot. You can – and should – get into the habit of always setting aside at least a *little* bit of money on a regular basis. If you can change your financial habits to the point where you're able to squirrel away a *lot* of money – say, 10% or more of your salary – then you'll really put yourself in a great position financially.

In addition to the benefits described above, here are five reasons everyone needs a cash cushion:

■ **To deal with emergencies and unexpected events**
You never know what can happen: if you get sick, suffer an accident, lose a job, or go through a divorce, having some savings will cushion the financial blow.

■ **To pay for future goals**

If you dream of starting a business, funding your child's education, going back to school to earn a degree, or retiring at a certain age, these all require money.

■ **To prevent yourself from amassing excessive credit card debt**

It's a bad idea to whip out that plastic in your wallet to satisfy your every whim; having cash on hand minimizes your temptation to overboard with credit.

■ **To avoid being a burden on your family and friends**

You don't want to have to call on your parents, siblings, or friends every time you face a financial crunch, right? Having some savings will help you avoid the embarrassment and awkward feelings of needing to ask others for money.

■ **To reward yourself when appropriate**

Saving money just for the heck of it, and living like a pauper, is no fun at all. As a reward for your diligent and responsible financial behavior, you should be able to enjoy your money and the fruits of your labor. Maybe you want to travel or splurge on a new suit. When you save up money for these purchases, it's fine to buy what you want.

If you plan to become a homeowner any time soon, you obviously have one more powerful incentive to establish a cash cushion: to save the money you'll need for a down payment and closing costs. Fortunately, there are some time-tested strategies you can use to pay yourself first, and make sure you always save money. I'm going to tell you about those later in this chapter. First, however, I want to give you a much better sense of exactly how much money you'll need to buy a home. Then I'll offer you some tips and techniques to accumulate whatever funds you need.

## How Big of a Down Payment Do You Really Need?

Many renters mistakenly believe that in order to become homeowners they have to put a large down payment on a home. I suppose this misconception stems from the realities of financing homes decades ago. Back then, banks required a 20% down payment and only those diligent enough to save up a big chunk of money ultimately got a home. Today, however, the entire mortgage market is drastically different. Gone are the days when banks only offered a standard 30-year fixed-rate mortgage. Now you can get an adjustable-rate mortgage, as well as any variety of so-called "hybrid" loans – those that combine features of both ARMs and fixed-rate mortgages. Plus, with relatively low interest rates and the steady rise in home prices over the past two decades, many lenders came to realize that if they required everyone to put down 20% on a home, millions of people would never become homeowners. Therefore, banks got creative and less strict in their down payment requirements. Today, you can buy a home with 10% down, 5% down, or even no money down. Believe it or not, according to the Mortgage Bankers Association, the average first-time homebuyer now puts forth a 3% down payment toward the purchase of his or her home. Surely you can save up a 3% down payment if you're committed to being a homeowner.

In dollar terms, here's what we're talking about. According to the National Association of Realtors, the median home price in America stands at approximately $230,000. (The median price means that half of all homes sold for above that price, and half sold for less than that figure.)

■ **Assuming you were to buy a $230,000 home, here's what you would have to save:**

| | |
|---|---|
| To have a 3% down payment, you must save: | $6,900 |
| To have a 5% down payment, you must save: | $11,500 |
| To have a 10% down payment, you must save: | $23,000 |
| To have a 20% down payment, you must save: | $46,000 |

Since these figures are based on the *median* national home prices, what if you live in a part of the country where homes are far less expensive, or perhaps far more costly, than $230,000? This wouldn't be uncommon, given the highly affordable cost of housing in many areas of the South, Midwest, and other regions. On the other hand, the East and West Coasts are much pricier markets. So let's look at those scenarios, too, with various price points in mind.

Assume you live in Texas, where the median home price is about $140,000 – way below the national average.

■ **With a $140,000 home, here's how much money you would need:**

| To have a 3% down payment, you must save: | $4,200 |
|---|---|
| To have a 5% down payment, you must save: | $7,000 |
| To have a 10% down payment, you must save: | $14,000 |
| To have a 20% down payment, you must save: | $28,000 |

Then consider your options if you live in California, where the average price tag of a home tops the $500,000 level – more than twice the national average.

■ **With a $500,000 home, here's how much money you'd need:**

| To have a 3% down payment, you must save: | $15,000 |
|---|---|
| To have a 5% down payment, you must save: | $25,000 |
| To have a 10% down payment, you must save: | $50,000 |
| To have a 20% down payment, you must save: | $100,000 |

I'm sure that to a lot of you those last set of numbers look very daunting. However, amassing the necessary down payment in high-cost areas like California, New York, or Washington D.C. becomes a lot more feasible when you realize that there are many down payment assistance and grant programs available for first-time homebuyers nationwide. Additionally, many lenders will allow you to use gift money – from family members or friends – in order to qualify for a mortgage. In the following chapter, I'll tell you about numerous first-time homebuyer initiatives that can provide you with financial assistance – some as much as $30,000 to $40,000.

For now, however, I want to focus on what you can do to come up with cash on your own.

So far, I've told you about national home prices and a few local markets. Now I want you to investigate average home prices in your own city – so you have a rough idea about your local housing market. Home prices vary based on size, location, desirability of the neighborhood, quality of the home, amenities, and other factors. Therefore, it's important to at least know the going rates. To find out the going price of homes in your area, or in any area you'd like to live, do a quick Internet search or contact a realtor. Some websites you can use include:

> http://www.zillow.com
> http://www.eppraisal.com
> http://www.realestateabc.com
> http://www.homegain.com
> http://www.cyberhomes.com
> http://www.propertyshark.com
> http://www.reply.com

Simply enter a street address, and these websites can offer you estimates on home prices, or give you actual pricing data on recent sales in a given neighborhood. Another way to get a quick insight into the price of homes in a specific city is to call a local realtor who specializes in an area of interest to you. Find a realtor in your local phone book, by doing a Google search, or simply by visiting the National Association Realtors' website at: http://www.realtor.org. Again, prices will vary from neighborhood to neighborhood, but at least you'll get a range of what homes are selling for before you start actively searching for your own house.

Lastly, housing markets can and do change from quarter to quarter, and year to year. Therefore you should also check to see the average appreciation rate in your city and state. A good realtor can tell you what's happening locally. Also, the Office of Federal Housing Enterprise Oversight tracks real estate appreciation at the state level. Go to the agency's website at http://www.ofheo.gov and click on the tab that says "Housing Price Index." This will take you to a state-by-state listing that illustrates the percentage change in housing prices for the most recent quarter.

## How Much House Can You Truly Afford?

Now that you have a rough idea about what homes sell for in your desired area, and how much of a down payment you might need, now's the time to think about other factors that impact how much you can truly afford to spend on a house. When you apply for a home mortgage, the down payment won't be the only cost consideration. You'll also be responsible for closing costs, which average about 3% of the loan amount. So if you buy a $250,000 house and put down 5%, or $12,500, your remaining mortgage loan balance will be $237,500. If closing costs totaled another 3%, you'll need to come up with an additional $7,125. As you'll learn in this book, there are lots of lenders and programs that allow you to fold your closing costs into your mortgage, so you might not have to pay the closing costs upfront. Nevertheless, let's operate on the assumption for now that you're trying to save enough money to cover both your down payment and closing costs.

When you put down less than 20% for a home, you usually have to pay for mortgage insurance. This is insurance that you buy to protect your lender against your defaulting on your loan. With conventional loans, mortgage insurance is called PMI, or Private Mortgage Insurance. If you take out a federally-backed loan, such as those insured by the Federal Home Administration (FHA), you pay a monthly MIP, or mortgage insurance premium. I'll explain mortgage insurance in detail in subsequent chapters. For now, it's important for you to realize that mortgage insurance is an additional factor in the cost of your home loan if you make a modest down payment.

## Why Smart Homebuyers Factor in Contingencies

I wish I could tell you that you'd be all set just by amassing a down payment and enough funds to cover your closings costs. However, that would be misleading and financially foolish. To get yourself off to the best possible start as a smart homeowner, you also need to save up money for what I call a "Home Expense Fund."

This represents the cash reserves you set aside for *after* you get into that house of your dreams. This money might be used on anything from buying new furniture, to paying the moving truck to haul all your stuff into your house, to painting that home and doing repairs. No matter what kind of house you buy, even if it's a brand new one, sooner or later something in the house will require maintenance or repairs. I don't want you to purchase a house that costs you so much that when you take possession of it you are totally broke, because as soon as that happens I can practically guarantee that something will happen. The roof might leak. The boiler might break. Or maybe some kids in the neighborhood will accidentally toss a baseball through your window. Whatever the case, you'd be wise to plan for contingencies and have some cash on hand to deal with unexpected home emergencies. This way, you won't have to charge those expenses, and run up unnecessary credit card debt.

How much cash reserves should you have? I recommend that your home expense fund be 2% of the value of the home you're purchasing. For a $250,000 home, you'd need to have $5,000 in savings put aside for potential expenses after you move into your home. If you think having adequate cash set aside for your Home Expense Fund will total too much money – think again. The true cost of homeownership far exceeds your principal, interests, taxes, and insurance costs. Be sure to check out Appendix A at the end of this book, where I spell out all the ongoing costs of owning and maintaining a home. This will help you understand why that 2% Home Expense Fund is a necessity.

If you've been following closely, you might have noticed something about the numbers I've used. No matter where you want to live, and regardless of the kind of home you plan to buy – be it a condo, townhouse, or single-family dwelling – I suggest that you plan on having a total of 10% of the total purchase price of the property available to you before you begin the purchasing process in order to cover the various costs. Your financial breakdown will look like this:

- 5% - for the down payment
- 3% - towards closing costs
- 2% - set aside for your Home Expense Fund
- 10% of purchase price needed to become a homeowner

Obviously, these are just guidelines. Yet these rules of thumb will help ensure that your home-buying experience will be a positive one from a financial perspective. Following these recommendations will steer you towards buying a home that you can truly afford.

Needless to say, I want to encourage you to become a homeowner – and I'd love for you to make the leap from renter to owner as soon as possible. However, I also advocate responsible, affordable, and sustainable homeownership. This means your goal should not be to do the least amount of work necessary, or save the least amount of money required, in order to get a home. If you have that mindset, you could wind up in foreclosure. Why? Because research shows that the #1 predictor of mortgage defaults isn't your income, or your credit history, it's actually the down payment involved in a home purchase.

Simply put, the bigger the down payment, the less likely it is that a buyer will become delinquent on his or her mortgage. That's why many people worry about no-down payment loans. They exist; and I'm going to tell you about those options as well. But the fact remains that putting some money down on a home – even if it's not your own money – means you're less prone to losing the home at some point down the road. When you think about it, that makes sense. The homeowner with equity of his or her own has a vested financial interest in keeping that property. That equity represents wealth and, for many people, a home is the largest asset they have. Additionally, when you have equity in your home, you have more options if you should run into trouble. For instance, you can refinance and take cash out of the home, or you can sell it. However, if you have no equity in the house, because you didn't make a down payment when you bought it, your financial options are limited.

Right now some of you might be thinking: "Lynnette, it could take me years to save up that 10% that you recommend. At the rate I'm saving, I'll never become a homeowner!" Well, I have some good news for you regarding the cash that you'll need: it doesn't have to come from you. The money can come from a variety of sources, including family members, your job, non-profit agencies, or even from builders and lenders. Again, Chapter 4 will explain the huge array of financial programs that are available to help first-time homebuyers and even move-up buyers. Understand that if even if you calculated that you need $25,000, the 10% required for a $250,000 home, it's very possible that more than half that money would come from other places, not directly from your own pocket. Additionally, you can tweak my recommended formula. Many loans, such as those insured by FHA, the Federal Housing Administration, require only a 3% down payment. Again, many lenders will permit you to finance your closing costs to eliminate that burden when you obtain a mortgage. Certain lenders even offer so-called 103% loans, meaning you borrow all the money you need to get into the house: including the down payment and all closing costs. The choice is up to you. Just begin by settling on a time table for how long you want to save for a house. Are you willing to sock aside money for the next six months, a year, or maybe 18 months? Whatever you decide, take comfort in knowing that when you start actively looking for a house, there are plenty of funds out there to supplement your own savings. Believe it or not, even if you are only able to save a few thousand dollars that might be enough to purchase the house of your dreams.

**How to Calculate Your Debt-to-Income Ratio**

By now, you've learned how much homes in your area cost, as well as how much savings you need to sock away – or get from other sources. To round out your knowledge of how much you can truly afford, you need to now take a hard look at your own finances, namely your income and expenses.

When you go to a bank, mortgage broker, or other lender to apply for a mortgage, one of the first questions they will ask is: what is your gross monthly or annual salary? Most of you know the answer to this question off the top of your head. If you don't, just multiply your salary by the number of times you get paid each month or each year. For instance, if your gross pay is $800 per week, and you get paid weekly or four times in a month, then your gross monthly pay is $3,200 a month. If you get paid 52 times a year, you'd multiply 52 by $800 for an annual salary of $41,600. In addition to your salary or wages, lenders will also consider overtime, commissions or bonuses that are guaranteed, plus alimony, child support, annuities, and any other income you receive on a regular basis.

Next, your lender will want to know what existing debts you have that will require 10 months or more to pay off. For instance, this might include your car payment, credit card bills, or student loans you are repaying. The lender will add up all your minimum payments for each of your debts and come up with something called your DTI, or debt-to-income ratio. Your debt-to-income ratio is calculated by dividing your monthly debt payments by your monthly income. (Don't try to fudge your debts on your loan application and say that your bills are lower than they really are. Once your lender pulls your credit file, they're going to see the total balances of what you owe to each creditor, along with the monthly payments you make to those creditors.)

### Front-End and Back-End Ratios Explained

Let's say your car payment is $285 a month, your credit card bills are $220 a month, and you pay $95 a month on your student loans. Therefore, your total monthly debts are $600. If your total income is $3,200 monthly, then your debt-to-income ratio is 18.75% ($600/$3200). This obviously excludes your housing costs. When you find a home you want to purchase, a lender will look closely at two things:

- your housing debt compared to your income
  Your housing expense is known as your "front-end" ratio
- your overall debt compared to your income
  Your total debt, housing plus other bills, is known as your "back-end" ratio.

Generally speaking, conventional lenders like to see maximum debt-to-income ratios of 28% for the front-end expenses and 36% for the back-end expenses. This means your housing costs take up no more than 28% of your gross income, and your housing expenses plus other bills should represent no more than 36% of your gross pay. There are many, many exceptions to this rule, however. Some lenders will allow your housing costs to be as much as 40% or more of your salary, and your total debts to be as much as 50% or more of your income. So don't get bogged down by the traditional 28/36 guideline for your debt-to-income ratios. Nor should you be discouraged and think that you won't qualify for a mortgage if your ratios don't conform to these numbers. Use them as a frame of reference to let you know how close or far off you are to meeting traditional lending criteria. Many banks have "expanded" criteria programs, meaning they offer loans with less stringent debt-to-income requirements and even easier credit requirements to allow you to get a mortgage.

Are you interested in knowing your own debt-to-income ratio to see how much you can afford to spend on a house by traditional lending standards? You don't need to go to a bank to do this. You can do it on your own, following these easy steps.

**Step 1:** Write down your estimated housing expense, including principal, interest, real estate taxes, and homeowner's insurance. This figure represents your housing expense, or front-end ratio.

**Tip:** use an online mortgage calculator for this estimate. At one site, http://www.bankrate.com, you just enter a loan amount, loan term and interest rate, and Bankrate.com can tell you the mortgage payment. For example, I used the site's calculator to find out the mortgage for the purchase of a $250,000 house with a $12,500, or 5% down payment. So I entered a $237,500 loan amount. The loan term I used was 360 months, or 30 years, at an interest rate of 7%. The result: the mortgage payment was $1,385 for principal and interest payments only. You can do a Google search on the Internet for other mortgage calculators that will let you plug in estimates for taxes and insurance.

**Step 2:** Tally up the minimum payments required on all your outstanding bills, then write the total number down. Remember: you don't need to add in expenses such as your cell phone, Internet service, or utilities, only debts which require 10 months or longer to repay.

**Step 3:** Add the number from Step 1 to the number from Step 2. This is your back end ratio, the total of your housing plus other expenses.

**Step 4:** Write down your total gross monthly income.

**Step 5:** Divide the number from Step 1 by the number in Step 4.

This figure is the percentage of income you will spend exclusively on housing, known as your front-end ratio.

As you can see, the figure you get from Step 5 is your front-end ratio; the number you come up with from Step 3 is your back-end ratio. How do your numbers look?

## Setting Realistic Expectations

Now I want you to take this process one step further to do something that the banks don't require, but which will help you nonetheless have realistic expectations.

**Step 6:** Add up everything else you have to pay for on a regular basis: food, utilities, insurance, childcare or school tuition for the kids, etc. Combine this number to the figure you arrived at in Step 3. Write down the total. We'll call this new number your "true total debt," because it indicates the truth about your personal financial situation. This "true total debt" gives you a much more realistic view of how large of a mortgage you can handle, regardless of what the bank says.

**Step 7:** Lastly, divide the figure you have from Step 6 with the income you recorded in Step 4. Write down the percentage. This is your "true total debt-to-income ratio."

What did you come up with for that last figure? If your "true total debt-to-income ratio" is extremely high, 90% or more, owning a home would be likely to seriously put a cramp in your budget – at least if your spending remains at its current level.

Why did I want you to calculate those last two figures? The reason is simple. Banks are in business to make money. They don't much care about your personal circumstances. They're not going to worry about whether you can buy your kids birthday gifts, spend money during the holidays, get your hair or nails done, or keep your cell phone service connected. Their primary concern is to make sure that can you repay your mortgage. That's why the bank's calculations are not "real life" or "true" calculations for most people.

Therefore, if you had a very high "true debt-to-income ratio" you have some tough choices to make. Among your options you can:

- buy the home anyway, keep your fingers crossed, and "hope for the best";
- seek out a less expensive house;
- cut back on other expenses so that every dollar you earn isn't being spent; or
- delay buying a home until you have a higher income, more savings, and fewer debts.

The first option strikes me as naïve and financially careless. There's no sense in rushing to buy a home if you'll wind up completely cash-strapped, with bills up to your eyeballs, and possibly at risk of foreclosure. The second, third, and fourth options are all viable, although the fourth one entails another risk you might not have considered. If you delay your active pursuit of homeownership, and stop preparing for it to happen sooner than later, you run the risk that home prices will appreciate, forcing you to come up with even more cash to buy the house of your dreams.

**Budgeting 101: Mastering Some Financial Basics**

Too often, we only think of one thing we can do with our money: spend it. In truth, though, there are four different things you can do with your dollars: save, spend, invest, or donate them. Consequently, I'd like to suggest that you create a budget for yourself that takes these options into consideration. Below I've described a range of categories that define typical bills that people pay. Use the list that follows to write down the monthly amount you pay for each expense and the percentage of your net income that the payment represents. For any expenses that you incur annually, add up the yearly cost and divide it by 12 in order to arrive at your monthly spending for that category. After you fill in the chart, look at where your money goes each month, and notice how much of your cash goes toward each area. Chances are, you're saving a lot less than you want and spending far more than you realize.

| Expense | Monthly Dollars Spent on This Category |
|---|---|
| **SAVE**<br>For Down Payment<br>For Closing Costs<br>For Home Expense Fund<br>For Cash Cushion<br>For Other Goals/Needs<br><br>**SPEND**<br>  **Food**<br>   o  Grocery Store<br>   o  Restaurants/Meals Out<br>   o  Breakfast, Lunch, Dinner, or Drinks<br>   o  Hotel and/or "On the Go" Food During<br>       Business Travel<br><br>  **Housing**<br>   o  Rent<br>   o  Renter's Insurance<br>   o  Repairs/Maintenance<br>   o  Furniture, Decorations, or Improvements<br><br>  **Transportation**<br>   o  Car Payment<br>   o  Gas for Car<br>   o  Car Registration<br>   o  Auto Insurance<br>   o  Daily, Weekly, or Monthly Parking Fees<br>   o  Vehicle Maintenance and Repairs (Oil &<br>       Fluid Changes, Tires, Car Washes, etc.)<br>   o  Bus/Subway/Public Transportation<br>   o  Taxis/Car Service<br><br>  **Debts**<br>   o  Credit Cards<br>   o  Personal Loans/Lines of Credit<br>   o  Family Obligations/Debts Owed<br>   o  Old/Past-Due Taxes | |

| Expense | Monthly Dollars Spent on This Category |
|---|---|
| **Utilities**<br>o  Electric<br>o  Water<br>o  Heat<br>o  Gas/Oil<br>o  Cable<br>o  Internet<br>o  Cell Phone<br>o  Home Phone<br>o  Business Phone<br>o  Fax Line<br><br>**Educational Costs**<br>o  Student Loans<br>o  Tuition, Registration, and Other Fees<br>o  Books and Supplies<br><br>**Childcare**<br>o  Babysitter/Nanny<br>o  School Tuition and Fees<br>o  Kids Birthdays/Parties<br><br>**Insurance**<br>o  Healthcare Insurance<br>o  Umbrella Liability Insurance<br>o  Life Insurance (Term)<br>o  Disability Protection<br>o  Business Liability Insurance<br><br>**Entertainment**<br>o  Movies (Rentals at Home or In-Theater Movies)<br>o  Tickets (Museums, Art Galleries, Broadway/Off-Broadway Theatres)<br>o  Parties/Holiday Celebrations<br>o  Other | |

| Expense | Monthly Dollars Spent on Category |
|---|---|
| **Hobbies**<br>o Leisure Activities<br>o Enrichment Classes<br><br>**Travel**<br>o Annual Vacations<br>o Holiday Travel<br>o Yearly Time Share Fees<br><br>**Personal Care**<br>o Manicures/Pedicures<br>o Hair Salon/Barber Shop<br>o Facials<br>o Personal Trainer/Nutritionist<br>o Clothing<br><br>**Miscellaneous**<br>o Annual Memberships<br>o Professional Organizations/Trade Groups<br>    Sorority/Fraternity<br>o Gym<br>o Discount Stores (Costco, Sam's, etc.)<br>o Newspaper Subscriptions<br>o Books<br><br>**INVEST**<br>401(k)<br>403(b)<br>Stocks<br>Bonds<br>Mutual Funds<br>IRA (Individual Retirement Account)<br>College<br>Fund Permanent/Whole Life Insurance<br><br>**DONATE**<br>Charity<br>Church, Synagogue, Mosque, etc.<br>Tithes<br>School/Other | |

Many people have never taken the time to truly itemize all their expenses. If you haven't ever tracked your spending, or if you have not done so lately, this exercise might be a real eye-opener for you. Add up your totals in each category. How much are you spending monthly? What about your monthly totals for saving, investing, and donating? Now think about the percentage of your income that you save, spend, invest, and donate. Do the figures seem unbalanced to you? If so, read on to discover how you can bring you budget into proper alignment.

**Two Easy Steps to Creating a Budget You Can Live With**

I know that most of you loathe the thought of being on a budget. The word "budget" alone conjures up images of deprivation – making us think about every thing we can't have, can't do, or can't buy. But creating a budget – and living with it – doesn't have to be so restrictive and it certainly need not be a painful process.

In fact, having a good budget offers a host of benefits. A well-made budget:

- Gives you power and control over your finances
- Keeps you from living paycheck to paycheck
- Allows you to save for future goals and dreams
- Helps you avoid going into debt

Here is my simple, two-step system you can use to create a livable budget that will help you achieve peace of mind and eliminate worries about your money.

**Step 1:  Make a list of your expenses**

Begin by itemizing all the different areas of your life in which you spend money. Some common categories are:

- Food
- Housing

- Entertainment
- Transportation
- Debts
- Utilities
- Educational Costs
- Childcare
- Insurance
- Miscellaneous

When you make your list, take a moment to think about how you really live your life on a daily and monthly basis. Do you have kids for whom you regularly buy gifts? If so, include a gifts category for things like birthdays, holidays, graduations, or other special occasions. Or maybe you're an avid reader, so you should add a category for monthly magazine subscriptions or books you routinely purchase. Your list can be handwritten, or entered on a computer spreadsheet.

### Step 2: Adjust to avoid budget-busters

If your expenses exceed your income, you'll have to cut back on areas that aren't necessities. Also, to avoid blowing your budget, remember that unexpected events and emergencies always arise. That's life. You can minimize the impact of these occurrences by adjusting your budget according to the principle of LIFE. **LIFE** is an acronym that describes the four ways that your budget gets out of whack – forcing you to spend more than you planned for the month, or causing you to live from paycheck to paycheck. The features of the LIFE formula are described below:

### ■ Listed items are under-calculated

The "L" in LIFE stands for expenses that are "listed" items in your budget, but the numbers you used are actually very inaccurate. For example, if your credit card bills show that you spend $250 a month on clothes, don't put $100 into the clothing category. Don't underestimate your spending. Enter a realistic number.

### ■ Impulse purchases seduce you

The "I" in LIFE refers to the "impulse" purchases that everyone makes now and again. Make sure you're not buying things on a whim week after week, month after month. That's a sure-fire way to kill your budget. Whenever you make an unplanned purchase – whether you're shopping online, buying something from a street vendor, or getting something from the mall when you were supposed to be "just window shopping" – that's considered an impulse purchase. Keep those to a minimum.

### ■ Forgotten bills surface

The "F" in LIFE is for those "forgotten" bills that pop up when you least expect them. Some bills get paid annually or perhaps twice a year – like your membership to the gym or perhaps your auto insurance. If you're not mindful of these expenses, you can forget them and then when the bills come due you'll be short of cash. To avoid this pitfall, do not omit them from your budget. Just factor them into your monthly budget on a prorated basis and put the money aside. For instance, if your auto insurance is $1,200 a year and it's due in December, enter $100 in your monthly budget for this expense. Then put $100 cash aside each month for 12 months – instead of trying to come up with all of the money at the end of the year.

### ■ Emergency or unexpected events occur

The "E" in LIFE stands for "emergencies." There are obviously times when emergencies – like a burst boiler unit – can ruin a budget. Try to minimize these events with preventative measures, such as regularly servicing your boiler, having routine maintenance done on your car to avoid breakdowns, and making periodic visits to the doctor to stave off serious medical conditions.

Once you realize that LIFE happens to everyone, you can take some steps to safeguard your finances and create a realistic, workable budget. For most of us, that's the first step to having fewer money problems and achieving financial freedom.

**Tips for How and Where to Save Money**

Now I want to offer you some money-saving strategies that will build up your bank account in preparation for homeownership.

■ **Save on Your Current Housing**

Some of the ways you can cut your existing housing costs are to get a roommate, rent out a room, and cut back on decorations and upgrades. Save your energy (and money) for making your new home exactly to your liking.

■ **Save on Your Car**

Lowering your transportation expenses isn't always easy, but it can be done. If you live in a city with reliable public transportation, like New York or Boston, and you don't actually need a car, consider selling it to raise cash. If you have a car and need to keep it, start following these cost-cutting tips.

Take account of all the expenses involved with having a car: your monthly car payment, gas and maintenance charges, insurance, parking, and so forth. See if you can renegotiate any of your current costs or shop around for better deals. For instance, if you're paying $50 a month for parking at your apartment complex, can you park it outside the building and get a $50 discount from your landlord? (Obviously, you only want to do this if it's relatively safe for your car to be parked on the street, as well as safe for you to enter your building from outside.) Then there's insurance. Ask your insurer about any discounts for which you might be eligible: good driver discounts, lower rates for taking a defensive driving course, or even decreased premiums for having an alarm system or antitheft device. Also, by raising your insurance deductibles, you can save 10% to 25% off of your annual premiums.

Even your car payment itself can be re-negotiated, through a process called auto refinancing, which allows you to get a lower interest rate and a smaller monthly payment than you currently have. Many people don't know that you can refinance your car loan just as you can refinance a mortgage. A car refinancing is faster, simpler to do, and costs virtually nothing. There aren't any closing costs or points, like you might have with a mortgage. Most auto refinancing companies do business online. Capital One Auto Finance (www.capitaloneauto.com) allows you to refinance your car loan in just 15 minutes, saving the average customer more than $1,300 over the life of the car loan. So if your car has a high interest rate, check out a lender like Capital One to knock down your monthly car note and save yourself some big bucks. I once refinanced my auto loan with Capital One and saved more $100 a month on my car payments. Two caveats though: don't try to refinance your car right before you go in to apply for a mortgage. You don't want extra inquiry on your credit report. Also, if you do refinance your car, don't extend the life of your payments. If you only have three years left to pay off your car, refinance with a lender that lets you keep a three-year payoff. Otherwise you'll stretch out your payments and wind up paying additional money in interest charges. When you do save money with auto refinancing, apply your savings toward your home down payment or build up your cash cushion.

■ **Save Money on Food**

Avoid wasting money on the things that can really blow your budget like eating out frequently. I'm not only talking about restaurants. I don't have to tell you the impact of spending $50 or $75 for dinner for two. I'm talking about eating out at fast food places, or spending what seems like small change on local delis and the like. If you're not careful, before you know it that "chump change" can really add up.

For starters, stop making your daily run for coffee and donuts or a bagel and juice before work. Many people spend about five dollars a day on these items, which equals $100 dollars a month, or $1,200 a year. Just as bad are those trips to the vending machine for junk food each day at work. If you spend $3 a day on these small items, eliminating those purchases saves $900 in a year.

At the grocery store, use coupons and choose your purchases based on the price per unit for everything from toiletries to food products, and take advantage of sales and reward cards from retailers who offer discounts to repeat customers.

■ **Save Money on Medicine**

I love to tell people to do a makeover to save money – not a personal makeover, but a makeover of their medicine cabinet at home! This is an area to which most people never pay any attention. You probably don't either. I'm sure many of you adore brand-name clothes and shoes, but when it comes to medicine, you don't need brand-name products. Get generic drugs from your doctor or pharmacist. By law, generic drugs have the identical chemical makeup and active ingredients as brand-name medications—without the hefty price tag. The typical brand-name prescription costs $100, while the average generic drug is just $30, a 70% difference. If you hit the pharmacy once a month, in the span of a year you'll save $840 just by using generic drugs instead of brand-name prescription drugs.

### ■ Save Money on Household Items

Get creative about stretching the stuff you already buy and use at home on a regular basis. We all need toothpaste, right? To save money reach for the tubes, not the pump toothpastes sold in many stores. Why? Pumps don't last as long as tubes, so they give you less bang for your buck. What about that deodorant you buy. Did you know that budget-conscious people purchase sticks or roll-ons because aerosols get used up faster? (Not to mention that aerosols are less friendly to the environment.)

### ■ Save Money By Kicking Bad Habits

If you have a habit that's hurting you, financially or health-wise, it's high time you kicked that habit. Take cigarettes as a case in point. The average pack of cigarettes costs $4, excluding state taxes. If you smoke two packs a day, that adds up to $10 daily (taxes included) just for the "pleasure" of sucking on a nicotine stick! Do your best to rid yourself of that bad habit. If you can, you'll save $300 dollars a month or $3,600 dollars a year, not to mention the savings you'll reap from fewer medical bills.

### ■ Save Money on Utilities

Being a lot more conscientious about your habits around the house can help you save thousands of dollars on utilities. Here's how to be savvier in this area. Unplug appliances when you're not using them. That goes for toaster, coffee maker, blender, and other appliances. Leaving them plugged in is just draining power and wasting money unnecessarily. If you make a habit of unplugging these items, you'll save 10% on your energy bills. The same thing goes for wasting energy by having so many lights on in the house. Turn off lights when you leave a room. Also, switch high-watt bulbs to lower-wattage ones or fluorescent bulbs to save even more money. Lower your hot water costs by up to 50% just by taking showers instead of baths. Only run your dishwasher, clothes washer, and dryer when they're full for additional savings on your utility costs.

### ■ Save Money on Clothes

Do you want to save money on clothes? Well, at the risk of being called a "traitor" by my own people (i.e. those of the female persuasion), let me start by making this suggestion, especially to you ladies: just stop shopping so much! OK … I've said it. I had to get that off my chest because so many people I know, particularly women, moan about how they don't have any money whatsoever. Somehow, however, they always seem to have the money to go shopping for clothes – either with cash or credit. If you must go shopping, go when there's a sale, or use those store coupons that come in the mail or that you can find in the newspaper in which your favorite retailer advertises. Additionally, save yourself money by simply shopping around. Take advantage of some really great deals you can find on the Internet. Quit always buying designer labels. Places like H&M and Target have really cute clothes, too, and usually no one will ever know that you bought that nice pair of jeans from a discount store or an outlet. If you make it a practice to avoid paying full retail price for your clothes, you can save yourself hundreds, if not thousands, of dollars in the course of a year.

### ■ Save Money on Entertainment

When you're building your cash cushion and trying to get a down payment together you might think that all things fun have to go out the window. Not so. You can enjoy yourself plenty if you do it the smart way – namely by sticking to free or low-cost forms of entertainment. For example, choose free museums and local cultural spots and historic venues over other activities that cost money. If you're dating, have picnics in the park or cook your sweetie dinner at home, rather than the traditional movie and restaurant thing. If you're a partier, get to the club early to avoid paying a cover charge. Better yet, go to someone's house party where there's no price for admission, except maybe an inexpensive bottle wine if you want to bring one to your host. The idea is to select fun diversions that won't bust your budget.

### ■ Save Money on Miscellaneous Expenses

Here are some other ways you can cut back on the dollars going out your door. This advice comes from AmericaSaves.org:

| Tip | Monthly Saving |
|---|---|
| Save $.50 a day in loose change | $15 |
| Cut soda/pop consumption by 1 liter a week | $6 |
| At work, substitute 1 coffee for 1 cappuccino | $40 |
| Bring lunch to work (saving estimated $3/day) | $60 |
| Eat out 2 fewer times a month | $30 |
| Borrow, rather than buying, one book a month | $15 |
| Comparison shop for gas (save est. $.25/gallon) | $4 |
| Maintain checking account minimum to avoid fees | $7 |
| Bounce one less check a month | $20 |
| Pay credit card bill on time to avoid late fee | $25 |
| Pay credit card bill on time to avoid late fee | $25 |

Notice that if you follow all these tips, you can save $237 a month – in addition to the many thousands of dollars saved annually using the strategies I recommended earlier. That's a nice chunk of change to set aside for your new home, isn't it?

**Tips From a Single Mom Who Saved $50,000 in Two Years**

I know many of you will say: "No matter how hard I try, I can't save money." Well, let me inspire you with the incredible success story of Debra Suzanne Payne, a single mother of two-year-old twins, who stashed away an amazing amount of money – $50,000 – in just under two years. Payne, 38, is a pharmacist who works for the government. In October 2007, she closed on a beautiful 3,400 square foot, five-bedroom, three and a half bath house – the home of her dreams – in Lanham, Maryland. She bought the $500,000 home after dramatically reducing her spending and saving nearly half of her take-home pay. "I took $1,200 out of every paycheck and I put it in the bank," says Payne. She also stashed away a $10,000 income tax refund. She did it by remaining steadfast in her focus that she wanted a home above everything else. That meant making "every sacrifice imaginable," including trimming her phone service to just the basics, and slashing her cable bill to the bare bones level of $13 a month.

"I was determined to get my home," Payne says. "I was on a mission."

When Payne first wrote to tell me about her home purchase, she let me know that while she read my books, *Zero Debt* and *The Money Coach's Guide to Your First Million*, she didn't buy them. Instead, she checked them out of the library. "I love your advice and took heed of it," she said, adding that she "couldn't afford to buy your books since I was squirreling away every penny I had." She didn't want her kids – a boy and a girl – to miss out on fun events. So she took them to every free activity, park, or library event she could to keep the children entertained. The result: Payne's diligent savings and single-minded focus allowed her to come up with a 10% down payment on her home, giving her substantial equity in the property. Plus the house was actually appraised at $620,000. It was a foreclosure, "owned by a relocation company for over a year, and they were desperate to dump it," Payne says. While you may not be able to come up with $50,000 in two years, you can adopt the same "save at all cost" mindset that Payne used to build your own savings. Isn't a new home worth it?

### The Special Account That Triples Your Savings: Guaranteed

I've given you lots of ideas about *how* to save your money. Now I want to tell you *where* to put those hard-earned dollars. This advice is geared specifically to those of you who don't earn a lot of money. What would you say if I told you there's a special account where you can stash away thousands of dollars and triple your savings? Even more amazing, this little-known account lets you build up your savings risk free, relatively quickly, and with a guaranteed return on your money. Do you doubt that such a savings account exists? Well, it's no fairy tale. I'm talking about Individual Development Accounts, also known as IDAs. If you open an Individual Development Account, you can turbo-charge your savings because IDAs are designed to help low and moderate income people reach their financial goals by encouraging them to save, and then matching the contributions that you sock away. Contributions come from government funding, non-profits, community-based organizations, churches, businesses, and private entities. These groups offer a "hand up," not a "handout," because they help people who help themselves.

Most IDAs provide you with a $2 or $3 contribution for every $1 you save. Some IDAs feature $5 to $1 and even $8 to $1 matching grants. This is free money that you earn just from being a disciplined saver! The extra, matching funds you get do not have to be repaid. You usually do have to take a brief money-management course, which emphasizes how to save. You also typically have to agree to save a minimum amount of money (an amount of your choosing) at regular intervals, and to leave your savings in the account for a set period of time (usually one year). You withdraw the money – and receive your matching funds, no strings attached – once you've reached your designated goal, which is most often savings for a home. Some IDAs let you save money for other objectives too, like paying for your kid's college education or starting a business. If you can triple your money in such an easy fashion, isn't it worth it? IDAs are presently available in nearly 500 communities across America.

Scott Guthrie is an administrative vice president at M&T Bank Corporation, a regional bank that has been in business for 151 years and services customers in New York, New Jersey, Delaware, Pennsylvania, Maryland, Virginia, West Virginia, and Washington D.C. In addition to offering "Get Started," a special first-time homeowners' mortgage program for which you only need to come up with a 3% down payment – 1% on your own and the rest from other sources – M&T has an Individual Development Account called First Home Club. It features home-buying counseling and a $3 to $1 match. Whatever money you put into a savings account, the bank will match your contribution up to $5,000. "There's a lot of assistance out there for first-time buyers," says Guthrie, who is based in western New York.

To learn more and to find out where you can open an IDA account in your area, visit this website of the Corporation for Enterprise Development at http://www.idanetwork.org. You can also write or call CED. Here is their contact information:

> Corporation for Enterprise Development
> 777 N. Capitol St., NE, Suite 800
> Washington, DC 20002
> 202-408-9788

## Alternatives When You Have Little or No Money

Some of you might cut your budget to the bone, forego every possible luxury, and still find that you're living paycheck to paycheck. Fortunately, even when you have little or no money from your direct savings available, there are other alternatives for you to come up with the cash necessary for a home down payment and closing costs. You can tap into funds you might have already accumulated in your retirement savings account, obtain cash gifts from family members or friends, take money out of an insurance policy, and even possibly get financial assistance from your employer. Let's look more closely at these options, so you can evaluate the pros and cons of each and decide if any of these alternatives are viable for you.

## Using Your Retirement Savings

If you have contributed money to an employer-sponsored savings program, such as a 401(k) or a 403(b), you can use funds from that account to help you buy a house. According to IRS regulations, money in your 401(k) is required to stay there until retirement. Otherwise, taking the money out means you'll face ordinary income taxes as well as a 10% penalty on any withdrawals. But the IRS does allow so-called "hardship withdrawals," and one acceptable hardship is making a down payment to buy a primary residence.

People often ask me whether they should take money out of their retirement plans to pay off credit card debt. In the majority of cases, I tell them not to touch that retirement money because it winds up costing them in more ways than they would have thought. In addition to the taxes and penalties, there's the "opportunity cost" associated with losing earnings on the money that is withdrawn. When you put away money for your Golden Years, don't touch it unless it's absolutely necessary. Plus, a lot of people use lump sums from home equity loans and retirement accounts to pay off credit card debt, then wind up running up those credit card bills again because they haven't learned how to handle their financial affairs. Therefore, it's better to pay off credit card debt organically, though good old fashioned hard work, saving, budgeting, and proper money management than making a 401(k) withdrawal.

Making a 401(k) or 403(b) withdrawal to buy a home is a more reasonable proposition. I don't recommend it as a first course of action, because you still are going to give up any potential interest that the money would have earned had you left it in your retirement account. But if you've already done everything you can to save money and you're still short of the amount you need for a down payment, closing costs, and your "Home Expense Fund," then it's fine to tap your 401(k) or 403(b) assets. One bonus is that, since you're using the money for a house, you'll be purchasing an asset that has the potential to appreciate over time, offsetting some or all of the lost earnings from your retirement fund.

A better way to access your retirement funds is by "borrowing" from them rather than making a withdrawal. Most employers allow you to borrow money from your 401(k). You then repay yourself, including interest, through automatic deductions from your paycheck. You are not taxed on the money you borrow, nor do you have IRS penalties for borrowing money in this fashion. Just be careful with money borrowed from an employer-sponsored retirement plan such as a 401(k) or 403(b). If you quit or lose your job, you must repay all the money you borrowed in a short period of time, usually about 60 days, or else the IRS will treat it as a withdrawal and will tax and penalize you on the funds you tapped.

## Cash Gifts From Family or Friends

If you're thinking about borrowing money from family members or friends, this can be a thorny situation. Some of you might have well-heeled relatives who would be all too happy to help you out and give you money towards the down payment of a new home. Alternately, maybe some of you have family members who have the money, but they're tight with it so you're reluctant to ask. Well, first of all, can you really blame them? They probably didn't get to be financially comfortable by doling out money to every person who asked.

You have to consider your own track record before you approach other people to ask for money. Have you borrowed money in the past, and not repaid it? Have you been irresponsible in managing your finances – and practically the whole world knows it? If so, realize that your request for a donation – even for a worthy cause like buying a home – might be rejected, or at the very least seriously questioned. By the way, I've used the words "donation" and "give" to describe what you'll have to ask for, because lenders that allow you to use money from others as a down payment require that the funds be in the form of a gift – not a loan. In other words, this is money you will not have to pay back. The bank may even ask you and your benevolent family member to write a letter or sign documentation to that effect, stating the money going from their pocket into yours is a gift, not a loan.

In most instances, I urge people to avoid going to family and friends for money. I know it feels like I'm telling you to "tough it out." In many ways that's true, because I'd prefer that you learned to handle your financial responsibilities on your own. That's part of being an adult. Additionally, getting a gift (or even a loan) can sometimes create a strain on a relationship. When you take money from someone, even if you pay it back, it can be awkward to deal with that situation. Surely you don't want to put someone you know, trust, or love in an uncomfortable position, financially or emotionally.

The exception to this advice is to those of you who actually have been very responsible with your money, are hard-working and so forth, and have a good reputation with your family or friends. If a relative of yours has the money (and only that person knows if they "have it like that," so don't assume that they do based on outward appearances) and wants to help you, he or she will say, "Yes." If the relative declines your request it doesn't mean that the person does not love you or support your dream of homeownership, so don't get mad and hold a grudge. Just keep it moving, and recognize that getting into your new home will be that much sweeter when you accomplish this major goal on your own.

**The Insurance Solution**

One source of cash you might not have thought about is money from a life insurance policy you own. You can't get money from a term insurance policy, but some of you have whole-life policies, which build up cash value over time. If you do have such a policy and you've been paying the premiums on it, you could have a significant source of funds to utilize for a down payment on your home. You can usually borrow up to 50% of the cash value of any whole life insurance policy in your name. If you think you have an insurance policy, but you're not sure because someone else opened it, call that person and ask them about it. In many families, parents and grandparents take out insurance policies for their children and grandchildren, and many have paid the premiums faithfully year after year. A lot of these are term policies, which won't offer you any cash value. However, if you think there's an insurance policy in your name courtesy of a well-intentioned relative, find out whether it's a whole-life policy.

**How Your Employer Can Help**

Lastly, think about whether your employer can come to the rescue. Many companies and organizations offer all kinds of benefits and perks to their workers. It's a way for businesses to recruit and retain the best employees. In addition to your standard employee benefits, like paid vacations and holidays, lots of firms offer more generous perks like bonuses, stock options, and other cash incentives. Ask whether you qualify for such a cash payment and find out what you have to do to receive it. Additionally, inquire with your boss or at the human resources department about whether your company offers down payment assistance for the purchase of a new home, as do 12% of companies nationwide. You might be pleasantly surprised to find out that such a program exists at your workplace – and all this time you never even knew about it.

## Why Big Business Wants You to be a Homeowner

Also advise your boss about how the business community is increasingly leading the charge for "workforce housing," which refers to single-family homes, townhouses, condominiums, and even apartments that are affordable and convenient for area workers. Why is big business gung ho about this topic? There is a growing recognition among cities, corporations, and other organizations that employees must have affordable housing with good access to their place of work, or else those employees will relocate to other areas. According to research from the Rutgers University American Affordable Housing Institute, employer-assisted housing increases productivity by slashing commuting time, and saves money on recruitment and retention, too. Chicago was a pioneer in promoting "workforce housing" initiatives with employers. Now, throughout the state of Illinois, about 65 large employers offer down payment assistance to their workers. In fact, in 2001, the Illinois state legislature passed a bill giving tax credits to employers that offer down payment assistance, as well as matching funds directly to qualified employees. The state's success led other legislators in Maryland, Nevada and Minnesota to also issue housing tax credits for employer-assisted housing programs.

## New Federal Housing Tax Breaks Might be on the Way

Happily, there is even national interest in this effort. New York's Democratic Senator and Presidential contender Hillary Clinton has introduced federal legislation called the "Housing America's Workforce Act" to Congress. The bill would provide tax incentives to employers that offered their workers either $10,000 or up to 6% of the purchase price of a home, whichever is less. That money would also not be taxable to employees. Under current law you must report any housing assistance you receive from your employer as taxable income. The Housing America's Workforce Act was reintroduced in both chambers of Congress in 2007 and appears to have broad support. As of this writing, the legislation was still pending. But rest assured, if the federal government starts giving tax breaks to companies that offer down payment assistance – and I predict that such legislation will pass in Congress – it won't be long before this nation witnesses a huge explosion in the number of employers helping their workers become homeowners and live the American dream.

# 4

## Take Advantage of First-Time Homebuyer Programs

Experts have long recognized that the biggest obstacle to homeownership in America is that many people lack the savings necessary to cover a down payment and closing costs. Fortunately, many non-profit groups, mortgage lenders, government agencies, and businesses are willing to provide you with the money you need to get a home. Each of these entities has a vested interest in seeing you become a homeowner. After all, when you buy a home, you stake down roots in a community, and you're more likely to care for that neighborhood because you now have a personal interest in seeing it thrive. Homeowners also pay property taxes, supporting the building and development of local schools, highways, hospitals, and other needed community services. In addition to invigorating communities and providing a tax base, homeowners patronize neighborhood stores, work at local businesses, volunteer in places of worship, and perform other civic duties.

### Aid is Available to Overcome the Down Payment Dilemma

For all these reasons, over the past decade there has been a surge in first-time homebuyer initiatives designed to give people like you a helping hand in overcoming the down payment dilemma. In fact, in every state in America there are a broad range of first-time homebuyer assistance programs, including:

## AID FOR FIRST-TIME HOME BUYERS

| |
|---|
| Free grants and cash gifts for down payments – with funds ranging from $500 to as much as $40,000 |
| Money for closing costs, prepaid escrows, and other mortgage expenses |
| Grants or loans to fix up homes in need of repair |
| 100% financing programs, so that you pay zero down on a home |
| Home loans that feature 0% interest, low interest rates, or below-market interest rates |
| Mortgages with loan forgiveness benefits or no payments for a set period of time |
| Federal and state housing tax credits |
| Homebuyer workshops to teach you about the rights and responsibilities of being a homeowner |
| Mortgage education classes that explain the mortgage process |
| Budgeting, credit counseling, money-management, and overall financial planning services |

No matter where you reside or where you're looking to settle down, if you're a first-time homebuyer, there's a program that can help you purchase a house. Virtually every type of residence is eligible under these programs, including single-family homes, condominiums, townhouses, modular homes, and manufactured housing. Many assistance programs have income limitations, particularly those that provide city, state, or federal funding, but other programs have no income criteria. Also, certain housing assistance plans impose caps on the purchase price of the property you can buy. Despite these restrictions, you'll find that taking advantage of a first-time homebuyers' program is one of the smartest things you can do. It will allow you to get into a home sooner, save money in the process, and simultaneously accrue wealth.

Even if you've already been successful at saving on your own, I highly recommend that you utilize a first-time homebuyer program for three reasons. First, if you can get down payment assistance, and you combine that money with your own savings, you'll walk into your new home with a greater piece of equity. Second, using funds from a first-time homeowners' initiative can allow you to keep some of your own savings in the bank as cash reserves – rather than depleting all of your money for the down payment and closing costs. Finally, many first-time homebuyer programs have a mandatory homeownership counseling component. The knowledge and skills you'll gain from this counseling will make you better-educated and more prepared for homeownership as you make the transition from renter to owner.

### How Move-Up and Repeat Buyers Can Benefit Too

One important feature about many "first-time" homebuyer programs is that most of them actually do not require you to have never owned a home. Almost all programs consider you a first-time homeowner as long as you have not owned a home in the past two or three years. Check the eligibility requirements for any program of interest to you. This eligibility clause could be important for those of you who owned a home in the past, but enough time has lapsed since you were a homeowner that you can now qualify for aid. Additionally, there are many homeownership programs across the country open to all buyers, including those trading up (or down) to a different home. Again, the reason for this is that it's a well-known fact that high rates of homeownership provide economic benefits to neighborhoods as well as tangible social benefits – ranging from fewer high school dropouts and less teenage pregnancy, to decreased crime and greater voter participation in the political process.

With this is mind, let's start with an overview of the eight sources of aid you can turn to for financial and educational assistance in buying a home of your own. The eight sources include:

- Federal and/or National Programs
- State Aid
- County Initiatives
- Local/Municipal or City Efforts
- Non-Profit and Community-Based Organizations

- Lender-Specific Programs
- Programs Based on Your Job or Occupation
- Employer Assisted Housing Initiatives

It's common for there to be overlap between programs. For instance, a state might offer aid to certain workers, such as teachers, fire fighters, or police officers or a community program might work closely with designated lenders or specific types of national mortgage loan programs. As you read about the staggering array of financial assistance initiatives available nationwide, keep in mind an important trend that is emerging in many communities. Lenders are starting to permit borrowers to layer two, three, or more first-time buyer programs. This means you get the benefit of multiple sources of aid – instead of just one – which allows you to offset higher home prices, and enter a new home in a stronger financial position. Let's look more closely, therefore, at the range of possibilities.

### Federal/National Programs You Should Know

A handful of federal home loan programs, as well as national mortgage programs offered by government-sponsored entities such as Fannie Mae and Freddie Mac, hold particular appeal for many first-time homebuyers. In this section, I'll tell you about some of the most popular homeownership initiatives currently available from these federal and quasi-government sources, and explain the pros and cons of each.

### ■ FHA Loan Programs

With the help of the Federal Housing Administration (FHA), you can buy a home with just a 3% down payment. The FHA itself doesn't lend you money. Instead, it "guarantees" your mortgage. This means that the FHA promises your lender – either a bank, credit union, mortgage banking company, or another institution – that if you default on the loan for any reason, the FHA will step in, pay off the mortgage, and take over the house. With FHA backing a loan, lenders are willing to make mortgages available to borrowers with modest down payments.

To qualify for an FHA loan, you need to have a steady income, one that is sufficient to support your mortgage loan. In fact, because the FHA has no maximum income limits, FHA loans are available to practically all working homebuyers. The house you select must be up to code and "suitably located as to site and neighborhood." Of course you must come up with the 3% down payment and your closing costs. On this last point, the FHA is quite lenient. Your down payment doesn't have to come out of your own pocket. You can receive gift funds from family members, housing grants from city housing programs, or down payment assistance from non-profits and other entities. Also, you can roll your closing costs into your mortgage, so you pay those expenses over time, rather than all upfront. Another advantage of FHA-backed loans is that they frequently carry lower interest rates than conventional, or non-governmental, mortgages.

Shane Backer is a New York real estate broker with Robbins & Lloyd Mortgage in Manhattan. In addition to doing business in the five boroughs of New York City, Backer has clients in New Jersey, Connecticut, and Florida. He says one huge plus concerning FHA loans is that you can get a mortgage even if you have poor credit.

"It's not a credit score program. It's based on DTI," says Backer, whose website is http://www.ezmortgage.com. The debt-to-income ratios that FHA allows are 31/43, meaning your front-end ratio, your entire housing payment, can't be more than 31% of your gross monthly income. Also, all of your other long-term debts, combined with your mortgage payment, can not exceed 43% of your gross monthly pay. "The good thing about this program is that you can literally get 100% financing with a 550 credit score," Backer adds because "the 3% down payment can come from a gift – and it doesn't have to be seasoned," meaning the money doesn't have to be sitting in a bank someplace like conventional loans require.

However, FHA loans have several drawbacks. One is the amount of paperwork required for these loans. Real estate agents, mortgage brokers, and bankers often complain that the mountain of documents required make FHA-backed loans far more complicated than other loan options. Additionally, experts say FHA loans are stricter when it comes to home appraisals. So, in some instances, you might agree to pay a seller's asking price, and then have an FHA appraiser say that the house isn't worth that price, throwing a monkey wrench in the whole deal. Another downside is that FHA mortgages require you to pay a mortgage insurance premium (MIP). As of this writing, the insurance totals 2% of the loan amount. You pay an upfront premium of 1.50% of the loan amount at the closing (which can be added to your mortgage). There is another monthly MIP amount of .50% added to the principal, interest, taxes, and insurance you pay. As a first-time buyer, however, you can cut your FHA mortgage insurance premium by .50% just by taking a housing counseling class.

Paying for mortgage insurance on FHA loans is no different than buyers with less than 20% down payments paying for PMI, or private mortgage insurance, on conventional, non-governmental loans. What is different, however, is the cost between the two forms of insurance. When you pay 10% down on conventional mortgages, private mortgage insurance often costs just .50% of the loan amount, and then can fall to as little as .30% of the mortgage during subsequent renewal years. One final disadvantage of FHA-backed mortgages is that they have loan limits. Until early 2008, those limits were set at $362,790. Therefore, people shopping for homes in more expensive markets typically did not obtain FHA loans. However, The Economic Stimulus Act of 2008 increased the loan limits for FHA-insured loans to a maximum of $729,750, for homes in high-cost areas. As of this writing, these new FHA loan limits were due to expire Dec. 31, 2008, although Congress is considering legislation to make the loan limits permanent as part of the FHA Modernization bill.

For more information about FHA loans, call the FHA in Washington D.C. at (202) 755-6600 or contact a local FHA office. They're listed in your phone directory under U.S. Government, Housing and Urban Development, which oversees the FHA. Also, the website for FHA is: http://www.fha.gov. You can also simply ask your lender if they process FHA loans.

### ■ VA Loans

The Department of Veterans Administration (VA) loan system is the other big federal home loan program in the United States. VA loans operate similar to FHA loans in that the VA does not make home loans; it protects private lenders against loss. If you are a veteran, reservist, an active-duty service member, or surviving spouse of a veteran and you haven't remarried, you can purchase a home with no down payment courtesy of the VA. Unlike other mortgage programs for which you must have mortgage insurance when you put down less than 20%, VA loans require no mortgage insurance. In addition, the VA offers other benefits, such as leniency for VA homeowners when they can't pay their mortgages. To get a VA-backed loan, you must have "acceptable" credit – not great credit, but not lousy credit either. Your debt-to-income ratio must also generally meet the VA's requirements. VA loans permit the seller to pay your closing costs, up to 6% of the purchase price of the home, which is good if you're short on cash. Additionally, VA loans boast competitive interest rates and no prepayment penalties if you pay the loans off early.

Despite these bonuses, VA loans do have drawbacks. Experts say VA loans can be more complex and take longer to close than traditional loans because of all the government paperwork. The loan limits on VA loans generally top out at $417,000, making these loans less practical in pricey communities. Finally, you must pay a "funding fee" of 2.2% of the mortgage amount to obtain a VA-insured loan (2.4% if you are a reservist). For more information, visit the VA's website at: http://www.homeloans.va.gov.

### ■ Rural Development Housing & Community Facilities Program (HCFP)

Special homeownership programs aren't just for those who want to live in condos in the city or big homes in the suburbs. You can also get financing – and great deals at that – if you live in a rural community or would like to move to one. That's where the Rural Development HCFP comes in handy, according to Daniel Bedford, a mortgage broker and owner of DB Commercial (http://www.dbedfordloans.com) in Richmond, Virginia. Bedford has been in the real estate business for 12 years and also works for the Rural Development agency, which is an arm of the U.S. Department of Agriculture.

Bedford touts the program's three-day approval process. "It's one of the few programs that are quick in the federal government," he says with a chuckle. All kidding aside, Bedford and others swear by the Rural Development program as a way to get a mortgage when other lenders won't touch a home in a rural area.

"Rural areas are hard to get financed," Bedford says "because it's hard to find comps (comparable sales) or to find people to do the work," that might be required to fix up a property.

That's why if you have a hankering to live somewhere rural (and no – it doesn't have to be on a farm), make sure you bone up on the Rural Development program, which can help you get into a home by providing you with a subsidy or by guaranteeing a no-down payment loan, commonly called a Section 502 loan. Learn more information, and the program's requirements, at: http://www.rurdev.usda.gov.

### ■ Fannie Mae's My Community Program

Fannie Mae is a government-sponsored entity created in 1938 to help make homes more affordable. Fannie Mae doesn't lend you money. Instead, it invests in mortgages that lenders originate, and then Fannie Mae sells those loans to investors on Wall Street. With Fannie Mae's My Community Program, it is easier than ever for millions of people to get into a home because of the more flexible requirements on the cash and credit front. For starters, the program offers 100% financing, so you don't have to make a down payment at all when purchasing a home. Additionally, if you lack the necessary funds to pay your closing costs, you can use gift funds from relatives, grants from non-profits or municipalities, or even employer-provided housing assistance. Additionally, Fannie Mae's My Community program is particularly helpful for people with thin credit histories or no "traditional" credit, meaning you've never had a credit card, car loan, or the like. If you can show that you're still creditworthy, based on paying rent on time and other bills, like your utilities, you will likely qualify for this loan program. Flexible income criteria add yet another dimension to My Community mortgages, a bonus for people who receive public assistance, get income from boarders, or derive other sources of income aside from standard wages. All major lenders, along with thousands of credit unions, banks of all sizes, and financial institutions, work with Fannie Mae. Virtually any lender you choose will have confidence issuing you a mortgage if you qualify for a home loan under Fannie Mae's guidelines. After you obtain a loan, in all likelihood, your lender will sell your loan to Fannie Mae.

As of 2008, the limits for single-family mortgages purchased by Fannie Mae were $417,000 for one-unit properties for most of the U.S. Limits for two-family loans were $533,850, three-family loans $645,300, and four-family loans $801,950. The maximum loan amounts for one-to-four-family mortgages in Alaska, Hawaii, Guam, and the U.S. Virgin Islands are 50% higher than the limits for the rest of the country. In 2008, Congress also temporarily increased Fannie Mae's loan limits to $729,750 in high-cost areas. These limits will expire Dec. 31, 2008 unless Congress makes the limits permanent. For more information about the My Community program, visit the agency's website at: http://www.fanniemae.com or call 800-7-FANNIE (800-732-6643).

Like Fannie Mae, Freddie Mac is a government-sponsored agency that also buys mortgage loans from lenders. In fact, since 1970 Freddie Mac has financed more than 50 million home loans. Today, one out of every six home loans in America runs through Freddie Mac. The company's Home Possible program, specially designed for first-time buyers, allows you to purchase a home with little or no money down. The 100% financing option holds particular appeal for anyone with decent credit, but who lacks the savings necessary for a down payment. Additionally, Home Possible mortgages allow someone else to pay your closing costs. Closing costs can be paid by a gift from a relative, a second lien, a grant from a local housing finance agency, nonprofit or employer, or even a contribution from the seller up to 3% of the loan amount. Lastly, Home Possible loans are available for up to 40 years, instead of just the standard 30 years. For more info on these loans, which are available in every state in the country, visit: http://www.freddiemac.com/homepossible.

## State Initiatives to Help Renters Become Owners

When housing prices are affordable, more people will buy their own homes. The opposite principle also holds true: the more expensive houses are, the less likely it is that renters will become homeowners. That's why states with high-cost housing, such as California and New York, have the lowest rates of homeownership in the nation. In California, only 58.4% of people are homeowners, compared with the national homeownership rate of 69%. Also, in the Golden State, 19.4% of residents spend 50% or more of their income on housing. Meanwhile, New York has the lowest homeownership rate in the country, at just 52.8%. Residents of New York also face a steep housing burden, with 19.3% of people in the Empire State spending 50% or more of their income on housing.

State officials everywhere are aware of the need for affordable housing. As a result, you can find state-sponsored housing programs not just on the coasts, but all across the country. Most of these first-time homebuyer programs actually serve two purposes: transitioning more renters into property owners, and also promoting the worthwhile goal of affordable home-ownership.

One such program comes from the State of New York Mortgage Association. If you are a first-time homebuyer getting a home in a targeted area, you can obtain a mortgage at an interest rate as low as 4.625% via the state's "Achieving the Dream Program." With this program, you also receive a minimum of $5,000 or 5% of your mortgage amount, whichever is higher, in order to pay your down payment and closings costs.

When you get state grants designed for first-time home buyers, you normally must meet income guidelines that vary based upon the median household income in your area. Some forms of government aid – from states, counties, and cities – are outright grants that you never have to repay. But most of them are actually loans that are known as "silent seconds." A "silent second" is a no-interest loan, and you make no monthly payments on the loan either. Many times, the loan is completely forgiven, as long as you live in the home for a set period of time (often five to 10 years). With other programs that do require you to repay a "silent second," you typically are not required to repay the mortgage loan until you sell the house.

Receiving government aid often boils down to three steps. First, you must prove that you are eligible, based on your earnings and the number of people in your household. Second, you must get approved for a mortgage with a lender that allows you to use down payment assistance as part of your loan qualifications. Third, you must meet the definition of a first-time homebuyer: someone who hasn't owned a home within the past three years. If you meet these three general criteria, you're practically guaranteed to receive available government funding to buy a home.

Realize, however, that you might not qualify to receive assistance from your state or local government if any of the following circumstances apply to you.

- Your income is too high compared with others in your area
- You owned a home within the past three years
- You had a bankruptcy discharged less than 24 months ago
- You have defaulted on a government or student loan
- You have outstanding tax liens
- You have past due child support payments
- You previously had a house that went into foreclosure

If none of these situations apply to you, you have an extremely high probability of getting state aid. If you do fall into one of these categories, your best bet is to first clear up the problem area. Alternatively, you can pursue other down payment assistance programs that won't disqualify you based on these conditions.

Here is a sample of the type of state aid available to first-time homebuyers available throughout the country:

- **In Texas**, you can get grant funds of up to 5% of your mortgage amount, along with two type of loans with interest rates that are typically 1% below current market rates, via the Texas First Time Homebuyers Program. For more information, call the Texas Department of Housing and Community Affairs at 512-475-3800 or toll-free at 800-525-0657 or visit: http://www.tdhca.state.ts.us.

- **In Illinois**, first-time homebuyers taking part in the Assets Illinois Homeownership Project can receive a dollar for dollar match up to $2,000 to help them save for the purchase of a first home. Funding for these matching contributions in these Individual Development Accounts is provided by the Illinois Department of Human Services. Participants also receive free homeownership counseling and advice on how to avoid predatory lending. For more information, call 312-793-3819 or visit: http://www.dhs.state.illinois.us/assets.

- **In South Carolina**, the Single Parent Program is open not just to first-time homebuyers, but to anyone renting, as long as the person has a child under the age of 18 and the homebuyer is divorced, has been separated for six months, or was never married. The program offers a forgivable loan up to $5,000, or down payment assistance of up to $4,000. For more information, call 803-896-9508 or visit: http://www.schousing.com.

- **In California**, the High Cost Area Home Purchase Assistance Program (HiCAP) offers up to $7,500 in down payment assistance in the form of a deferred-payment second loan. For more information, call 877-922-5432 or visit: http://www.calhfa.ca.gov.

- **In Georgia**, the Dream Homeownership Program offers 100% financing via low interest rates with a 30 or 35 year mortgage, and a second loan ranging from $5,000 to $20,000 that can be used for a down payment and closing costs. The down payment assistance loan has no interest, no monthly payments, and no payment is due until the house is sold, refinanced, or no longer used as the buyer's primary residence. For more information, call 877-359-4663 or visit: http://www.dca.state.ga.us.

- **In Pennsylvania**, the HOMEstead Down payment and Closing Cost Assistance Loan features up to $20,000 in down payment and closing cost assistance in the form of a no-interest second loan. Funds up to $14,999 are forgiven at 20% per year over five years. Funds between $15,000 and $20,000 are forgiven at 10% per year over a decade. For more information, call 800-822-1174 or visit: http://www.phfa.org.

- **In Nevada**, you can get up to $10,000 in down payment and closing cost assistance, and a below-market interest rate on 30 and 40 year loans with the Nevada Housing Division First Time Homebuyer Program. For more information, call 702-486-7220 or visit: http://www.nvhousing.state.nv.us.

As you can see, a broad range of programs exist for all potential homebuyers. So where can you find these state programs? Start by turning to State Housing Financing Agencies (HFAs). These are state-chartered authorities established to help meet the affordable housing needs of the residents of their states. Although they vary from state to state, most HFAs are independent entities that operate under the direction of a board of directors appointed by each state's governor. Their purpose is to help homeowners like you, so they can often point you in the direction of incredible housing and development programs you never dreamed existed. There is a National Council of State Housing Agencies (NCSHA) active in Washington D.C. to keep the issue of affordable housing high on the government's list of national priorities. Housing Finance Agencies and the NCSHA (http://www.ncsha.org) can help you tap into three federally authorized programs: Mortgage Revenue Bonds, Mortgage Credit Certificates, and the HOME Program.

### ■ Mortgage Revenue Bonds

State and local housing agencies also offer loans to first-time buyers via mortgage revenue bond programs. Mortgages funded with these instruments often feature low down payment options and have interest rates as much as 1.5% to 2% below conventional 30 year fixed rates.

### ■ Mortgage Credit Certificates

The Mortgage Credit Certificate (MCC) Program is another perk available through states to qualified first-time homebuyers. This benefit is in the form of a federal income tax credit of between 10% and 20% of the annual interest you pay on your mortgage.

### ■ Home Investment Partnership Program (HOME)

Available from the U.S. Department of Housing and Urban Development, the HOME program is the largest federal block grant available to state and local governments. The HOME program allocates roughly $2 billion to local governments each year in an effort to create affordable housing for low-income households. One component of the HOME initiative is the American Dream Down Payment Initiative (ADDI).

Through ADDI, you can receive down payment assistance, money for closing costs, and even funds to fix up a home you are buying. Cash is offered in the form of a loan equal to 6% of the purchase price or $10,000, whichever is greater. The loan carries a 0% interest rate and a maximum loan term of 10 years. For each year you live in the house, 10% of the loan amount will be slashed. If you stay in the home 10 years, the entire amount will be forgiven. If you sell your home before 10 years – and most first-time buyers do sell their homes after an average of four or five years – the remaining amount of the loan must be repaid. This program is open to all first-time buyers who haven't owned a home within the past three years. The money provided via ADDI can be used to purchase a one-to-four family house, condo, cooperative unit, or manufactured housing. To qualify, your income must not exceed 80% of your area's median income. Get more information about this initiative through your state housing finance agency, or by visiting HUD's website at: http://www.hud.gov. Also, if you find out about a program like this one that receives federal money, but the money hasn't come through yet to your state, put your name on the list to be notified about a change in status ASAP. That way you'll be ahead of many other people who are also seeking housing grants or forgivable loans.

■ **Housing Redevelopment Offices**

In addition to state housing finance agencies, contact the Housing and Redevelopment Office in your state, county, or city. Members of the National Association of Housing and Redevelopment Officials (NAHRO) (http://www.nahro.org) champion the cause of adequate and affordable housing for all Americans – especially those with low and moderate incomes.

Be mindful that state housing agencies and redevelopment offices across the country can use lots of different names. One might be called a "Housing Finance Agency," as is the case with the Vermont Housing Finance Agency, while another one is dubbed a "Housing Development Authority," as is true of the Virginia Housing Development Authority. Any agency with the name "Home" "Housing," "Community Development," "Mortgage Finance" – or similar words – is a good place to inquire about homebuyer assistance programs.

The importance of state programs can't be emphasized enough. I think so highly of these initiatives, that I've provided you with housing and development agencies for every single state in the country. Their names and websites are provided in Appendix B of this book. A few states have multiple listings.

## County Programs for First-Time Homebuyers

Just as there are a myriad of state programs designed to help first-time homeowners, so, too, are there scores of county housing programs that can offer money and other resources to transition you into homeownership.

In Florida, you might be surprised by what's available in Martin County. Via the State Housing Initiative Partnership, also known as SHIP, Martin County provides down payment and closing cost assistance of up to $50,000 to eligible first time homebuyers. The program also offers up to $25,000 to eligible existing homeowners for home repairs. For more information on the SHIP Program, contact the Martin County Community Development staff via the Martin County web site: http://.www.martin.fl.us.

Needless to say, great offers can be found across more than a thousand counties nationwide. Here's a sampling:

- **In Arlington County, Virginia**, the Live Near Your Work Program provides a forgivable loan of up to $5,400 for all homebuyers, not just first-timers, if you or a member of your family works at least 30 hours a week for Arlington County or the Arlington School Board. This program has no income requirements. The money can be made available to you before, at, or after your home closing. If you remain employed with the county or school board for three years, and the property remains owner occupied, your loan becomes a grant. For more information, call the Housing Information Center at 703-228-3765 or visit: http://www.arlington.va.us.

- **In Johnson County, Kansas,** you can obtain a grant of up to 6% of the purchase price of a home, up to $10,000 if you are a low to moderate income resident of the county or you've worked there for at least two years. For more information, call the Johnson County Housing Authority at 913-715-6616 or visit: http://www.jocogov.org.

■ **In Maricopa County, Arizona**, under the Home in 5 Program, you can get a grant of 5% of your loan amount, up to $10,000, for down payment or closing costs. This program is available to first-time buyers and anyone purchasing a home in designated areas. For more information, contact the Industrial Development Authorities of the County of Phoenix and Maricopa County at 602-262-6602 or visit: http://www.phoenix.gov/housing.

You'll have to do a bit of homework to track down county-initiated or county-sponsored homeownership programs that can help you as prepare to go from renting to owning. To make your job easier, though, here are two organizations you can contact to locate county housing initiatives in your area:

■ **The National Association of Counties**; visit their website at: http://www.naco.org. Click on "About Counties" then click "Find Counties" to locate a county of interest.

■ **The National Association for County Community and Economic Development**; visit their website at: http://www.nacced.org and click on "County Websites" to find links to certain member counties, as well as cities and other development agencies near you.

## Tapping Into Local and City Housing Resources

Lots of people who work in New York City commute from neighboring New Jersey. Many live in Jersey City, which is right across the Hudson River from Manhattan. It's a fast-developing area that offers speedy access to the Big Apple, great views along the waterfront, and a robust business environment. Yet, lots of people rent in Jersey City; 72% versus a 34% rental rate throughout the entire state of New Jersey. I'll bet relatively few potential homeowners – from there or other parts of the Garden State – know about a great Jersey City program designed to turn renters into owners. It's called the Golden Neighborhoods Homeownership Program, and it grants first-time homebuyers (those who haven't owned a home in the past three years), with up to $40,000 for down payment assistance and closing costs. This program is administered by the Division of Community Development. Applications are accepted on a first-come, first-served basis.

So if you've ever dreamed of living near the Big City – with the "Big City" in this instance being Manhattan – Jersey City is a great option. For more information about the Golden Neighborhoods program and to find out about other eligibility requirements, call the Division of Community Development at 201-547-5916 or visit: http://www.cityofjerseycity.com. This program is a little tricky to find online, so here's what you do: Click on the "City Government" tab, then click on "Department of Housing Economic Development & Commerce." Go to the link for "Community Development" and scroll to the bottom of the page where you'll find another hyperlink that says "assistance to first-time low and moderate income homebuyers." It's there where you'll finally find information about the Golden Neighborhood Program. Good luck – and enjoy that New York skyline!

**The Latest From NY to the Windy City & Washington D.C.**

If the New York metro area isn't your cup of tea, perhaps Chicago sets your heart racing. I know I love Chicago with a passion: the Magnificent Mile district, the great restaurants, fun activities, the shopping, and interesting people to boot. Even though I currently endure some pretty rough winters residing on the East Coast, I don't think I'm up to living in Chicago and braving the city's notorious winter weather. Don't blame me: I was raised in Los Angeles, and still haven't quite acclimated to colder climates. But I digress. My point was that Chicago is a fabulous city, and I know lots of you would love to own property there. Fortunately, the City of Chicago represents perhaps one of the best examples in the nation of how municipalities are working hard to improve housing affordability and access to homeownership. Just take a review of the city's website (http://egov.city.cityofchicago.org) and you'll find a slew of grants, special mortgage programs, and other homeownership initiatives designed to assist a vast array of homebuyers and unique circumstances. Two quick highlights:

- In September 2007, the city launched an affordable homeownership program for artists. It involves purchasing and rehabilitating the former Strand Hotel and converting it into 36 live/work loft spaces for artists in the Woodlawn community on Chicago's South Side. Eligible buyers will qualify for $10,000 subsidies too. This is the kind of program that represents government at its best – recognizing the needs of *all* citizens and meeting those needs.

- Along with Chicago Public School teachers, Chicago police officers, firefighters, and paramedics are eligible to receive grants of up to $7,500 when they purchase a home in the city. And since 1996, the city of Chicago has provided roughly $2 million in grants to help nearly 500 public service officers become first-time homeowners citywide.

Outside of Chicago, other opportunities abound. Consider yourself lucky if you're in the market for a new home in or near the nation's capital. That's because first-time homebuyers benefit from tax abatement initiatives, low-interest loan programs, lots of government investment, and plenty of private development in the greater metropolitan Washington D.C. area, according to Jesse Kaye, a mortgage broker with Ken Taylor Real Estate (http://www.ktrealestate.com).

"There's a (government) mandate to create 30,000 affordable homes, which makes for an even stronger market," says Kaye, who also writes an informative daily blog (http://www.DevelopersAgent.com) about the mortgage market and development issues in Washington D.C.

No doubt you'll want to find out what's happening on the homeownership front in your own city. To locate your city's website, or that of another city where you are interested in buying a home, visit the National League of Cities at: http://

www.nlc.org. This is the oldest and largest group in America dedicated to promoting cities as viable places of opportunity, leadership, and governance. The NLC is an advocate before Congress for more than 1,600 cities, towns, and villages in the United States.

Whether you live in the Windy City, Washington D.C., or elsewhere, you can find local housing programs via the National League of Cities' website at http://www.nlc.org. Just click on "About Cities," then click "Link to City Websites." You'll be taken to a state-by-state listing of NLC member cities and their websites. By taking advantage of city funding, you'll make the home-buying process far less financially burdensome.

### ■ Community Development Block Grants

One of the most widespread sources of funds through your city, town, or village is Community Development Block Grants. In addition to your city itself, the most relevant organization for you to know about when it comes to these grants is the Community Development Block Grant Coalition. Its purpose is to stimulate and revitalize local neighborhoods – chiefly through boosting quality, affordable homeownership. Members of the CDBG Coalition include American Federation of State County Municipal Employees, Council of State Community Development Agencies, Enterprise, Habitat for Humanity International, Housing Assistance Council, International Economic Development Council, Local Initiatives Support Corporation, National Association for County Community and Economic Development, National Association of Counties, National Association of Development Organizations, National Association of Housing and Redevelopment Officials, National Association of Local Housing Finance Agencies, National Community Development Association, National Conference of Black Mayors, National Housing Conference, National League of Cities, National Low Income Housing Coalition, National NeighborWorks® Association, National Rural Housing Coalition, and the United States Conference of Mayors.

If you contact any of these entities to ask about first-time homebuyers programs, they'll point you in the right direction.

■ **0% Loans With No Payments for Five Years**

Here's another exciting example of what's happening at the city level in municipalities all across America. In San Diego, California the Centre City Development Corporation has created the Downtown First-Time Homebuyer Program to help people realize the dream of homeownership. The Program provides financing, in the form of a second trust deed loan, which allows moderate income first-time homebuyers to purchase a primary residence in the downtown area. Qualified buyers get an incredibly good deal. They can obtain a maximum $75,000, 30-year, zero-interest loan – and they have absolutely no payments at all for the first five years! This initiative focuses on downtown homes priced into the mid-$200,000s. Already, many first-time homebuyers have taken advantage of this program, including new owners at Western Pacific Housing's Union Square condo complex, and Citymark Development's Doma Lofts and Towns development.

If you happen to live in downtown San Diego (or would like to!) get an application for this program or obtain more info here via this contact:

Lucy Contreras, Assistant Planner
Centre City Development Corporation
225 Broadway, Suite 1100
San Diego, CA 92101
619-533-7132
email: contreras@ccdc.com

**Popular Non-Profit and Community-Based Programs**

As fabulous as many government-sponsored programs are to help renters become homeowners, some people say the down payment assistance programs are even better in the non-profit arena. Without a doubt, non-profits and community-based organizations have actively stepped up to the challenge of promoting affordable housing over the past 15 years or so. The activity in this sector within the past two or three years has been nothing short of explosive. As a result, you can find non-profits in every part of the country that will help you secure incredible amounts of assistance to purchase your dream home. Often tines, as much as $25,000 or more is available, completely free, as a grant to you. Let me first explain how these programs work. Then I'll give you highlights of what's being offered by some of the best-known non-profit agencies and other civic groups at the forefront of boosting homeownership.

In the early 1990s, federal housing laws were changed to allow nonprofit housing groups to give money to individuals and families who lacked the necessary savings to buy a home. The laws stipulated that funds could be used for down payments, closing costs or other upfront expenses to help low-to-moderate income people achieve the American dream of homeownership. In the wake of the new federal laws, non-profit groups have helped assist well over one million people in purchasing homes. Further, 85% of all buyers who receive down payment assistance are purchasing their very first home.

What most people don't understand is how it's possible for charities and non-profit organizations to supply all this money. The answer is simple: they're getting a lot of the funding from home sellers. Here's how it works.

When you find a home you'd like to buy, you can ask a seller to agree to "concessions" or price reductions, through which you negotiate with the home-owner and agree upon a sales price. In a buyer's market, it's common for sellers to agree to give buyers anywhere from 2% to 5% off the asking price as a concession in order to facilitate a speedier sale. Assume a couple offering their home for sale put it on the market for $200,000. After some negotiating back and forth, you reached a deal to buy it for $190,000 – along with a seller concession equal to 3% of the purchase price. The seller concession therefore would amount to $5,700. That money gets credited to you, and you can use it to pay for your closing costs at the settlement table when the deal is finalized. In this example, the seller winds up making $184,300, before paying real estate commissions and other expenses. This is an example of a traditional negotiated sale.

When a non-profit gets involved, however, the seller must agree to make a "donation" to the charity, which in turn the charity/non-profit funnels to you. The bigger the donation, the more money you have for a down payment and closing costs. Technically, most non-profits don't – or aren't supposed to – only use the money the seller agrees to donate as a way to give you a grant. Instead, the seller's money goes into the charity's coffers at or after closing. (The seller also must pay an "administrative" or "service" fee to the non-profit; it can be a flat fee, ranging from $500 to $1,000 or approximately 1% of the purchase price). The donation and administrative fee paid to the non-profit helps cover its operating expenses, and provides charitable funding that the agency will use to help the next homeowner. Through a myriad of other fund-raising activities, reputable non-profits will have additional monies available to make grants, not just funds collected from home sellers.

By now, some of you might be asking: why would a seller agree to all of this? The answer is: down payment assistance programs increase the pool of eligible buyers, translating into a faster sale for the seller – and sometimes a higher-priced sale too. As a result, these programs can be a win-win situation for all involved. Clearly, they're helpful to homebuyers, by letting them get into a home faster. However, these deals also benefit sellers – by helping them unload their homes faster, and often at the full asking price. Consider the example I explained before, with the couple asking $200,000 for their home. Instead of their waiting for the buyers to get approved for a mortgage, or going through the hassle of back and forth negotiations, they might be glad to have a buyer request that they make a donation to a charity as part of the home deal. Assume you made an offer of $200,000 – their full asking price – and included a provision that the purchase was contingent upon their donating 6% of the sales price ($12,000) to a charity or non-profit. Under this scenario, the seller would pocket $188,000 before paying their realtor's commission and other expenses. If they negotiated with another buyer, lowered their asking price, and made a concession as explained above, they'd wind up with just $184,300. So it can actually be a better deal financially for a seller to agree to your purchase offer, and make the charitable donation. That's why every month, more than 25,000 homebuyers purchase homes using non-profit down-payment assistance programs.

To finalize these deals you need four things:

- a real estate agent skilled at presenting home offers that contain requests for concessions and donations from sellers
- a seller who is willing to make a donation to charity
- your own ability to qualify for a mortgage
- a lender and a loan officer accustomed to issuing mortgages that feature down payment assistance programs from non-profit sources

Lenders who originate FHA loans are very familiar with non-profit down payment assistance programs. In fact, 40% of all loans insured by FHA included some level of down payment assistance. So if you use a charity as a way to secure cash and buy a home, make absolutely sure that you pick a lender accustomed to doing FHA loans or conventional loans that feature down payment help from charitable organizations. (Note: Only lenders approved by the FHA can process FHA loans. Find an FHA lender by using the FHA lender search engine, which is available online at: http://www.locator.fha.gov.)

Many lenders put a 6% limit on the amount of down payment assistance you can receive – regardless of whether the funds come from non-profits or any other source. You can often combine assistance, too. For example, you're allowed to get government aid as well as charitable assistance. The main difference between the two is that the amount of government aid you can receive is largely dependent upon your income. When you get money from a charity for a down payment and closing costs, the amount you can receive is mainly limited by the size of the donation the seller is willing to make. Other limitations might be special rules imposed by the non-profit or maximum loan assistance amounts set by your lender.

To learn more about this process and for additional advice, visit: http://www.downpaymentsolutions/com. It's one of the single-best resources I've come across to help buyers, sellers, lenders, and others learn about down payment assistance programs via charities. As you investigate charitable organizations that offer help to first-time homebuyers, another group you should know about is called HAND, which stands for The Homeownership Alliance of Nonprofit Downpayment Providers. HAND was formed in 2002 to increase public awareness of the availability of down payment assistance from its members to low and moderate-income Americans.  Among HAND's members are:

- The AmeriDream Charity, Inc., of Gaithersburg, MD
- Consumer Debt Solutions, Inc., of Highland, NY
- Fair Housing Assistance of Orem, UT
- The Genesis Program of Austin, TX
- Home Buyers Assistance Foundation of Alpharetta, GA
- Homes for All, of North Fort Myers, FL, and
- Neighborhood Gold of Orem, UT

If you pursue down payment assistance from a non-profit group, I suggest you investigate at least one of these organizations because HAND has a set of best practices and a code of ethics by which its members must agree to abide. Also, each one operates at a national level so you can use their services no matter where you live. Now let's look at what these and other reputable non-profits are offering, so you can tap into this source of cash and more quickly purchase a home.

### ■ AmeriDream

The AmeriDream Down Payment Gift program provides you with down payment assistance of up to 10% of the purchase price of a home. You never have to repay the funds and the program helps you get a single family home priced up to $417,000, or two, three, and four-family units priced at a maximum of $533,000, $645,000, and $801,000, respectively. To qualify, you don't have to meet any income, asset, or geographic conditions. Aside from offering cash grants and recommending homeownership counseling, AmeriDream provides services and programs to help you throughout your experience as a homeowner. For instance, the agency's DreamKeeper Mortgage Payment Relief Program helps homeowners keep their homes by offering protection against involuntary unemployment and disability. Also, the Home Retention Program counsels people behind on their payments on how to stave off foreclosure. For more information, contact the organization at:

AmeriDream Inc.

18310 Montgomery Village Avenue, Third Floor

Gaithersburg, MD 20879

866-263-7437

http://www.ameridream.org

### ■ Consumer Debt Solutions

Consumer Debt Solutions (CDS) runs a private gift trust fund, which can give you a grant of up to $25,000, depending on your needs. To qualify, you must have less than $15,000 in cash reserves and attend a free homebuyer education course, in person or online. CDS grants are available nationwide, including Alaska and Hawaii. One unique feature about the program offered by CDS is how the fees are paid. With CDS, any third party can make the donation to the charity, including the seller, a private corporation, your employer, or another source. For more information, contact the organization at:

Consumer Debt Solutions, Inc.

158 Vineyard Avenue

Highland, NY 12528

845-691-9697

http://www.cdsgrants.com

### ■ Genesis Foundation

The Genesis Foundation will give you up to $22,500 to cover the down payment and closing costs associated with buying a home of your own. Like other programs, there are no income restrictions on buyers and you can buy a home wherever you want in the country. You need only find a seller willing to participate, and a lender who accepts gift funds as part of the mortgage application process. For more information, contact the organization at:

The Genesis Foundation

8834 N. Capital of Texas Highway, Suite 110

Austin, TX 78759

512-231-0270

http://www.thegenesisprogram.org

### ■ Homes For All

Through the Homes For All charity, you can receive up to 7% of the purchase price of any home you'd like to buy. Moreover, this program is available to first-time and repeat buyers of all income levels throughout the country. You do need decent credit and the ability to get a mortgage. For more information, contact the organization at:

Homes For All, Inc.

13180 North Cleveland Avenue, Suite 136

North Fort Myers, FL 33903

941-656-4633

http://www.ezdownpayment.com

### ■ Neighborhood Assistance Corporation of America

The Neighborhood Assistance Corporation of America (NACA) is a non-profit organization at the forefront of promoting affordable homeownership and fairness in housing and mortgage lending. NACA takes an activist approach: it often goes after predatory lenders and challenges the notion that credit-challenged people in urban and rural communities are riskier borrowers than others. True to its philosophy, NACA focuses on helping people who often get locked out of the financial mainstream: low to moderate income individuals, those with poor credit or no credit history, and borrowers with little to no savings. NACA emphasizes that consumer education works in promoting successful homeownership. Therefore, NACA uses flexible guidelines to make affordable loans to borrowers. With a NACA mortgage, you can obtain a loan with no money down, and get an interest rate that is 1% below prevailing market rates. To qualify, you must meet income guidelines for your area and attend homebuyer counseling. For more information, contact the organization at:

> Neighborhood Assistance Corporation of America
> 3607 Washington Street
> Boston, MA 02130
> 888-297-5568
> http://www.naca.com

### ■ Nehemiah Foundation

The Nehemiah Foundation is the down payment assistance arm of the Nehemiah Corporation of America, a non-profit community development organization. Nehemiah bills itself as "The Most Trusted Name in Down Payment Assistance," and indeed Nehemiah enjoys a stellar reputation among housing advocates and lenders nationwide. Through Nehemiah, first-time and repeat homebuyers can get online homeownership education counseling, learn about avoiding predatory lenders, and buy new or existing homes using gift funds from Nehemiah of up to 6% of the home's sales price. The program is free of income and asset restrictions and can be used anyplace in the country. For more information, contact the organization at:

> Nehemiah Corporation of America
> 1851 Heritage Lane, Suite 201
> Sacramento, CA 95815
> 877-634-3642
> http://www.getdownpayment.com

### Federal Rules Impacting Down Payment Aid Programs

Now I have two caveats about using non-profit down payment assistance programs, and since the first one has to do with Uncle Sam you need to pay close attention.

An IRS ruling in May 2006 shook the entire down payment assistance universe. In essence, the IRS said many organizations that provide down payment assistance weren't following the letter of the law, and didn't qualify as tax-exempt charities. At issue was the practice of non-profits essentially playing middle men, obtaining seller donations and passing along the exact amount of that contribution at or before closing to homebuyers. The IRS said such activities don't adhere to the standards of organizations operating as non-profits under the law. To meet the definition of a tax-exempt charity, a non-profit housing agency should offer a complement of educational services that go beyond just providing grants. Another critical point, the IRS said, is that non-profit housing organizations must have a broad-based fundraising program, securing gifts, grants, and contributions from a multitude of sources, like foundations, businesses, government agencies, and the general public – not just donations from home sellers. When non-profits only get money from a home seller in order to pass along that money to a home buyer, that serves a private interest (i.e. the parties involved), and not the public's interest, which is a key part of the definition of a charitable organization.

This IRS ruling resulted in many non-profits shutting their doors, discontinuing down payment assistance programs, or changing their organizational structure. The Neighborhood Gold Program (http://www.neighborhoodgold.com) is a case in point. Previously, if you want to buy a home with no money down, the Neighborhood Gold Down Payment Assistance Program could help you do it. Neighborhood Gold worked with The Buyers Fund, Inc. a non-profit organization, to offer first-time homebuyers grants. Now those grant-making activities have ceased. While the Provo, Utah-based Neighborhood Gold organization still offers homebuyer education, it discontinued its down payment assistance program as of July 3, 2007.

Also, American Family Funds (http://www.affdpa.com), which had been a non-profit, is now operating as a government grant program. Interestingly, Neighborhood Gold and American Family Funds were both founding members of HAND.

**Will Government Grant Programs Replace Non-Profit Aid?**

In explaining its shift from a non-profit to a government grant entity, American Family Funds president Joel Pate said in a letter on the company's website: "AFF has secured an agreement with the Penobscot Indian Nation (PIN) through an alliance with the owners of the Grant America Program (GAP). Collectively, we have the only down payment assistance program that will survive as the IRS begins to enforce last year's revenue ruling."

"Several non-profits have already shut down and you should expect many more to follow suit over the next weeks and months," Pate added.

Some observers expect government grant programs to start replacing non-profits, at least in part, in the down payment assistance arena. Government housing grant programs operate similar to non-profits, except that the origin of gift funds come from a government source, not a charity. HUD guidelines permit a cash gift of down payment funds from a government entity. Also, government grant programs are not subject to the IRS ruling that impacted non-profits.

As you can see, you must be careful in selecting potential non-profit agencies from whom to obtain down payment assistance. You don't want to go through the mortgage process expecting to get free money – only to see those funds evaporate at the last minute because the charity is having IRS problems or no longer qualifies as a non-profit and subsequently stops offering grants. So pick carefully, and ask a charity pointed questions, such as:

- Are you an IRS approved non-profit? (If they say "Yes," it's perfectly acceptable to ask if they will verify their tax-deductible status by letting you see the organization's IRS letter recognizing it as tax-exempt. Tip: note the date of the letter. It should be recent, not five years old!)

- Is your status as a charitable organization currently under review or in question at all? (A "Yes" answer isn't necessarily a bad thing; most housing non-profits are under IRS review. The key to ascertain is whether the non-profit has received any letters from the IRS or adverse rulings concerning the organization's 501(c)(3) status.)

- What kind of homeownership education do you offer and what fund-raising efforts do you undertake to accumulate the money necessary to provide grants to homebuyers like me? (You want to hear them talk at length about lots of education projects and a variety activities or sources from which they derive money).

■ How much seed money, or other funds, do you currently have in place to fulfill grant requests this year? (Hint: if they don't already have an existing war chest, that's reason for concern. Some groups first offer money to homebuyers, then worry about fundraising later, which is a big red flag.)

It's also a smart idea to double check a non-profit's status. Sure, they may say they're legit, but what do the feds say? The IRS is currently examining 185 organizations that offer down payment assistance programs. You can verify a group's tax-exempt status by calling the IRS at 877-829-5500. Alternatively, you can confirm a non-profit's status online at http://www.irs.gov. Just click on "Charities & Non-Profits" and then click on "Search for Charities." So far, the IRS has revoked many agencies' non-profit status; it has also denied applications for dozens of organizations that sought 501(c)(3) status as a way to provide down payment assistance.

Finally, here are a few other reputable non-profit down payment assistance programs you can explore:

■ The Affordable Housing Alliance, of Everett, Washington – gives gifts of up to as much as 5% of a home's purchase price, up to $10,000. For more information, you can call 425-353-7131 or visit: http://www.housinggrants.org.

■ The Community Housing Assistance Program of America (CHAPA) in Fairfield, Iowa – provides gifts totaling 6% of your home price up to $24,000. For more information, call 888-218-0180 or visit: http://www.chapagifts.org.

■ Family Home Providers, of Cummings, Georgia – offers up to 3% of a home's purchase price for houses under $166,000. For more information, you can call the organization at 770-887-4578 or visit: http://www.familyhomeproviders.org.

■ Liberty Gold, located in Cleveland, Ohio – offers up to $18,000 for your new home via The Buyer's Dream program; get more information by calling 216-320-0870 or visiting the group online: http://www.libertygold.org

Each of the aforementioned programs is available nationwide, no matter where you'd like to live. You can also do a Google search entering the words: "down payment assistance," "home," and your city or state for additional leads to programs in your area.

**Do Non-Profit Assistance Programs Really Help or Hurt?**

The IRS threat to non-profit down payment assistance programs isn't the only federal challenge these initiatives face. In October 2007, a HUD ruling was issued that could have negatively impact millions of potential homeowners nationwide. Essentially, HUD said it would ban borrowers using FHA loans from receiving down-payment assistance offered from charities and non-profit agencies that give homebuyers grants based on money received from home sellers. Currently, 40% of all FHA loans feature some form of down payment assistance, either received from charities and non-profits or as gift money from family. However, HUD wasn't playing fair with its proposed new rule. It would only have stopped down payment aid that comes via non-profits, as opposed to also placing restrictions on money a potential homebuyer can get from well-heeled relatives or friends. The effect of this would be problematic because, generally speaking, many minorities and working class families are less likely to have wealthy family members and friends able to help them out by supplying a down-payment gift. Fortunately, there were legal challenges to HUD's proposed ban on non-profit down payment assistance, including a lawsuit filed by AmeriDream to block HUD's actions. On October 31, 2007 – the day HUD's proposed ban would have gone into effect – U.S. Federal District Court Judge Paul Friedman issued an injunction against the HUD regulation. The judge said the rule lacked a "reasoned analysis," was based on "flimsy" support, and that there was a "substantial likelihood" that the regulation violated applicable law.

So why did HUD pursue this course of action? Some people worry that giving grants to low to moderate income people might result in homeowners with above-average default rates. In fact, in 2005 HUD twice published reports suggesting that very idea. HUD also said that people who received down payment assistance from non-profits were endangering the FHA insurance pool. Other research, however, doesn't support concerns that these borrowers are any more high-risk than others and bankers don't seem to believe the claims either. "The default rate is a lot lower when homeowners have gone through counseling. That's why we require it on certain programs." says Scott Guthrie, of M&T Bank.

In response to the HUD survey, members from HAND – the Homeownership Alliance of Nonprofit Downpayment Providers – published their own research study on the matter. According to HAND's findings, about 75% those receiving down payment gifts get their money from relatives, while roughly 25% get money from non-profits and community-based organizations. However, HAND concluded that the default rate is no different between the two groups of buyers: exactly 5.1% for each. Clearly, just getting money from a non-profit won't automatically make you more likely to fall behind on a mortgage.

Additionally, a study by the University of Georgia Family & Consumer Services College found that many families earning as little as $30,000 annually can become successful homeowners if they are aided by down payment programs. Interestingly, minorities benefit most from such aid. A study from the Federal Reserve Bank of Minneapolis found that more people are likely to become homeowners if they receive direct cash payments and down payment assistance, rather than 100% financing programs which feature no money down.

Programs that require no down payment result in 2.5% more renters becoming homeowners, according to federal research. In contrast, a cash payment of $5,000 dramatically boosted the rate of homeownership, by increasing the percentage of renters who can own a home by up to 13% for African Americans, and 7% for Hispanics. When the cash payment is $10,000 those percentages double.

## Build Sweat Equity in a Home with Habitat for Humanity

There's one other extremely important non-profit program I want you to know about – and it's unlike any other initiatives mentioned thus far. If you're very low on cash but are willing to work hard for a home – and in this case, I mean putting in some intense physical labor – you might try your hand at getting a new home through Habitat for Humanity. This is an international, non-profit Christian group whose mission is to help eliminate poverty housing and homelessness around the world. With Habitat for Humanity you won't get luxury digs, however you will get a very nice home – and it will be structurally sound, decent, and affordable housing too. Habitat affiliates operate independently, and are locally run. A local affiliate can tell you whether or not you qualify, and what you'd need to know in terms of the availability of a new home, the costs involved, and how much "sweat equity" you'd be required to invest to help build your own house. On average, a typical Habitat home in the U.S. costs about $60,000 – a price far below the national average because of volunteer donations of material, money, and labor – including your own hard work. Expect to spend hundreds of hours of your time and labor to get your house built. The house prices are also kept affordable because Habitat does not make a profit when selling the home to you.

With the Habitat program, the criteria by which homeowners are chosen include: your level of need, your willingness to become a partner in the program, and your ability to repay a no-profit, no-interest loan. Neither race nor religion factor into the selection process. To learn more, call 800-422-4828 ext. 2551 or 2552 or visit: http://www.habitat.org. At the group's website there is an online search tool where you can find a local affiliate in your desired area. In addition to operating in 90 countries around the world, Habitat affiliates exist in all 50 states, as well as Washington D.C., Guam, and Puerto Rico.

**Lender-Specific Programs for Which You Might Qualify**

As you piece together the money necessary for your down payment and closing costs, don't forget about the programs offered by lenders themselves. In many instances, credit unions, banks, and other financial institutions have their own special offerings designed to help first-time buyers more readily qualify for a mortgage. For instance, you can get a zero-down payment loan from the L & N Federal Credit Union in Louisville, Kentucky. It offers 100% financing for purchases up to $175,000, and its First-Time Home Buyers Program features no discount points, no origination fee, and reduced closing fees. For more information, call 502-368-5858 or visit the credit union online at: http://www.lnfcu.com. The Wright-Patt Credit Union in Fairborn, Ohio offers a handful of mortgage loans that allow you to put either no money down, or just 1% or 3% down. In addition, its Home Rebate Program is designed to help put cash in your pocket after your home sale is finalized. For more information, call the credit union at 937-912-7000 or visit: http://www.wright-pattcu.org.

Membership in a credit union is often based on where you live or work, or is tied to civic, social, academic, or professional affiliations. If you already belong to a credit union, you probably know the benefits: free or low-cost savings and checking accounts, competitive rates on loans, personalized service, and a host of consumer education programs and other financial offerings. If you've never explored membership in a credit union, you can learn more about them or find a local credit union from the groups listed below:

- Credit Union National Association; log onto the association's website at: http://www.cuna.org and click on the "Consumer Information" button.

- National Credit Union Administration; find this group on the web at: http://www.ncua.gov and click on the "Resources for Consumers" tab.

- National Credit Union Foundation; visit the group on line at: http://www.ncuf.coop.

Needless to say, regional financial firms and big banks also offer very attractive, highly competitive programs that appeal to first-time homebuyers. As of this writing, all of the following large, national banks listed below had programs of interest to renters looking to become homeowners:

| | |
|---|---|
| Chase | http://www.chase.com |
| Citigroup | http://www.citigroup.com |
| Countrywide | http://www.countrywide.com |
| GMAC | http://www.gmacfs.com |
| HSBC | http://www.hsbc.com |
| SunTrust | http://www.suntrust.com |
| Wachovia | http://www.wachovia.com |
| Washington Mutual | http://www.wamu.com |
| Wells Fargo | http://www.wellsfargo.com |

In addition to resources like online calculators, financial tools, and homebuyer education materials, here are several examples of special mortgage products available from some of these lenders:

- At **Chase**, you can purchase a home with no money down using its "Dream Maker" mortgage program, which is popular among low and moderate income borrowers who require assistance with down payments and closing costs. For more information, call 800-873-6577.

- **GMAC** has the "HomeStrength" plan, which provides you with a second loan for up to 4% of the property value, which you can use for the down payment and closing costs. You simply contribute $500, and finance the rest of your mortgage. As an added bonus: that second mortgage requires no monthly payment and is forgiven after 10 years of on-time payments. For more information, call 877-355-4622.

- **HSBC**'s product offering features a "Less-than-perfect Credit" program to help you overcome past credit problems and get a mortgage loan with no money down. For those of you who fall in love with an historic or old house that needs updating or repairs, HSBC also provides "Home Renewal Mortgages" that make it easy for you to acquire and subsequently renovate a fixer-upper of your choosing. For more information, call 800-622-7759.

- **Washington Mutual** offers a program called "Community Access Home Loans" to enable those of you without a credit score or cash reserves to more easily qualify for a loan. For more information, call 877-800-9268.

- **Wells Fargo**'s most popular offerings include the "Home Opportunities" program, which offers 100% financing and flexible credit guidelines. Wells also has loans with special incentives for fire fighters, EMTs, police officers, healthcare workers, teachers, and other qualified public employees. Finally, the bank's Military Mortgage Express® program features nice deals for military personnel, including "no documentation" loans, special loan pricing, reduced fees, and super-fast handling of purchases or refinancing if you get called into active duty and need to close a home loan in a hurry. For more information about the Home Opportunities loan, call 877-937-9357. Service members can call the bank's military relocation specialists at 877-337-9405.

No matter which lender you ultimately choose to finance your mortgage, make sure you ask whether they offer any special deals or incentives for first-time homebuyers.

## Special Homeownership Programs Based on Your Job

When you're in the market for a new home, find out whether your work qualifies you for special perks as a fist-time buyer. In many regions nationwide, there are unique housing programs for municipal, county, or state workers, as well as others who perform services of value to the general public. The goal of these programs is to ensure that there is no shortage of local police officers, teachers, fire fighters, healthcare workers, and so on in local neighborhoods. If you work in any of these fields, be sure to investigate first-timer homeowners programs designed especially for you.

In addition to the jobs mentioned above, working in many other professions can qualify you for a first-time homebuyers programs that offers down payment and closing cost assistance. For example, are you a member of a union? If so, you might qualify for a good deal. The American Federation of Labor and Congress of Industrial Organizations (AFL-CIO) is a voluntary federation of 55 national and international labor unions, representing 10 million working women and men from all walks of life. The AFL-CIO is steadfast in its promotion of homeownership for its constituents, which run the gamut: many writers, television actors, and taxi drivers are union members, as are factory workers, musicians, engineers, painters, and others. The AFL-CIO has a program called HIT Home that has helped thousands of people reach their dream of homeownership. HIT stands for Housing Investment Trust. The HIT program is an initiative among the AFL-CIO, Countrywide Home Loans, and Fannie Mae to help union member buy or refinance homes, get educated about mortgages, and prepare for homeownership. Participants also save money by gaining access to lower-cost mortgages and getting benefits such as free appraisals and credit reports, which lowers closing costs. All members of AFL-CIO affiliated unions and the UBC are eligible for the HIT Home Program. (UBC is the United Brotherhood of Carpenters, a 550,000-member union that split off from the AFL-CIO in 2001). For more information on HIT, plus referrals to bilingual program representatives, call 866-HIT-HOME. You can also write, email, or call the organization's local number, as well as learn more online. Here is the contact information:

AFL-CIO Housing Investment Trust

1717 K Street, NW, Suite 707

Washington, D.C. 20036

202- 331-8055

http://www.aflcio-hit.com;

email: info@aflcio.com

## The Rise of Employer Assisted Housing Programs

The Society for Human Resources Management reports that 12% of employers now offer homeownership assistance programs, compared to just 7% in 2002. Additionally, 8% of employers provide down payment help, compared to 4% in 2002. Companies in the financial services and manufacturing arena represent the organizations most likely to offer mortgage assistance. Also, some of the most common entities that offer down payment help are so-called "land-locked institutions," places like colleges and hospitals that don't have the choice to relocate. Other employers with deep roots in a town, or in need of a vibrant or specialized workforce, also provide aid.

If your company doesn't have a down payment assistance program in place, you can always ask them to create one. Tell your employer about Freddie Mac's Workforce Home Benefit program, through which Freddie Mac designs employer-assisted housing (EAH) initiatives. Since 2003, Freddie Mac has been working with employers around the country to make homeownership possible for employees.

Freddie Mac's Workforce Home Benefit program is a turnkey solution, mainly suitable for companies with at least 1,000 employees. Under this initiative, Freddie Mac links employers with lenders, local non-profit housing counseling agencies, and local down payment assistance programs. The program also features homebuyer education, financial literacy training, down payment, and closing cost assistance. Some of the entities that have signed onto Freddie Mac's Workforce Home Benefit program are Tyson Foods, Allegheny General Hospital in Pittsburgh, and Jackson State University, a historically black college in Jackson, Mississippi. Needless to say, Freddie Mac has designed an employer- assisted housing program of its own, which is made available to the company's full-time and part-time workforce.

## The Money is Out There – Just Go Get It!

I hope by now I've convinced you of the vast sums of money out there – literally billions upon billions of dollars for first-time homebuyers and, in many cases, repeat buyers too. I don't want you to fall victim to "information overload" and feel paralyzed by all the options presented here, however. So here's what I want you to do: whittle down all your choices and decide which first-time homeownership programs make the most sense for you. Follow these easy steps to get the job done:

### How to Select the Best First-Time Home Buyer Aid Program

**Step 1**: Create a written list of a dozen different types of homeownership aid programs for which you are eligible.

(**Tip**: make sure they're not all the same type. They should not all be community-based grants, or city housing funds, etc.)

**Step 2**: Prioritize your list by the dollar amount of the resources offered, then trim your list in half. Narrow down your list to the top six programs you could pursue. Make sure your list includes at least two programs from non-profit groups, and two that offer government aid (i.e. from state, county, or city resources).

**Step 3**: Get applications, any other necessary paperwork, and documentation about program requirements from your top six programs. You'll collect this information by going online, visiting the offices of the entity offering aid, or writing or calling to have them send you what's required.

**Step 4**: Eliminate two programs from your top six list. Make sure that your final list includes at least one government and one non-profit program. Weed out the less desirable programs by selecting the initiatives that appeal the most to you. For example, you might drop the following:

- Programs that offer fewer dollars in aid versus other homeownership programs you like better

- Programs with contingencies or criteria you don't like or for which you might not meet the requirements

- Programs that requires far more work or time than you can reasonably devote

**Note**: Expect to put in some time at a homeownership class to receive government aid; virtually all programs require this. Anyhow, taking a class for a few hours, or even a few weeks, is worth it to gain several thousand dollars. However, if a program requires an exceptionally long commitment – in terms of either time or effort – that you can not or are not willing to make, scratch that one off your list.

**Step 5**: Prepare the applications to receive down payment and closing cost assistance from four sources. Don't submit these applications just yet. At this point, you're simply getting a jump on the process, which will expedite things later on.

It's OK if you simultaneously apply for more than one source of financial assistance, as long as it's allowed by the programs themselves. Also, many banks will let you do this. If it turns out later that you're working with a lender or a program that will only allow you to use one aid source, simply take the best one. In the end, even if you apply for four aid programs, I would expect you to wind up with two, perhaps a government grant and a non-profit profit grant. Or maybe you will only use one of these along with another form of aid – such as down payment assistance from your employer.

Congratulations! You're well on track to getting your first home! Remember: these funds are readily available and most first-time homebuyer programs do not require you to jump through an inordinate number of hoops just to get the money. In fact, in some cases, the funds are just sitting in a bank account, waiting for a prepared, qualified, and responsible would-be homeowner like you to come along and stake your claim. Since the money is out there – shouldn't you go get it? Of course you should! It's high time you grabbed your own slice of the American Dream.

# CHAPTER

## 5

# Make Yourself Attractive to a Lender

At this point in your quest for homeownership, you're just about ready to approach a lender. What can you do to virtually guarantee your success in getting approved and receiving a great deal on a mortgage? Actually, there are plenty of things you can do – and they all center around shoring up your personal and financial profile so that you will present yourself in the best possible light. In this chapter, I'll share with you lots of strategies I learned straight from underwriters, bankers, brokers, realtors, and other mortgage pros who've seen many thousands of applicants seeking home loans. Their insights and eye-opening tips will stack the deck in your favor, making you irresistible to whichever lender you choose. Wouldn't you like to be in the enviable position of having your pick of lenders – instead of the other way around, where you're feeling so overwhelmed by the mortgage process that you would be grateful to have any old institution give you a mortgage? This section is where you learn the inside skinny that will put you in the driver's seat when it comes to getting a home loan.

### The Importance of Cash, Credit, and Character

I've already discussed strategies for boosting your available cash and improving your credit, each vital factors when it comes to sealing a deal for a mortgage. Let's turn our attention now to another area – your *character* – to see how that can impact your ability to get home financing. For a lot of you, this may be a touchy maybe even offensive area. I know many people think "who are they to have the nerve to judge me?" but it's not about their "judging" you on a moral level; the bank has to size up your track record to determine how much of a risk you'll be if they give you a loan. So if you want to get that loan, you have to learn how to play by the bank's rules. Fortunately, you can demonstrate solid character to the bank in a way that gives a lender confidence in approving your mortgage application.

## Why and How Banks Assess Your Character

The primary way that banks sum up your character is by looking at your FICO credit score. For many lenders, this tells them a lot – although not everything – about what they need to know about you. Your FICO score gives a lender a snapshot of how you've handled your finances in the past. Think of your three-digit FICO credit score as the chief tool your banker will use to quickly grade your financial behavior – and, yes, your character, too.

Before you start protesting that your FICO credit score is "just a number," and not reflective of your character, consider the fact that, in other areas of life, you do the same thing the bank loan officer does. For example, most of us make certain judgments about students when we hear their grade point averages, right? Chances are, you're more likely to think a student with a 4.0 GPA, or "A" average, is harder working, more studious, smarter or somehow better in school as opposed to a student with a 2.0 GPA, or "C" average. By the same token, a bank is viewing your credit score as a fast or shorthand way of grading you. The person with the 750 FICO score is always going to be viewed more favorably than the person with the 620 FICO score – and in the vast majority of cases, it's entirely justified.

The reason the banks place so much emphasis on your credit score is because they know it's the numerical summary of how you've dealt with other creditors. To a banker's thinking, you're likely to treat them just like you've treated others you owe. If you have a negative mark in your credit file – say because you were 30 days late in paying a bill – that blemish damages your financial reputation. In the worst of situations – say you've had a multitude of late payments or very serious marks in your credit history – like a foreclosure, repossession, judgment, or charge-off – this can brand you as financially irresponsible in the eyes of the financial community. Even if you fell into financial distress because of circumstances beyond your control, as can happen due to a divorce, layoff, or big medical bills, failure to pay your bills on time will signal to a creditor (rightly or wrongly) that you might not be financially trustworthy.

## The Character Trait That Can Bolster Your Application

Please understand that I'm not judging you based on previous mistakes or past economic troubles. But poor credit nonetheless implies that you can't (or won't) honor your obligations, that your word is not your bond and, from a financial point of view, you're a bad risk. This can lead to banks not wanting to touch you because, frankly, if your credit is horrendous because you didn't pay your bills on time, you have the economic equivalent of a scarlet letter. It's sad but true: Once your financial reputation is damaged, it can be so very hard to restore it. This is obviously the case in the credit industry, where one mistake can hurt your credit for seven years. The good news is that with the passage of time those blemishes on your credit report will be less important and will play a much smaller role in your FICO than your more recent credit behavior.

Even if you don't have great credit, you can demonstrate solid character to a bank through other means. Several other ways that banks judge your character are by your personal life, professional background, and financial habits. If you can show just one trait – *stability* – in each of these areas, it will go a long way towards bolstering your loan application and convincing a lender that you are a borrower of good character. Let me give you some specific examples of how stability – or the lack thereof – can make a difference in how others view you.

Once, when I was a guest expert on "The Dr. Phil Show," one of the people on the program, a woman named Lynette (ironic, I know), was a shopaholic. Lynette admitted on national TV that her freewheeling spending had landed her about $38,000 in debt. She shopped whenever and wherever she wanted, without regard to price. According to Lynette, she'd purchased 10 cars in five years and had also moved several times during that period. She said she got bored easily with her purchases, and wanted "nicer cars and homes." This constant need for change astonished me! After analyzing her behavior, however, Lynette went to Dr. Phil because she had to finally acknowledge that her reckless spending was taking a toll on her marriage and setting a bad example for her teenage daughters. Lynette also represented an extreme case of how you can show poor "character" to a bank with your actions.

Besides having a positive credit score, one of the best ways to demonstrate a solid character to a lender is to create stability in your personal and professional life. Maintaining order and stability in your world is a powerful way of investing in your financial reputation. Yet it's something that most people overlook.

Think for a moment about how bankers and others view you when you have no stability and zero permanence in critical areas of your life. Are you constantly changing important things – like your place of residence or home telephone number? If so, realize that you're hurting your prospects with a lender. Instability just doesn't look good. Why do you think it is that on loan applications they often want to know *how long* you've lived at your present location, or *how long* you've worked at a certain job? The bank is looking for stability or, even better, longevity. Longevity is a sign that you're settled and will be responsible in meeting your financial obligations.

The same theory is held by employers. When you apply for a job, prospective bosses want to know *how long* you've been at your previous workplace. It's great to have career advancement and to learn new things. But switching companies every year and engaging in constant job-hopping is unattractive to most employers because it does not indicate a stable track record.

To create stability in your universe, consider implementing these ideas:

■ **Maintain continuity in your residence address and other contact info**
As mentioned, in the financial world, bankers look for stability in your home life. I know some people for whom I have to double check if they have the same phone number, email, or street address practically every time I try to contact them. Trust me: your relatives, friends, and associates might not tell you to your face, but they'd

appreciate some continuity in your life. Behind your back, they're probably murmuring about how you've "moved again."

### ■ Quit changing jobs so frequently

Some of you might say "my job is boring" or "I'm looking for a better-paying position." If that's the case, explore your options within your current company before you hop to another firm. See if you can get a promotion, a transfer to a different, more exciting department, or simply earn a merit-based raise if it's more money you're after. In other words, don't think you automatically have to quit your job and land some new position just to meet your needs.

### ■ Stop getting new cars every year or two

Lots of people like to lease or trade in vehicles to have the latest, greatest model car on the market. Quit trying to "keep up with the Joneses." It's not worth it and it makes you look fickle and unstable. Besides, leasing a car means you don't own it, and even when you purchase/finance a car, remember that any vehicle you buy instantly depreciates in value the minute you drive it off the lot.

### ■ Don't let your love life become a revolving door

Realize that breakups are expensive. They can take their toll in a number of ways. Divorce is financially costly – not to mention emotionally painful. Unfortunately, I've been through a divorce. In the process, one of the interesting statistics I learned was that whenever a couple divorces, assuming it takes a year to go through the court proceedings, the economic recovery period is two and a half years, as each party adjusts to the costs of running two households instead of one. If a divorce drags on for two years, then it typically takes five years for the parties involved to fully recover financially. You should also realize that instability in your personal life can also have a much longer and much more severe impact on your personal finances. For instance, if you split with your spouse, depending on your individual circumstances and the state in which you live, you might have to fork over half of your assets that it took you years to build, like 401(k) monies, real estate, and other property.

Therefore don't think that being stable is boring. Having some degree of perma-nence, or even longevity, will actually put you in good financial stead – and help you avoid a lot of unnecessary drama. Perhaps most importantly, cultivating an air of stability will demonstrate your positive, responsible character to a lender.

A final way you can show good character to a lender is through your finan-cial habits. Are you the type of person who has the discipline to sock away some cash each month – even if it's just a little bit of money? If so, you'll get brownie points from lenders for your efforts. What if you have absolutely no discipline what-soever when it comes to money issues? Realize that such fiscal mistakes will hurt your prospects when a bank considers your overall loan application.

"If your credit is shaky, at least have money in a 401(k) or some type of savings to show us. That says a lot about your character," says Olayinka "June" Olomo, Assistant Vice President and Sales Manager at Chase Home Finance in Houston, Texas.

### Tipping the Scales in Your Favor

Olomo's comments about having some savings to offset a spotty credit record high-light a little-known secret to getting a mortgage. That secret can be summed up in two words: "compensating factors." Simply put, compensating factors are positive attributes or strengths in your overall application that can make up for any negatives or drawbacks you might have in your record. For instance, if you have so-so credit, then having a strong history of saving money – as evidenced by cash in your sav-ings, checking, brokerage, or retirement accounts – will definitely count in your favor as a compensating factor. Or maybe you have little or no money for a down payment. A strong income or a proven history of steadily rising wages could help you compensate for your low-cash position. Even having a guarantee of a higher income in the immediate future could be a compensating factor. For example, say you're in the market for a mortgage and you know that you'll be getting a raise soon. It's possible that with your current income you might not qualify for a loan. Yet if you can get a letter from your boss stating that in 60 days or less you'll be getting a raise, your higher expected income could be considered a compensating factor and help you qualify for a loan. If you do pursue this route, just know that such a letter from your employer can't have any strings attached. In other words, it can't have contingencies or indicate that you have to meet certain criteria to get the raise; if so, a lender won't consider that a "guarantee" of immediate future income.

### Turning a "No" Into a "Yes" With Compensating Factors

Remember: to get that mortgage, you want to make the most favorable impression you can, get your cash position as strong as possible, do everything in your power to improve your credit, and be mindful of how certain personal and professional habits impact your character in the eyes of a lender. So if you feel like your application is less than perfect, don't despair. You can definitely tip the scales in your favor by knowing what "compensating factors" will help your mortgage application. To show you how powerful compensating factors can be, listen to a few stories about loans that were approved although you might have assumed that the person would be laughed out of a lender's office.

### How to Get a Loan with $1 a Month in Income

Matt Fitzgerald is a vice president with Fidelity and Trust Mortgage, a full-service residential mortgage banking firm. His company does business in Pennsylvania, Maryland, Washington D.C., Virginia, West Virginia, North Carolina, and South Carolina.

"In our market, the average loan amount is $180,000," says Fitzgerald, referring to Raleigh, North Carolina, where he's based.

"I had a customer once who listed his income as $1 a month and he got approved," Fitzgerald reveals. Sound impossible? Not so, according to Fitzgerald and other experts. Like most mortgage professionals, Fitzgerald uses an automated, computer-based underwriting system called "Desktop." (Lenders use a program called Desktop Underwriter and mortgage brokers use a program called Desktop

Originator). This Desktop electronic underwriting tool, which was created by Fannie Mae, is now used by virtually every major lender in America. Freddie Mac, another quasi-government agency, provides its own automated underwriting program, called Loan Prospector, which is also commonly used in the mortgage business. Desktop analyzed the customer's details and recommended that the mortgage be approved.

## How Computers Help Grade Your Loan Application

Desktop Underwriter was launched in the mid-1990s and it has drastically changed the landscape of how mortgage applications get processed, analyzed, and ultimately approved or rejected. Before the advent of electronic underwriting, manual underwriting was the norm, making the process much more labor intensive, time-consuming, and subjective. An individual underwriter, or sometimes a committee of underwriters, would manually review each and every loan application and determine whether or not to grant a mortgage. Often, underwriters would review written letters of explanation from potential borrowers with credit blemishes. These would-be homeowners were explaining a multitude of past transgressions – everything from why they were late making a credit card payment to why they had an account in collections from an overdue medical bill., The mortgage underwriting process often took weeks, and sometimes months to wade through all the paperwork. Today, with electronic underwriting, a loan officer enters some key data into the computer system – i.e., your credit, debts, assets, and details about the property you want to buy – and within minutes Desktop Underwriter will generate a recommendation stating whether or not your loan should be approved.

How does all of this relate back to Fitzgerald's buyer? When you look at it on the surface, you might ask: how could anyone get a mortgage with only a dollar a month in income?

"The answer," Fitzgerald says, "is unbelievably good credit, a huge down payment, and lots of cash in the bank after closing."

In this case, Fitzgerald explains, the buyer actually had a whopping 80% down payment for the property being purchased. "What's the risk to the lender?"

Fitzgerald asks. "There's absolutely no risk when a person makes an 80% down payment," because with that much equity it's highly unlikely a person will ever default on the loan. Therefore, Fannie Mae's automated Desktop program recommended that the loan be approved.

"I've also gotten loans through where the loan applicants had 60% or higher debt-to-income ratios," Fitzgerald notes. "It used to be the case that [front-end and back-end debt to income] ratios were 28/36 or 29/41, but today that's really not the rule," he explains. "Your qualifications are really based on all factors: credit, cash, payment shock, and other things." Payment shock measures the difference between your current housing expenses and what your new housing payment would be if a lender gave you a mortgage.

Fitzgerald's cash-rich buyer is an extreme case, to be sure, however this example goes to show you how you can "tweak" the system and use positive compensating factors in your favor. Electronic underwriting programs automatically take compensating factors into consideration when they give lenders an answer about whether a loan should be approved, denied, or looked at more closely to get further information. When it comes down to the specific guidelines or exceptions to be made, realize that compensating factors can vary from lender to lender. Once you settle on a lender, if you have any doubts about your ability to qualify for a loan ask your lender or mortgage broker upfront what compensating factors you could use to help turn a possible "no" into a "yes."

### Insider Tips From an Underwriter

Tim Rawlinson is the vice president of Residential Loan Origination at Fox Chase Bank in Hatboro, Pennsylvania. The bank has been in business for 140 years and, like other lenders, it tightened its credit qualifications in the wake of the 2007 mortgage crisis, when hundreds of thousands of borrowers defaulted on their loans and scores of lenders went out of business. At Fox Chase Bank Rawlinson reviews all the credit files that come in with mortgage applications. He works with one other underwriter, and he's seen it all.

Rawlinson emphasizes that while your credit standing is important when he considers your application, so, too, are other factors. "We also look at assets, and at the monthly cash flow that you have in the bank," says Rawlinson. "We look at your highs and lows for your balances. Are you going week to week where all of a sudden your balances are running really low?" If so, that could be viewed negatively if you have a borderline application.

Although your credit history is an indication of your financial past, Rawlinson calls getting a new mortgage a "lifestyle change" and a "life changing event." Fortunately, "[t]he past is the past," he notes. "Going forward is what I have to work with." That's why he also looks closely at assets in the bank as a compensating factor. His goal is to make sure that you have the income and assets on hand to substantiate carrying whatever mortgage you request.

You might be wondering how much you need in cash reserves. It varies from lender to lender but, in general, expect to show at least two months' worth of mortgage payments – including principal, interest, taxes, and insurance – as cash reserves in order to have it count as a positive compensating factor. Depending on your application and other areas of weakness, a lender might require as much as six months' worth of cash reserves. Many lenders will accept reserves from any source – including gifts from family members or friends. Some lenders, however, have stricter requirements that mandate that your reserves be "seasoned" assets," meaning they've been in the bank for at least two months. Consequently, you must prove the source of your reserves by providing a few months' worth of your recent bank statements.

### Let Non-Traditional Assets Boost Your Qualifications

"I'll generally look for two months in reserves. It can be in retirement accounts as well," Rawlinson says, adding that he might be inclined to ask whether you have any other assets you wish to disclose. Sometimes, he says, prospective homeowners don't reveal – or don't think about – certain assets they own, when in reality those assets could help them qualify for a loan. "Their grandmother might have given them $5,000 in savings bonds that they have sitting in a firebox somewhere," Rawlinson says. "And because the person isn't going to sell them or use it for the down payment, they don't think it matters. But it can help their loan application."

In the final analysis, Rawlinson says he puts equal weight on four criteria:

- credit (he likes a minimum score of 660)
- assets (he recommends two months' cash reserves)
- income (he prefers debt-to-income ratios of 40/50 or better)
- loan-to-value ratio (he typically offers low LTV mortgages of 70% to 80%, meaning you need a 20% to 30% down payment)

"If one [factor] is bad, then I'll look for the other three to be stronger than usual," he says. "If I have two that are bad, then there's a good chance that the file isn't going to be approved."

To summarize, compensating factors can be any or all of the following:

- high checking account balance
- low monthly mortgage payment
- large down payment
- strong cash reserves in any account, including a 401(k)
- low debt-to-income ratio
- very good credit rating
- low loan-to-value ratio on the property
- long length of time working at the same job
- long length of time living at same place of residence
- near-term and guaranteed future income increases

### Intangibles Can't Hurt

In addition to "compensating factors," you can make a whole set of "intangible" factors work for you. The "intangibles" are the simple, but powerful, factors that enter minds of bankers, mortgage officers, or underwriters when they're evaluating your loan application. If you can create an overall positive impression in their minds, you improve your chance of getting approved. How do you make a positive impression? Here are a few ideas:

### ■ Be nice

Don't laugh. I'm totally serious here. Simply being nice to a loan officer can help your loan get pushed through – and sometimes faster than the next guy's application. By "pushed through" I mean expedited in the loan process. Don't think you can charm your way into a loan approval. You'll only get approved on the merits of your overall application. However, imagine the harried loan officer who's fielding numerous phone calls a day. Some folks call because they want loans for new purchases and others want to refinance their homes. This loan officer has to deal with all kinds of people, including some irate customers who balk at providing certain sensitive financial information or who generally are not-so-pleasant during the application process. If you're courteous, respectful, and nice, you'll be remembered and appreciated by the loan officer. Don't be fake and try to force small talk; that's not going to get you a loan. Just be pleasant, and thank the loan officer for his or her efforts. The officer will appreciate your consideration – and may even help you out by putting your application at the top of the stack, telling you specifics about their lending policies, or advising you about what to expect next.

### ■ Be prompt

If you have an appointment with a loan officer, banker, or underwriter, respect the person's time and show up to the appointment on time. You'll get off on the wrong foot by being late. By the same token, if they ask you for additional information, supply it in a timely manner. Don't prolong the approval process by dragging your feet when it comes to providing requested documents. That won't make a favorable impression. On the contrary, if you get a request for a document and by day's end you've faxed or emailed exactly what was asked for, wow, the loan officer will think, that's a fast response! You'll stand out as someone who immediately takes care of business and doesn't procrastinate – two good qualities in a loan applicant.

### ■ Be thorough and honest

Some people want a house so badly that they'll say and do virtually anything to get it. Don't succumb to that temptation. Make sure everything you put on a mortgage application is 100% accurate and thorough. Let's say you claim to have $10,000 in assets in three different accounts. Be prepared to give the names of those three financial institutions, their addresses, and your account numbers and balances for each. In instances like these, the more detailed the information you can supply, the better; it lets a bank know that you don't have anything to hide, which might give a lender more confidence in loaning you money. Lisa Alley, managing partner of Five Star Capital, a mortgage brokerage firm based in Huntington Beach, CA, says: "Do not exaggerate your earnings. Do not inflate, nor underscore other financial responsibilities either. Give your mortgage broker the truth and nothing but the truth!"

### ■ Be professional

If you go in to a bank to fill out an application, dress nicely. Don't feel like you have to go out and buy a fancy designer suit. (Save that money for your closing costs later!) Just wear something clean, nice, and professional. Many of you, of course, will fill out loan applications over the telephone or online, so your appearance won't matter. However, even when you talk to someone via telephone, be professional, not casual or overly chatty. This is a business transaction, after all.

### ■ Be educated and informed

Many bankers are impressed when they encounter a customer who is educated about mortgages, informed about the loan process, and able to speak a banker's language. When they started talking about "DTI," "back-end ratios," "escrows," or "private mortgage insurance" and you can converse with them intelligently about these and other topics, they know you've at least done your homework and have taken the time to understand what your responsibilities will be as a homeowner. I'm not saying that you should devote a ridiculous amount of time trying to learn the ins and outs of the mortgage world, and you'll likely never surpass their level of knowledge, since they do this for a living. However, do learn enough lingo to be conversant and to demonstrate that you take this process seriously.

**Red Flags Bankers Don't Like**

Just like there are tangible and intangible ways that you can impress a banker, there are some things you can do, or some elements of your loan application, that can send up a red flag. Negative items in your credit report are obvious causes for concern, but so are other things you might not expect. If you have past due child support payments, if you've co-signed on anyone else's loans, or if you are currently being sued for any reason, you'll have some explaining to do.

An inability to provide standard documentation will likely raise some eyebrows. Let's say you claim to have paid your rent on time for the past year. You don't live in a big apartment complex, rather you live in a place that you rent from your aunt. You might think a simple letter from that aunt attesting to your timely payment record is enough. However, the bank is likely to ask for more solid proof – in the form of the canceled checks you wrote for that rent. What they'll be looking at primarily is the date on your checks, to see if you really made on-time payments. If you say you "can't find" your old checks or are missing a few, chances are that will raise doubts about the veracity of your payment history and you'll be dinged on the interest rate. Likewise, unexplained gaps or frequent changes in your recent employment picture can be a cause for concern to some lenders.

**Looking Good on Paper**

Now that you know how to tilt the scales in your favor when applying for a loan, and also know what kind of things set off alarm bells in the minds of bankers, how can you best use this information? It's easy. Do something that 99% of all other mortgage applicants don't do: make yourself look good on paper to your banker. By this I mean, type up a one-page summary about you as a loan applicant and submit that with you loan application.

By typing up a brief, clear synopsis of why you represent a good credit risk, you make a powerful case for yourself that's hard to ignore. There's something about the force of having something in black and white that's always very compelling to the reader. At this point, if you think you're ready for homeownership, it's time to really demonstrate it: show your banker that you care about your loan application and that you are professional and about business when it comes to getting a mortgage.

Any person who is truly ready for homeownership can look good on paper. I don't care what your circumstances are, or where you might have deficiencies. You can make yourself look good on paper by literally emphasizing your positive attributes in writing. I'm not talking about your physical attributes or the fact that you love babies and are kind to stray dogs. I'm talking about your positive personal, professional, and financial attributes that relate to your ability to get a mortgage, and which can bolster your assertion that you can handle that mortgage and pay it back as agreed. The positive attributes that could demonstrate this to a lender include:

- Your credit history and current FICO credit score
- Your financial habits and savings track record
- Your employment track record
- Your educational background
- Your personal and financial stability
- Your understanding of a homeowner's obligations – as evidenced by a homebuyer's counseling certificate
- Any other compensating factors that put you in a good light and present you as a serious, qualified borrower who is ready for homeownership

The idea is to accentuate the positive and, if there are any negatives, minimize them in your one-page, typed customer profile. For instance, let's say you got into trouble with your credit cards four years ago, but managed to pay many of them down, have since taken a credit counseling class, received a $5,000 grant and a certificate of completion after successfully finishing a first-time local homeowners education program, have saved $15,000 for a down payment and closing costs, have a 675 FICO credit score, and have been at your job for seven years. You would create a summary about yourself that looks something like this:

| Loan Applicant: | Mary Jones; Age 34; DOB: 3-20-73 |
|---|---|
| SSN: | 555-55-5555 |
| FICO Score: | 675; no late payments in the past 3 years |
| Job/Career History: | Employed as a teacher, at the same school for the past seven years; have worked in education for 13 years |
| Education: | B.A. degree, early childhood education |
| Income: | $57,000 annually |
| Debt to Income Ratio: | Currently 35%, including rent |
| Savings: | $15,000 in savings account; $13,600 in 403(b); and $2,800 in checking account |
| Additional Resources: | $5,000 housing grant from city |
| Other Information: | Have lived at the same residence for 9 years, been through credit counseling, and taken homeownership classes |

Can you see how you can highlight the positives about yourself? Just by reinforcing the better, stronger parts about your loan application upfront, you create a more favorable first impression with a loan officer – making your chances of receiving an approval greater than they might otherwise be.

# CHAPTER

## 6

## Get Pre-Approved for a Mortgage

Armed with the information in the first five chapters of *Your First Home*, you are now ready to approach a bank and get a powerful tool – a pre-approval letter – that will put you one giant step closer to obtaining the home of your dreams.

If you've already been looking at houses or talking to realtors, you might have been asked whether you've been "pre-qualified" or "pre-approved" for a home loan. It's important to know the difference between the two because although some people use the terms interchangeably, in reality they're very different.

### The Difference Between Pre-Qualified and Pre-Approved

A pre-qualification letter is a bank's rough guess about how big a loan you might qualify for, based on preliminary, unverified information you've told them about yourself. The prequalification letter, in today's market, is largely useless in the eyes of most home sellers and realtors. That's because a pre-qualification letter is basically yours for the asking. It's very easy to get one because when a bank issues this letter, it doesn't have to do any homework to substantiate that what you say is true. There's no real process to double-check that you will ultimately qualify and be approved for a loan. Since "pre-quals," as they're known in the mortgage industry, are a dime a dozen, you can even get one over the Internet. I recommend that you don't even both with one. A much better use of your time and energy would be spent obtaining a pre-approval letter.

**What to Expect During the Pre-Approval Process**

In contrast with a pre-qualification letter, a bank will only issue a pre-approval letter after it has done a detailed assessment of your ability to repay a mortgage. This means the bank will pull your credit file and check your FICO score (likely all three credit scores from Experian, Equifax, and TransUnion), verify your employment, confirm the amount of debts you owe and the assets you have, and calculate your debt-to-income ratios.

The bank will also take a full loan application from you, request any additional needed documentation, and run your application through the automated underwriting system. To make this process easier, fill out and have handy Appendix C, the Mortgage Pre-Approval Checklist, found at the end of this book. An underwriter will then "pre-approve" you for a loan at a given amount. When you get your pre-approval letter, it is definitely cause for celebration, because you know you've jumped through some major hurdles on your way to becoming a homeowner. Now all you have to do is go out and find the house you want to buy!

The only thing the bank will be missing to complete your loan application is the appraisal on the property, which they'll do once you give them the address and a title search on the home. A title search will likely show that the current homeowner has a mortgage, and maybe even a home equity loan, or a home equity line of credit on the property. The title search should also prove to the bank that the home is clear of any liens or other "encumbrances." After all, banks don't want to issue a mortgage loan to you on a house and then have some one else come along and "lay claim to the title" by asserting that they have an ownership right or interest in the property.

**The Benefits of Getting Your Loan Pre-Approved**

Because of this more rigorous process, a pre-approval letter puts you on equal footing with a cash buyer. The seller knows that you won't have any trouble getting a mortgage – so long as the title is clear and the house appraises for at least the selling price upon which you and the homeowner agree. Therefore, the pre-approval letter serves many important functions:

■ It shows home sellers that you are a qualified buyer; this will result in any offer you make being taken into careful consideration

■ It shows realtors that you are a serious house-hunter; this will make a real estate agent work harder on your behalf; in fact, some agents won't even show you homes unless you first have a pre-approval letter

■ It makes your final mortgage application process much smoother since you've already been screened

### A Pre-Approval Letter Saves Time, Money, and Effort

For first-time homebuyers, there are additional benefits to getting a pre-approval letter. It gives you flexibility to seek out and compare various loan options, which could save you money. For example, when you deal with a bank for the first time in connection with a mortgage application, you might be asked some questions that will help determine which loan product is best for you. Some of the questions you might be asked are:

■ Are you looking for a fixed rate loan or an adjustable rate loan?
■ How long to you intend to reside in the home?
■ How much of a down payment can you make?
■ Do you want to avoid mortgage insurance?

If you're not asked these questions at the pre-approval phase, volunteer the information so that the loan officer can tell you about what offerings the bank has to fit your needs. Your pre-approval letter should indicate the type of mortgage you'll get (i.e. 30-year fixed or adjustable, etc.), along with the interest rate on that note. However, you are not obligated to get your home loan from the lender that supplies your pre-approval. When you finally find your house if you can get a better mortgage deal from another financial institution, you have the right to go elsewhere.

Getting a pre-approval letter will also reduce your stress because you won't have to fret over whether you'll qualify for a mortgage. It also cuts down on unnecessary time and effort spent house-hunting. After all, there's no point in looking at $450,000 homes if you'll only qualify for $300,000 homes. You'll wind up frustrated and disappointed if you shop for houses that are clearly outside your price range. A pre-approval letter can also save you money, potentially thousands of dollars, because you can use it as a negotiating tool with the seller of the home you want to purchase. Let's say the seller is offering his home for $275,000, and another would-be buyer offers $270,000 on the house, but that buyer lacks a pre-approval letter. Then you come along, love the home, and make an offer of $265,000. With your pre-qualification letter in hand, the home seller might be more inclined to accept your bid – even over the higher offer – simply because you're virtually guaranteed to a mortgage, and will get that loan faster because you've already been pre-qualified. The seller might want to move quickly and not waste time or run the risk that the other buyer won't be approved.

I hope by now you see the range of benefits you get when you obtain a pre-approval letter. It's empowering to go home shopping with one of these letters from the bank backing you. Besides, getting a pre-approval is free and takes some of the hassle out of the home-buying process.

**The Limitations of Pre-Approval Letters**

As wonderful as pre-approval letters are, don't think that getting one means your loan is a 100% done deal. Pre-approval letters aren't binding on lenders, meaning banks don't have to be bound by pre-approvals if new information comes to light that changes your application. For one thing, as previously mentioned, the bank still has to do an appraisal on the house you want. If you over-bid on the property, or if for some reason it just doesn't appraise for your purchase price, your loan will be affected. Pre-approvals also contain time limits, usually 60 to 90 days maximum. So you can't just go house hunting for six or nine months and then run back to a bank that has issued you a pre-approval letter and expect it to stand. You will have to do the whole process all over again. For starters, interest rates will likely have changed, so your loan will now have a different rate than what was originally promised.

Additionally, if the bank hasn't heard from you in three months, they might have closed your file because, for all they know, you might have gone to another lender for a mortgage. So don't expect a bank to just sit on your application and keep all your records on file for an unreasonable amount of time. Lastly, if anything changes regarding your loan application – say you run up credit card bills or decide to buy a car – these factors can change the amount of the loan for which you qualify. Moreover, if something major changes, like your losing your job, that will probably derail your entire loan application.

**What to Do if You Don't Get Approved**

It's not uncommon for first-time home-buyers to be surprised at the dollar figure the bank comes up with for a pre-approval letter. Sometimes would-be homeowners are stunned at how big a mortgage they qualify for, and other times prospective buyers are convinced that the bank is wrong, and has under-estimated how large a mortgage the borrower can repay. Realize that this estimation is what bankers specialize in, as a way to make profits and minimize lending risks. So if you go through the process of getting a pre-approval letter and want to buy a $500,000 home but the bank says you can only qualify for a $250,000 mortgage, the bank's assessment of what you can afford is the only opinion that really counts. In this case, understand that the bank is not saying "No." The bank is actually saying "Yes," – just not in the loan amount for which you'd hoped.

What if the bank does say "No" or approves you for such a paltry loan amount that you can't possibly afford to buy a home in your area? Now you have an entirely different dilemma to solve. In my opinion, if you get a flat-out "No" from a bank, you should take that as a serious sign that you are not ready to become a homeowner because of one or more shortcomings. Don't take a "No" personally and don't feel like the bank is forever rejecting you. Look at a "No" as if they bank is saying: "No – not today." That doesn't mean you can't come back later – in six to 12 months – with a much stronger application. If you are turned down for a pre-approval, take the opportunity to ask the bank directly what deficiencies you have as a potential borrower and work at correcting them. Once you find out what areas you need to shore up, and take steps to do that, you'll substantially increase your odds of getting approved down the road. In the vast majority of cases, you should be able to get that pre-approval in one year or less, if you do what is necessary to strengthen your mortgage application.

Let's say the bank told you "No" because you have bad credit. Now you know that you need to pay off delinquent bills, reduce debt to boost your FICO score, fix any lingering errors on your credit report, or possibly negotiate with your creditors to have negative information deleted from your credit file. I also suggest you seek help from a reputable, free, or low-cost credit counselor. "If you get denied because of your credit, first go to a credit counseling agency, because sometimes in three to six months they can help you fix any credit problems you have," says Bob Schultz, president of New Home Specialist Inc. in Boca Raton, Florida. Schultz started selling new homes in South Florida in 1968, and has been in the business for nearly 40 years. He now works with builders and realtors, and has been recognized by *Builder Magazine* as one of the "50 Most Influential People in Home Building."

"Get your credit back on track, and while doing that, start disciplining your-self to save more money toward a down payment," Schultz advises. "Six months later, when your credit is improved and you have more money in the bank, that looks good to the bank."

"The American dream is to have a home," Schultz notes. "But where in the Constitution is it written that everybody is entitled to a new home with no money down?"

"First-time buyers are going to have to buy their homes the old fashioned way: they have to earn it," he adds.

Take heart in knowing that by waiting just a short time to fix any problems in your loan application, you'll actually wind up saving yourself many thousands of dollars. That's because even if you did get approved for a mortgage with a weak application, you'd be forced to pay a higher interest rate and probably additionally fees just to get the loan.

If you absolutely dread the thought of waiting six months or more, here's another possible strategy that Schultz recommends: "Get a strong co-signer: Mom or Dad, or someone who trusts you enough so that they're willing to make the payments if you can't." Should you take this route, be absolutely certain that you can make your mortgage. If you don't, you'll jeopardize your own credit standing, and your co-signer's – something that could ruin a relationship for life.

# Part II: The Fun Part: Becoming an Active House-Hunter

# CHAPTER

## 7

# Find Your Dream Home

If you've made it this far, pat yourself on the back because you've survived the hardest part, which is preparing for homeownership. Now I want to walk you through the fun part, the stage where you'll start actively house-hunting.

This is a process you don't have to do alone – and indeed you shouldn't look for your dream home all by yourself. The best way to find a home that will suit your needs is to get some help right away, in the form of an experienced real estate professional.

**Enlist the Assistance of a Good Real Estate Agent**

A great real estate agent can help you in numerous ways, especially by saving you time, effort, and money. An agent saves you time by pre-screening homes and helping to narrow your search only to houses that fit your requirements. An agent saves you effort by gathering information about a neighborhood's school district, or getting answers to your questions about a property's utilities and zoning, thereby reducing the amount of homework you have to do on your own. An agent also saves you money by helping you bid appropriately for a home, and negotiating on your behalf. Good real estate agents will be very familiar with local "comps" – the actual prices of comparable homes that have sold in your area. By comparable, I mean homes of similar age, size, style, location, and condition. If you have a handle on comps, this tells you more than just recent sales data. It also gives you an indication of how a market is trending: is it flat, appreciating, or depreciating? You might not know this information, but a seasoned agent will. How else do you benefit by using a real estate agent?

- You have an advocate at the closing table, or settlement, to make sure nothing goes wrong at the last minute.
- You gain access to properties you don't know about. In certain cases, homeowners don't want "For Sale" signs outside on their front lawns. Agents will know about such homes for sale even if those properties aren't being overtly advertised.

- You get referrals to other experts you need. A good agent will know of reputable home inspectors, title companies, and real estate lawyers.

Finding any old real estate agent is easy. There are more than 2.5 million of them nationwide because getting a real estate license isn't terribly difficult. Depending on the state, agents typically only need 30 to 60 hours of training, and then must pass an exam. However finding a really great, experienced agent – and one with whom you "click" – can be more difficult. Part of the reason for this is that during boom real estate periods, lots of people jump into the property business, figuring that they can make a quick buck. Whenever a real estate downturn hits, though, the market tends to wash out those less experienced and less committed individuals. You obviously want to team up with someone who is knowledgeable, professional, and takes the business very seriously. An agent can demonstrate his or her level of commitment to the profession in a variety of ways: through numerous years of service in the business, continuing education and credentials, focus in specific areas or niche neighborhoods and properties, or other means. Whatever the case, you want to work only with the best.

To find a qualified real estate agent, drive around a neighborhood and see which professionals have property listings in an area in which you're interested. You can also ask friends, family members, or colleagues who have bought homes to give you referrals. Nonetheless, make sure you feel that the real estate agent is a good fit for you; just because your cousin liked an agent doesn't necessarily mean that you will.

You can also opt to find a Realtor through the National Association of Realtors (http://www.realtor.com). Only about 50% of real estate agents are designated as Realtors through the National Association of Realtors. This means they belong to the NAR, a trade group of 1.3 million professionals who work in all aspects of residential and commercial real estate and who agree to abide by a strict code of ethics.

If you can't find an agent through people you know, and you don't want a referral through the National Association of Realtors, there is another way you can track down a good real estate agent – and best of all you can do it from the comfort of your home or office, thanks to the Internet. A free website, http://www.Homethinking.com, is a fabulous resource for both homebuyers and sellers looking for real estate agents. Homethinking.com can show you which agents are most active in a particular neighborhood. This is a great time-saver for those of you who don't necessarily want to drive all around an area to find an agent. The tools on Homethinking.com can probably give you a glimpse into how good a negotiator the agent is too, since the site lets you see the original listing price of a home, as well as its finally selling price.

Best of all, though, Homethinking.com has consumer reviews and comments about real estate agents. These reviews are posted by buyers and home sellers. Each agent is rated on a five-point scale, and evaluated according to eight categories, including knowledge of the neighborhood and how much the agent helped the buyer (or seller) in getting the home for less than, at, or above the asking price. The more transactions an agent has, and the more positive comments he or she gets from consumers, the higher his or her ranking. Lastly, there's a neat question-and-answer tool on Homethinking.com, where you can pose housing questions and get online advice from a real estate agent. If you do post a question, and someone gives you a great answer, that might be a potential agent to interview.

Set up appointments to meet at least two – preferably three – prospective real estate agents, and have a list of questions handy. Be sure to ask the following:

■ **How long have you been in business?**

Look for someone with a minimum of three years experience; five years is even better.

■ **Are you a full-time agent?**

It's not necessarily a red flag if the person answers "No." Just realize that people with other day jobs might have less time to devote to you and your house-hunting efforts.

■ **In what communities or neighborhoods do you specialize?**

It's important that the agent is very familiar with the neighborhoods that you can afford and that would be of interest to you.

■ **If we sign a contract, how long will the term last?**

Many agents will want you to sign a contract allowing the agent to represent you for a set number of months, such as three, six, or 12 months. Opt for the shortest period possible. That way if you get nowhere with the agent after, say, three months, you can turn to a different agent. The flip side is also true. If everything is going well – and you simply haven't found your dream home yet – you can always extend the term of your contract with your original agent. (Caution: Don't sign an open-ended contract which has no expiration date; such contracts can be legally unenforceable.)

■ **Can you give me three references from home buyers with whom you've worked in the past?**

Getting references is vital. Anyone with a successful track record in the real estate business should be able to supply you with the names and phone numbers of satisfied customers. Be sure to ask for references who are not family members. Believe it or not, many agents will give you the names of relatives as references. Even if the agent did handle a family member's home purchase, you want a more objective opinion.

■ **How do you handle multiple offers?**

At times, you might not be the only person bidding on a home. Therefore, you need to know what the agent will do if another client also wants the home you are interested in buying. Is it first-come, first-served, or are offers presented on some other basis?

■ **Do you present offers yourself?**

You want to hire someone who is personally confident and skilled at presenting their own offers, not someone who has to get the broker in the office or a more senior agent to actually submit your bid.

■ **Why should I use you as an agent instead of one of your competitors?**

Ideally, the agent should emphasize his or her unique skills, negotiating ability, or some facet of knowledge or expertise that differentiates this individual from the competition. It certainly doesn't hurt if you get a good vibe from the person, too. After all, you will entrust him or her with helping you to get through one of the biggest financial transactions of your life.

■ **Will I be able to review documents beforehand that you want me to sign?**

No reputable real estate agent will put you on the spot by insisting that you sign a slew of documents without having some time to go over them in private, at your own leisure. Get certain documents upfront from an agent – including Agency Disclosures, a Buyer's Broker Agreement, and Buyer Disclosures – so you can analyze them and know what you're getting into.

■ **What is your company's policy about canceling a contract if you or I am unhappy with the agreement?**

If the agent says there is no formal policy, insist on adding some kind of exit clause to the agreement. It can be as simple as you or the agent inserting a written statement into the agreement that dictates what happens if things don't work out or if you don't find a home by a certain date in the future.

## ■ How much do you charge?

Many agents will tell you that their services are absolutely free, and that's true. In most cases, the seller pays the real estate agent's commission – which is yet another reason for you to use a real estate pro during your house hunt. Still, in some instances, you might opt to use what's called a "Buyer's Agent." This is someone who works for you and represents your interests exclusively. In most cases, even when you use a Buyer's Agent, the seller will still pay your agent's commission. In some instances, though, you might have to pay a fee to a Buyer's Agent; if so, this fee is negotiable.

**Should You Use a Buyer's Agent?**

You've probably been past lots of homes for sale, often advertised with signs outside, right? Unless it was a "For Sale By Owner" property, you also likely noticed the name and phone number for a real estate agent you could call to get more information about the property. This agent is known as a "Listing Agent," because he or she represents sellers by listing their homes and marketing them to the public. A listing agent might charge a seller a commission anywhere from 1% to 6% of a home's listing price. Assume a house is listed for $300,000, and the listing agent is scheduled to receive a 6% commission. If the home ultimately does sell for that $300,000 asking price, and the listing agent sells the house on her own, that agent would get $18,000, or the full 6% commission. What happens, however, if another real estate agent brings a buyer to the table – or more accurately – to the front doorstep of the seller? In that case, the listing agent usually agrees to split his or her commission with the second agent. So that 6% commission gets divided in half, with 3% (or $9,000) going to the agent representing the seller, and 3% (the other $9,000) going to the agent representing the buyer.

Now here's where a "Buyer's Agent" comes into the picture. When you buy a home, you have the option to decide what kind of working relationship you will have with your real estate agent. Your options are based on what type of agent you select.

■ **Buyer's Agent:**

A buyer's agent, sometimes known as a "Buyer's Broker," works only for you and is legally bound to represent your best interests, first and foremost. This is the optimal agent for any homebuyer and the one I strongly urge you to choose. In fact, 64% of all homebuyers use a buyer's agent, according to the National Association of Realtors. One reason for this might be that when you work with a buyer's agent, he or she will usually agree to represent only you, as opposed to other buyers in the market for the same house.

As you interview real estate agents, try to find someone skilled as a buyer's agent. That person might be a licensed real estate professional or a Realtor. To find a Realtor who specializes in representing buyers, look for someone designated as an ABR, an Accredited Buyer Representative. Individuals with the ABR mark are Realtors who have advanced training in negotiation, and have completed at least five transactions in which they served solely as a buyer's agent. The NAR's Real Estate Buyer's Agent Council (REBAC) awards the ABR designation. You can find a list of REBAC members online at: http://www.rebac.net.

If you sign an agreement to be represented by a buyer's agent, your agreement will spell out the agent's compensation. The agent can be compensated by the seller, the buyer, or both. In most cases, the seller will pay the agent's commission. Even when the seller pays your agent, a buyer's agent is still obligated to represent your interests exclusively. In certain instances, though, you might want to really motivate your agent and agree to pay that person yourself for his or her efforts. If you do agree to pay the broker, you can either negotiate a flat fee, or a commission that is based on a percentage of the home's selling price.

Finally, if you do work with a buyer's broker, you can limit the agreement to homes for sale in the Multiple Listing Service. This way, you're still free to buy a home directly from a seller who has a "For Sale By Owner" sign outside in the yard and who might refuse to work with agents.

■ **Seller's Agent:**

A seller's agent works only for the seller of the home, so his or her job is to look out for the seller's best interests above all. Clearly, this is not the agent to get you the best deal on a home since he or she is trying to get the highest price for the seller.

■ **Disclosed Dual Agent:**

A disclosed dual agent works for both the buyer and the seller. This could be the case if an agent is listing a property for sale, and you call the agent because you're interested in the home, then wind up buying that property. I suggest that you refrain from buying your home through a dual agent. There is too much at stake, and you don't want your agent to have a conflict of interest. How can this person effectively represent both your best interests and the seller's? It's impossible. As a result, many states don't even permit dual agency.

■ **Designated Agent:**

Under the terms of designated agency a broker can appoint one agent affiliated with that broker to represent the seller and another agent employed by that same broker to represent the buyer in the same transaction. By having two separate agents involved in the deal, you technically avoid a dual agency relationship. Still, I think designated agency can also be problematic. If two agents are working in the same office, there's a possibility that they will talk about the deal – even if accidentally. A little comment like "Oh, my client just loved that house!" from the buyer's agent could signal to the seller's agent that his client should hold firm on the price because the buyer is really interested. Fortunately, whenever dual and designated agencies are allowed, this status must be disclosed to you, the buyer, and the seller. Also, all parties involved in the real estate transaction must agree to the relationship. Again, because of the potential pitfalls inherent in dual agency and designated agency, I suggest that you avoid these arrangements when buying a home.

**A Few Final Words About Agents**

No matter what type of agent you select, there are a couple of do's and don'ts you should follow in working with this person.

- Do expect the agent to be responsive to your needs and requests, but don't be unreasonable in your demands.

- Do sign an agreement before you go out looking for homes together, and once you do, don't violate the agreement by working with another agent; that will only cause problems, and potential legal headaches too.

- Do give your agent a conservative price range you'd be comfortable with, but don't disclose everything about your finances to the agent. It won't help you and, in some cases, it can hurt you. The best strategy is to hold your cards "close to the vest" and not completely tip your hand about how much you can or would spend on a new home.

- Do request that the agent perform his or her homework in showing you properties and telling you about the area, but don't expect the agent to do 100% of the due diligence you might want on a community. By law, agents are not able to tell you about crime or the ethnic make-up of various neighborhoods. They can, however, point you in the right direction to acquire such insights on your own.

Pat Massenberg, a licensed real estate agent from West Orange, New Jersey, says, "The best agents aren't those who know everything, because no one can know everything. But top real estate agents do know where to find information, and they can tell you where to get the info you need."

In the end, pick the agent who is most professional, knowledgeable, and experienced to handle your needs. Also make sure you select someone with good communication skills. You want a person who can explain lots of things to you in laymen's terms – as well as listen and hear your point of view, hopes, wishes, and fears.

If you get stuck with a bad real estate agent who keeps showing you properties well outside your price range, or who doesn't seem to understand what you're looking for, don't get rid of the person immediately. Perhaps there's been a miscommunication and the individual doesn't understand your needs. First take the time to communicate clearly about any issues of concern. After that, if the situation doesn't change, the agent clearly isn't listening, is incompetent, or is just trying to get a bigger commission – all of which are grounds for severing the relationship. Waste no time with an agent like this. Cut your losses and move on as quickly as possible. Also, don't stand for a real estate agent who insists on steering you into certain neighborhoods on the basis of your race. Report the person to HUD, which enforces the Fair Housing Act, a law that forbids discrimination on the basis of race, religion, color, and other factors.

**Getting the Most out of the MLS Database**

Real estate agents in most markets nationwide use an electronic database known as the MLS, or Multiple Listing Service, to share information about properties for sale. The MLS can tell you plenty of information about houses on the market, including a home's asking price, the square footage of the residence, how many bedrooms and bathrooms it has, and the annual taxes on the home. Traditionally, the MLS system was accessible only to real estate brokers and licensed real estate agents who were Realtors, affiliates of a local real estate board, or members of a trade group, such as the National Association of Realtors or the CREA, the Canadian Real Estate Association.

However, MLS systems operate independently, on a state-by-state basis, with local rules and practices governing how information is accessed and shared. Consequently, and due to the fragmented nature of the real estate market, you can often get good access to the same MLS data that real estate brokers and agents use. For example, many brokers and online services allow sellers of FSBO (For Sale By Owner) properties to pay a flat fee and list their homes in a local MLS database. The same structure works for buyers. For example, Redfin, an online firm, lets you access the MLS to search for properties in different markets across the country. Redfin (http://www.redfin.com) bills itself as a home-buying program that combines the best of the Web with the services of a local, experienced real estate agent. The company says that by using its service, you can save around

$10,000. How so? Well, if you find a home on your own, 67% of Redfin's commission is refunded to you at closing – even though a Redfin agent still handles your paperwork and negotiations and works with you during inspections and the closing process. As of this writing, Redfin agents were available in Boston, Chicago, Seattle, Washington, D.C., and several markets in California, including the greater Los Angeles area, Orange County, San Diego, and the San Francisco Bay region.

Other ways for you to access MLS information are to use Realtor.com, visit a real estate website called – appropriately enough – Multiple Listing Service (http://www.mls.com), or just do a "Google" search for a local MLS. For instance, in northern New Jersey, where I live, there's the Garden State Multiple Listing Service, at http://www.gsmls.com, which has information on 98% of all homes on the state's MLS.

Whichever site you use to access the MLS, leverage this database most effectively and avoid wasting time by signing up, if the option is available, for daily or weekly email updates about new homes coming on the market. You can also get electronic alerts when homeowners drop their asking prices on homes listed in the MLS.

### Using the Internet for Your Search

Experts estimate that 80% of homebuyers launch their search for a new house by using the Internet. As wonderful as the Web is, you also need to be aware of its limitations. Sometimes, the data you get online can be outdated. Other times, people are enormously creative in describing properties over the Internet as a way to lure you to come see a house. For instance, a "cozy" three bedroom might really mean a super-small home – or worse, a tiny shack. A "handyman's special" or a home "in need of a little TLC" might actually need to be totally gutted and renovated or a home built in 1960 with "newer" appliances and fixtures might be "new," but in 1990s-style new.

Pre-screen a property visually – look at its exterior and interior on the Web before you make an appointment to see the home in person. Many buyers find that pictures on the Web are truly worth a thousand words. If the outside of a home or its interior layout is flat-out unappealing to you, it's probably a waste of your time to go see it. You can preview homes first on sites like Realtor.com, where numerous photos are posted along with descriptions of homes for sale. Realtor.com even has an advanced search tool, under the "Find a Home" menu, that lets you sort your results based on the number of photos shown for a home.

Also, when you use the Internet to get comparable sales data, make sure you're looking at current listings and recent sales – not old information from a year ago. In many markets, housing prices can change quickly, and you don't want to rely on stale data to make your purchasing decisions.

In addition to Realtor.com, a slew of other consumer-friendly websites have emerged in recent years to help make your home shopping process a lot easier. These websites give you a peek into everything from how much a given home sold for or what the average sales price is for houses on a specific street, to data about price appreciation and equity in a home.

For this type of information, try the following sites:

| |
|---|
| http://www.eppraisal.com |
| http://www.cyberhomes.com |
| http://www.homegain.com |
| http://www.homevalence.com |
| http://www.propertyshark.com |
| http://www.realestateabc.com |
| http://www.reply.com |
| http://www.zillow.com |

Be warned, though, that none of these sites are as "in the know" about home prices and regional conditions as a good local real estate agent. In fact, in a *Wall Street Journal* article, Zillow executives acknowledged that their home price estimates – while dead-on for some houses and certain areas – can also sometimes be way off the mark. The company, therefore, suggests that you use its "Zestimates" as a starting point, and not regard the numbers as gospel. This is good advice for any homebuyer (or homeowner for that matter) using an online site to estimate a home's value.

If you think appraisals that you get from real live humans will always be more accurate and consistent, think again. In August 2007, my husband and I had four professional appraisers do separate appraisals on our home. The four appraisals came back as follows: $620,000, $650,000, $714,000, and $725,000. There was a $105,000 difference between the lowest and highest appraisal! That's a lot of variation. Are you curious to know how those detailed, in-person appraisals stacked up to online appraisals? And were online appraisals better? I'll let you be the judge. Here is what we found online:

- Eppraisal.com gave the following range for our home:
  - $525,632 for a low price
  - $618,390 for a middle price; and
  - $711,148 for a high price.

- Zillow's Zestimate concluded that our home was worth $511,644, with a value range of $450,247 - $634,439.

- Realestate.com returned these prices:
  - $605,000 – Low estimate
  - $672,500 – Median estimate
  - $740,000 – High estimate.

- Cyberhomes.com produced this estimate: $697,910, based on an estimated value range of $628,119 - $802,596.

- Reply.com said our house was worth $618, 931.

- Homegain.com estimated the home was valued between $698,261 - $819,698.

Realestateabc.com didn't have enough information for an estimate, and

PropertyShark.com doesn't give users a specific estimate. Instead it tells you what other homes in the neighborhood sold for and lets you draw your own conclusion. A quick look at the numbers from the online sources above shows the very lowest estimate at $450,247 and the highest estimate at $819,698. That's an incredible price difference of nearly $370,000!

The lesson here is to take these online estimates with a grain of salt. Use them as an initial reference point, but don't make the mistake of under-bidding or over-bidding on a house based solely on property values or estimates you find on the Internet. Also, if you already have an agent, don't fill out any forms online requesting that someone contact you. If you do, multiple real estate agents will reach out to you – either by phone, email, or snail mail. Moreover, you could find your inbox clogged with tons of unwanted housing-related solicitations and emails – everything from moving services to mortgage banks might begin to spam you.

**Leverage for "For Sale By Owner" Networks**

In your search for the perfect home, don't think that houses listed on the MLS are the beginning and end of the home-sale universe. In fact, during any given month, hundreds of thousands of homes are available for sale which might not be listed on the MLS at all. Many of these are "For Sale By Owner" properties. The owners of these homes often do not want to pay any commission to an agent. However, some homeowners are more than happy to compensate a buyer's agent if your agent brings you to the home and facilitates the deal. Some of the most popular FSBO (pronounced fiz-boh) websites you should explore include:

| http://www.fsbo.com |
| http://www.forsalebyowner.com |
| http://www.fsbosearch.com |
| http://www.homesbyowner.com |
| http://www.owners.com |

All these sites contain photos of houses for sale, have detailed home descriptions, and are free for buyers to browse. Sellers typically pay a fee to have their homes listed and advertised online. As a buyer, you can also get property alerts and save listings of interest. So make sure you don't skip the vast FSBO network of potential homes while you are house-hunting. If you do, you could miss out on an entire group of homes – one of which might be waiting just for you.

## Do's and Don'ts During the Open House Process

An open house is a like a beauty pageant to showcase a home's finer qualities. Savvy buyers will look past the glitz and glamour and know how to use an open house advantageously. Here's what you should do – and not do – in order to get the most out of those numerous open houses you'll undoubtedly attend.

First, let me tell you what to avoid; then I'll give you tips on how to work an open house like a pro.

### ■ Don't waste time on homes you know you won't buy

If you walk into a home and it instantly turns you off, you won't offend a real estate agent by taking a rapid look at the property, minimizing questions about it, and quickly leaving. Real estate pros have seen it all – from prospective buyers who speed through a home in one or two minutes flat – to potential buyers who linger in a home for 30 minutes or more. If you fall into the prior group, no need to apologize for your hasty retreat. If asked directly, "Do you like this home?" feel free to be honest, though gracious, about saying that the home isn't what you are seeking. A simple line like: "It's nice, but I'm afraid it doesn't suit my needs," will suffice.

### ■ Don't lose your mind over a home – even if you would give your right arm for it

Have you ever been to an auction where people get caught up in the emotion and frenzy of the event? Sometimes, auction bidders find themselves so swept away by the charged atmosphere that they lose all commonsense, and wind up bidding reck-lessly for something they absolutely "must have." This can be a dangerous thing if you get caught up in the beauty and appeal of a home, particularly if you see lots of other buyers clamoring for that property.

No matter how phenomenal the home – in terms of aesthetics, price, condition of the home, or other features – it's always a bad idea if you think only with your heart, and not with your head at an open house. Sometimes, first-time buyers and even move-up buyers will walk into a home and simply lose their minds. They gush over the open layout. They ooh and ahh over the newly-renovated kitchen. And they practically plunk down on the owner's nice big king-sized bed in that grandiose master bedroom suite. Needless to say, these are all big mistakes. I'm not asking you to put on the world's best poker face, but don't look like a kid in a candy store either. Have some restraint even if you're looking at a trophy home. I recently toured a $1.5 million estate in the next town over from where I live. It was a phenomenal, 6,400 square-foot home, complete with a pool and cabana, floor-to-ceiling windows, and a to-die-for view, set on two-and-a-half acres. Was it glorious? Of course it was! But I didn't let my jaw drop when I walked in the place – not even when I marveled (to myself, of course) about the home's dramatic 25 foot-high ceilings.

### ■ Don't criticize homes you love or homes you hate

Sometimes when buyers really love a house, to hide their true emotions they'll nitpick over the smallest defects, or quibble over inconsequential things. While you might think you're masking your interest in a home, many real estate agents know this ploy. In fact, some agents say they love it when a buyer fusses over little details, because it means the person is picturing him or herself in the home – a sure sign of interest. Your best bet: keep negative comments to yourself. You can certainly ask questions about material flaws or defects, but make your inquiry a matter of fact-finding. Don't take issue with the homeowners' décor or the fact that the house smells like pet dogs or cats. Trust me: if it's smelly in the house, the agent (and the homeowner) already knows it.

### ■ Don't disclose your buying power

When you walk into a home, be prepared to sign a sheet for potential buyers, and indicate whether you're working with an agent. Of course, if your agent is there with you, it will be obvious that you have representation. Nonetheless, it is common for listing agents showing a home to pepper buyers with questions. The ones to watch out for are: "What's your price range?" or "Does this home fit your price range?" That's the seller's agent's way of fishing around to find out if you're interested in the home, and – more importantly – if you can actually afford it. If an agent poses such a query, just deflect the question with a noncommittal reply like: "I'm still looking, so the price I'm willing to pay really depends on the quality of the home and how well it suits my needs." If they push further, inquiring about whether that specific home is in your budget, you can simply say: "Well, I'm looking for a home that's a great value." Another option: pause (for a long time) and give a one-word answer – "Possibly."

OK, now let's talk about what you should be doing when you attend an open house. All of these ideas are designed to help you find the home of your dreams as quickly as humanly feasible, and get the best possible price on the home too.

### ■ Do ask why the homeowner is moving

You'd be surprised the juicy tidbits of information you can learn simply by asking: "Why is the owner selling this home?" Some listing agents will gloss over the question, and give you a generic reply like: "They're just ready to move on." Well, duh, any home on the market signals the owner is ready to move. Don't let that answer halt you in your tracks. Restate your question, if necessary, asking about the owner's motivation for selling – based on your observation of the house. For instance, if you see that the house is empty, or nearly empty, it's probably safe to assume that the homeowners have moved out or are in the process of doing so. Therefore, you could ask something like: "Have the owners bought a new home already?" In response, the agent might tell you yes, a fact that could give you some bargaining power down the road.

Let's say you notice that the photos all around the house show elderly people with their kids and grandkids. You might comment, "Looks like they've retired. Are the owners downsizing or relocating to a warmer climate?" Again, an agent's reply could be telling. In fact, you'd be shocked at what you might learn just by asking, "Why is the owner moving?" Sometimes, you might learn of an impending divorce, a job transfer taking place, an out-of-state relocation for personal reasons – all sorts of things. I've known some agents and even homeowners themselves to be honest enough to tell prospective buyers that the sellers simply didn't like the neighborhood anymore; that it has changed and, for whatever reason, the homeowner is fed up living there. Go figure! In any event, knowing the owner's rationale for leaving is one of the key tidbits of information you'll obtain if you use your time wisely during an open house.

### ■ Do find out how long the home has been on the market

One of the best ways to gauge how open a seller might be to a reduced offer is to find out how long the home has been for sale. Generally speaking, the longer the home has been on the market, the more desperate sellers become. This makes them far more willing to negotiate – especially if time is of the essence for the seller. They might have already bought another property, or have a home under contract, and want to avoid carrying two mortgages. Note: this isn't always the case. Remember that luxury estate I mentioned that I visited during an open house? Well, it turns out it was on the market for an entire year! However, the owners could probably care less. They were an ultra-wealthy couple who had retired after years of owning their own business, and when they moved out of the home, they didn't downsize like many older folks do. Instead, they actually bought their ultimate dream home: a 25,000-square foot mansion on nearly two dozen acres. With that kind of money, carrying that second note wasn't a problem for them.

### ■ Do ask if the owners have received any offers

In response to this question, you might learn that there have been no takers, or that the seller has rejected offers deemed too low. Such information could help you to position a bid if you're interested in the home.

### ■ Do bring a notepad and/or a digital camera with you

After seeing house after house, week after week, everything will become a blur. It will be difficult to remember which house had that nice master bedroom with the walk-in closet, and which one had the kitchen that needed updating. A camera – even one from your cell phone is fine – will help you to recall these things. Also, a notepad will be useful for you to record your overall impressions and gut feelings. Write down whether or not you like the neighborhood, how much curb appeal you think a home has, and what you think of neighboring properties (or even the next door neighbors themselves if you see and/or meet them). Also note unique characteristics about a home, such as nice moldings or special architectural features. By the same token, if you have serious concerns about a property you like – say about a large crack you saw in a ceiling, or a basement that appeared to have suffered water damage – write that down too. A good idea might be to rate each home you see, giving it a score of 1 to 10 after you leave the house. When you start to narrow down your search, or if you want to go back and look at homes a second time, scratch off anything on the list ranked 6 or lower. Only look at homes with a 7 or 8 ranking, or higher. After all, your new home might not be perfect, but you do want to buy a house you absolutely love, right?

**The Importance of Cruising the Neighborhood**

I've told you already about how you can use the Internet to jumpstart your home search. Now I want to tell you about the importance of getting out there and looking at a home and it's neighborhood in person. While the Web is great for giving you preliminary info about a home or a community, it's certainly no substitute for what you can see with your own two eyes just by driving around a neighborhood of interest. Before you make an offer on a home, it's critical that you scour the neighborhood carefully.

Just because all is peaceful and quiet on a Sunday afternoon when you first saw the house, doesn't mean it's the same way on Saturday nights or weekday mornings. Drive around a neighborhood at different times and different days of the week to get a feel for whether or not it's a place you'd really like to live. Take a lunch break from work if you have to, and visit the area during the middle of the day. Hit a local coffee shop or diner to see how people in the area treat you. When you walk down the street, do people look the other way or do they greet you with a hearty "hello"? Do neighbors and community members seem snooty and stuck up, or are they warm and friendly? A good place to experience the locals is to go to the local supermarket – again, during the middle of the day – and do a little people watching. First eyeball the cars that you see in the parking lot. Are people shopping for basic groceries in fur coats, and is the parking lot full of luxury cars and convertibles? Also, take notice of what kind of stores are in the neighborhood. Do you see any pawnshops or payday lenders nearby, or do high-end retailers dominate the area?

Visit your intended area from different routes. People are creatures of habit and tend to travel the same route over and over. You need to know, however, if there's a penitentiary or a psychiatric ward just three minutes away on the road less traveled. Also, where are essential services? How far away is the closest hospital and what is the quality of that hospital? Ditto for schools in the area. If you have kids, or intend to, you definitely want to check out the local school district.

Just because you're cruising a neighborhood in your car – looking for homes the old-fashioned way –doesn't mean you can't use new-age technology to aid you in your property search. Be sure to take a cell phone or PDA with you. If you have one handy, you'll be able to use sites like http://www.housefront.com, Realtor.com, or PropertyMap.com to your advantage. Say you're out driving around one Sunday and you see a home of interest. Simply text the home's address to 46873 (HOUSE) and Housefront.com will text you back a message to your mobile phone with details about the home. It can give you an estimate of the home's value, provide you with its sales history, and tell you the size of the property, along with how many bedrooms and bathrooms it has. The company's online website also accepts comments from the public about properties, which allows you to see what other house-hunters think about a house.

No matter what other people think, you have to go with your gut instincts and select the home that is most appropriate, affordable, and best-suited for your needs. Nevertheless, I want to offer one final recommendation for you to keep in mind when searching for a house. Simply put, there are some places you should not buy your first home. Avoid buying a home in any area that is:

- economically depressed (perhaps because of a lack of decent transportation, inadequate infrastructure, or a shortage of good jobs and local businesses to hire people)

- completely crime-ridden (even if the community is "coming back," that renewal could take many years)

- situated in a poor location (like near power lines, a very busy intersection, or adjacent to noisy commercial businesses)

All of these situations can negatively impact your home's value. Plus, you have to think about the prospect of selling your home down the road. Even though you might not be bothered by living right next to a major highway or a street with a lot of traffic, many other prospective buyers will. So no matter how much you love a house, if it's in a terrible location it will be far more difficult to sell in the future.

### Five Reasons to Hire a Competent Home Inspector

Let's fast forward things a bit and assume you've finally found a property you're interested in buying. Congratulations!

Before you agree to make one of the biggest financial commitments of your life, however, you'd be wise to get the home properly inspected – no matter how nice it appears to be. Even brand new homes can, and do, have problems. It's foolish to make such an enormous investment if you're not willing to spend the time and money necessary to protect it. That's what an inspection is: protection of sorts against things that might not be apparent to the untrained eye. To a seasoned home inspector, though, problems stick out like a sore thumb.

With this in mind, here are five reasons you definitely need to have a home inspector:

- **You'll get important details about your home**

Most lenders mandate basic inspections to make sure a house is free of termites and all kinds of nasty, wood-destroying insects. Additionally, you might also want to inspect for other things, like asbestos, the quality of the roof, or the status of a septic tank on the property. The most vital inspection, though, is optional, although you should regard it as mandatory. It's a general home inspection, which you should insist on doing before finalizing any house purchase. In this inspection, a professional will evaluate your potential home in detail, giving you a report that is 20 to 50 pages long about the structure of the house, its electrical, plumbing, and heating systems, as well as information about its roof, doors, windows, and other structures. How else would you know if the home's electrical work was shoddy or the plumbing system problematic?

Another tip: Go with the inspector on the day that he or she evaluates the property. You'll learn a lot about the home, which will make you a much more informed homeowner, should you go through with the purchase. Plan to spend at least three hours with the inspector. Depending on the size of the house and the condition of the property, some inspections can take as long as five hours.

### ■ An inspection could help you negotiate a better price

If the home inspection turns up significant problems – say, the air condition units in the house don't work – you could use this as a negotiating point to get a better price from the seller.

### ■ You'll minimize problems down the road

Even if the home seems like it's in tip-top condition, you should get an expert opinion to back up your hunches. Chances are, a pro will find things you never imagined were wrong with the house. Some issues could be minor, but there might be major safety issues. Either way, you'll know what needs to be done – and how quickly the situation should be addressed – if you hire a competent home inspector.

### ■ Your Uncle Joe can't do it

Some homebuyers try to cut corners and have a family member or friend do a home inspection. Please don't do this – at least not unless your uncle is a licensed home inspector. If you get a friend or relative to do it on the cheap – or even free of charge – what's your recourse if they mess up and miss something? You'll have a strained family relationship, and a lemon of a house to deal with, too. For these reasons, only hire someone who is a professional and is designated as such. Find a competent home inspector through referrals or through a home inspector association, such as ASHI, the American Society of Home Inspectors (http://www.ashi.com).

### ■ You'll have peace of mind

Sometimes homebuyers see problems in a home, such as a hairline fracture in a wall or a little bit of water in a basement, and fear the worse. All of a sudden that crack in the wall looks like damage to the house's foundation, or you're absolutely certain that the water in the basement is from constant flooding. A certified home inspector can put your fears to rest, by explaining to you what problems are serious and which problems can be readily fixed. Even if the inspector comes back with a laundry list of little things that could or should be handled, those small items probably aren't worth scuttling the deal. Most times you're better off getting a price break from the seller, then using the money you saved to fix any problems. Sometimes, however, a good home inspection can save you from buying a home that would've been nothing but headaches.

Listen to this story from J. Paige Clowser, who moved into her very first home this past Memorial Day weekend. Paige and her husband, Tony, were both 26 and married for three years when they bought their 3-bedroom, 2-bath split level in a suburb of Cleveland.

"We probably looked at more than 30 houses before we settled on this one," Paige says. The couple actually came close to buying two previous homes – before inspections of the properties turned up significant problems.

The first property was a foreclosure. It was on the market for $149,000, but needed major work – like foundation repairs, a whole new kitchen, and even basic appliances, like a stove and refrigerator. Walking away from that deal was relatively easy. It was the second home that Paige almost bought that resulted in what she calls "homebuyer's heartbreak."

"It was such a cute, quaint house, and it was in a city with a good school district. The house listed for $159,000 in a neighborhood you can't get into for under $200,000," she recalls. "We went to the house at first, and the next weekend my husband's parents went with us," Paige says. "We were so infatuated with the pretty things about the house, like the great kitchen layout, that we didn't notice major issues with the house, like foundation problems in the basement. My father-in-law actually pointed those out."

Soon after, other problems turned up, including mold in the attic, as well as water damage to foundation walls, beams, and floors in the basement. "The first time you're in a house, you're so excited to get a place of your own that you over-look things, because you're thinking about decorating and entertaining," Paige says. Fortunately, they didn't buy that lemon of a house. In fact, after living in an apartment for three years, being in their own 1500-square foot home, complete with its deck, backyard, and basement, is a dream come true. "We definitely think it's one of the best things we ever did," Paige says about buying her first home, adding, "It's certainly nice to have privacy, a garage, and just little things; like, in our old apartment building, we weren't allowed to have a dog. But this past weekend, we got two puppies."

As Paige's story illustrates, doing a serious inspection of a home is always worth your time and money.

## Questions to Ask Before Choosing an Inspector

Since most states don't license or regulate inspectors, be careful to avoid retaining the services of individuals who simply hang out a shingle and call themselves "professional" inspectors. Before you hire an inspector, pose the following questions:

■  **Are you certified?**

"No" is automatic grounds to eliminate that person from your list of potential inspectors. Only go with a certified inspector because it shows at least a minimum level of commitment to the profession and basic proof of the inspector's industry knowledge and expertise. Besides, with so many home inspector associations out there, it says volumes about a so-called "professional" inspector if he or she hasn't gotten certified by at least one organization. The best known association for inspectors in the U.S. is ASHI, the American Society of Home Inspectors. Others include the National Association of Home Inspectors (http://www.nahi.org) and the International Society of Home Inspectors (http://www.ishionline.org).

### ■ Where were you trained?

Ideally, the inspector should indicate relevant formal training, continuing education courses taken in the past or currently being attended, or having learned the trade through lots of hands-on work experience. Pick someone who's been inspecting homes at least three years.

### ■ Do you belong to a professional organization?

"Yes" is a preferable answer. Just be aware that some professional groups are little more than window-dressing. They don't require much of their members – other than a membership fee to join.

### ■ Do you have "Errors and Omissions" insurance?

This is malpractice insurance which kicks in if the inspector fails to spot a major problem which later emerges. Sometimes, however, any damages you recover based on E&O coverage are limited to the amount you paid for your home inspection.

### ■ How long will the inspection take?

If an inspector says anything less than three hours, he's probably not going to do as thorough a job as should be done.

### ■ How much do you charge?

Depending on where you live, expect to pay between $250 and $500. Also, if additional services are included – say the inspector is also qualified to inspect a septic tank – your inspection will cost more. (Termite inspections are separate, though, because home inspectors aren't licensed to do pest inspections.)

The answers to these questions should help you find a competent home inspector.

Again, this person's services are crucial. I encourage you to not take shortcuts. Pay what it takes to hire a professional; otherwise, you might soon regret your mistake.

## Lining up the Best Lawyer for You

The last member of your real estate team you might need to get is an attorney. Whether or not you need a lawyer largely depends on the part of the country in which you live and local customs in your area. Some real estate deals go off without a hitch without the presence of a lawyer at any stage. Others have attorneys involved from the get-go as a matter of routine practice.

A lawyer can help you at several points in the home hunting and home purchasing process. If you're working without an agent, a lawyer can help you draft a contract or a written offer to purchase a home. Most often, of course, you will have a real estate agent. Then the purpose of having a lawyer would be to represent your interests at closing, perhaps to do a title search, review the title on a property, prepare a title insurance policy, and negotiate any issues that might arise with the seller's attorney.

As is the case in hiring any professional, you want to get someone competent to do the job, an effective communicator, and an individual skilled in handling situations like yours. Don't hire a corporate lawyer or a divorce attorney – or worse, your cousin, the personal injury lawyer – to represent you during this transaction. Stick with an attorney who specializes in real estate law. Ask people you know for referrals to good property attorneys. Your real estate agent should also be able to recommend someone. Additionally, you can find a qualified lawyer through the American Bar Association (http://www.abanet.org), as well as websites like AllLaw.com, Lawyers.com, FindLaw.com, or LegalMatch.com. Lastly, you have the option of using the attorney that your bank is using. Whatever you decide, a good lawyer will probably cost you at least $250, and could be as much as $1,000. In the end, it will be money well-spent, especially since it will give you the confidence in knowing that should any problems arise, those issues will be handled by a trained professional and an advocate who's in your corner.

# C H A P T E R

## 8

## Negotiate the Best Possible Deal From a Seller

To make a smart transition from renter to owner, it's not enough to simply find a home you really want. You also have to get an affordable house at a price you can live with. Fortunately, there are ways to reduce your cost of homeownership from the outset – just by obtaining the best possible deal on any home you buy.

### Tips to Secure the Right Price From a Seller

To effectively negotiate a great deal from someone who's selling their home, you must start with having a very good idea of local market conditions. This is where you real estate agent should really earn his or her money. By giving you a sense of recent comps, you'll know how active the market is, and where pricing trends seem to be heading. When you have a good handle on comps, you'll also know how the home you want to buy stacks up against similar homes. If your place has fewer bedrooms, is smaller, lacks a garage that other similar homes have, or is substantially lacks in any way compared to the competition, all those factors should weigh into the offer you make on the house.

Getting the best deal doesn't rest solely on comps either. What you ultimately pay for a new home will also be determined by a whole host of other issues to be negotiated – everything from when you will take possession of the house to what fixtures will remain in the property. Even such matters as inspections and contingency clauses can impact what you spend on a home.

### Strategies for Buying in a Seller's Market

If you happen to buy a house during a seller's market, you have to be smarter than ever about getting a good deal. In a seller's market, there might be relatively few homes for sale, a glut of buyers all vying for the same houses, or economic circumstances that make it relatively more attractive to unload a house – rather than buy one. Whatever the case, in a seller's market, existing homeowners are generally in the driver's seat. That doesn't mean, however, that you can't use some savvy strategies to minimize your cost of home ownership. Try these techniques to leave a little more money in your pocket when you get that new home.

■ **Include a Pre-Approval Letter With Your Offer**

Remember all that hard work I had you do in order to prepare for homeownership? You had to learn about budgeting, saving, improving your credit, and other money-management techniques in order to get that pre-approval letter from a lender. Well, here's where some of that hard work starts to pay off. When you submit your purchase offer, forward a copy of your lender's pre-approval letter to the home seller to stand out from other buyers who lack pre-approval. With a pre-approval letter in hand, you come across as the more serious, committed buyer. Even if your bid is lower than a competing offer, with a strong pre-approval letter on the table (especially from a reputable financial institution) a seller is likely to look at you as a better prospect than someone who only then has to start the loan process – and might not get approved.

■ **Pick a Seller-Friendly Closing Date**

If you offer to close when the seller wants to settle, that could help you beat out competing offers – even if someone has a slightly higher bid for a home. The reason? A seller-friendly closing date satisfies the existing homeowner's needs. Maybe they need to wrap things up fast, in just 30 days or so, because of a planned cross-country relocation. If so, tell the seller in your purchase offer that you'll agreed to a speedy closing. In some cases, sellers might want to delay a closing, perhaps because they have kids in school and don't want to uproot the family before the end of the academic year. In this case, tell the seller you can wait to take possession of the home. Again, if you can be flexible on the closing date, this might make the seller more flexible on price.

### ■ Go Easy on Contingencies

Most offers to purchase homes contain contingencies, or so-called "weasel clauses" that let you back out of a deal if things don't go as planned down the road. For instance, it's common to have contingencies based on your getting a mortgage approval, on the house being appraised at the agreed-upon price, or on the property having a satisfactory inspection. I'm reluctant to tell you to forgo these contingency clauses in your agreement, however, you might omit other contingencies. For instance, according to federal law, you have 10 days to inspect a house for signs of lead paint contamination. You can waive your right to do so, and leave a lead paint contingency out of your offer, signaling to the seller that closing with you won't be a time-consuming, arduous process.

### ■ Provide a Serious Good Faith Deposit

When you make an offer on a home, it's customary to offer a "good faith deposit," which is also sometimes called an "earnest money deposit." The purpose of this deposit to is to show the seller that you're serious about your offer, even ahead of your providing your total down payment. In many markets, a good faith deposit is a nominal amount of money, perhaps just $500 to $1,000 or so. In a seller's market, however, you might consider making more than just a token deposit. To really demonstrate your intentions, particularly in high-priced markets, you could leave a much heftier deposit, of maybe 1% to 3% of the home's asking price. Even if you wind up sticking to your guns and not over-bidding on a home, leaving an initial good faith deposit that is relatively high puts the seller in a better mood to negotiate with you because you appear to be a more serious buyer. Your good faith deposit ultimately contributes to your overall down payment. If negotiations with a seller don't go through, you get your good faith deposit back. Remember, two things about your earnest money deposit. Never give it to the seller directly. Instead, let a real estate brokerage, law firm, title company, or escrow company hold the money in a trust account. Also, beware that if you default under the terms of your contract and your state has "liquidated damages" the seller might be entitled to keep your deposit.

### ■ Make a Large Down Payment

If you can swing it, make a bigger down payment in a seller's market in order to get the home you want and stand out from other potential buyers. Again, your down payment doesn't mean you have to pay more for the house. In fact, you can hold firm during negotiations. However, making a larger down payment – just like making a bigger good faith deposit – tilts the scales in your favor because psychologically sellers perceive you as more serious, which ultimately could mean you get a better deal on the house.

### ■ Include a Hand-Written Personal Note to the Seller

It may sound sappy, but many real estate agents will tell you how – in the middle of bidding wars and other heated contests for a given property – sometimes the buyer with the winning offer is the one with the personal touch. When you submit your purchase offer, also send the seller a hand-written note telling why you love the home so much, and why they should sell it to you. Even if someone tops your offer, in some situations you can tug at a seller's heart strings by letting the seller know that this is your dream house, you grew up in the neighborhood, you have always wished to live in that area, or you would care for the home in the same loving manner that the seller did. Whatever you say, be sincere and write from the heart. That way you might generate empathy and positive feelings from the right seller.

### ■ Bring out the Big Guns: An "All Cash" Offer

If you happen to be in the fortunate (and rare) position of being able to pay "all cash" for a home, don't hesitate to let a seller know this. The "all cash" offer is attractive to sellers because it means fewer worries about a buyer qualifying for a mortgage, and raises prospects for a speedier closing, too. The irony is that even when you put a down payment on a house, and a bank finances the rest of the cost, in the end the seller is still getting "all cash" at closing. When someone has cash up front, independent of a bank loan, that will always peak a home seller's interest.

## Strategies for Buying in a Buyer's Market

A buyer's market exists anytime there are more homes offered for sale than there are willing buyers. This might occur when the overall economy is poor, local economic conditions have taken a downturn, or real estate prices are flat or falling because of interest rates, credit conditions, or other factors like excessive development by home builders. Under any of these circumstances, the market is soft – which puts you, the buyer, in the driver's seat. This is the time when you can really get a bargain on a home – if you understand and apply some savvy strategies that will save you big bucks.

### ■ Consider Buying a Newly-Built Home

Sometimes, one of the best ways to knock the price off a dream home is to buy a property from a builder – instead of an individual. In a soft real estate market, new-home builders are often inclined to give you a dizzying array of freebies and sweeteners to entice you to seal a deal. Moreover, many will drastically slash prices to reduce their inventory and avoid having numerous unsold homes. Such was the case in 2007, when home builders nationwide dropped their prices by as much as 20%, and threw in a host of perks like luxury appliances, in-ground pools, and upgraded kitchen amenities. In fact, the National Association of Home Builders reports that 56% of builders offered financial incentives to homebuyers in 2007. Several of them, including Red Bank, N.J.-based Hovnanian Enterprises Inc., even gave home-buyers six-figure discounts off luxury homes. Hovnanian called its rock-bottom sales prices "The Deal of the Century."

"Every month that a new home sits there unsold, after it is finished, costs a builder money in taxes, insurance, interest, and so on. That's why they're inclined to lower the price, just to get rid of the carrying costs," says Bob Schultz, a sales expert on new homes from Florida.

Here is a list of the 10 largest new-home builders in the U.S. Visit their websites provided below to find new properties:

| |
|---|
| Beazer Homes USA Inc. of Atlanta, GA (http://www.beazer.com) |
| Centex Corp. of Dallas, TX (http://www.centex.com) |
| D.R. Horton Inc. of Fort Worth, TX (http://www.drhorton.com) |
| Hovnanian Enterprises Inc. of Red Bank, NJ (http://www.khov.com) |
| KB Home of Los Angeles, CA (http://www.kaufmanandbroad.com) |
| Lennar Corp. of Miami, FL (http://www.lennar.com) |
| NVR Inc. of Reston, VA (http://www.nvrinc.com) |
| Pulte Homes of Bloomfield Hills, MI (http://www.pulte.com) |
| Ryland Group Inc. of Calabasas, CA (http://www.ryland.com) |
| Toll Brothers Inc. of Horsham, PA (http://www.tollbrothers.com) |

Even if you don't buy a new home, you can use the fact that new-home builders are offering great prices as a negotiating point with sellers of existing homes. Sooner or later, in a down market, those sellers will have to lower their asking prices to keep in line with the competition.

■ **Attend a Property Auction**
Real estate auctions are becoming increasingly popular among home sellers, build-

ers, and even banks that own foreclosed properties. The big appeal of an auction – for both sellers and buyers – is the speed with which a transaction can be finalized. As a buyer in a soft market, auctions also give you an opportunity to snatch up a property at a nice discount. In 2007, I was interviewed on *Good Morning America* about the rise of real estate auctions. In that television segment, a newlywed couple, Sonny and Flerida Zaragoza, got their first home – their dream home – at a California auction for a steal: They paid $355,000, which was more than $100,000 off the market rate for their 2,000-square-foot house. According to the National Auctioneers Association, residential real estate auctions are the fastest-growing segment of the auction industry. Find a home this way via RealtyBid.com (http://www.realtybid.com), a rapidly-expanding online real estate auction firm, or through America's largest real estate auctioneer, Sheldon Good & Company (http://www.sheldongood.com),

### ■ Leave A Token Good Faith Deposit

Of course, most consumers won't buy through auctions, but rather directly from sellers. When a seller hasn't received many (or any) bites for his or her home, if you come along and make an offer, you can certainly give a small good faith deposit. This is the exact opposite, of course, of what you'd do during a seller's market. Leaving a nominal good faith deposit in this situation signals to the seller that you're interested in the house – but only if you can get it at a great price.

### ■ Provide a Modest Down Payment

Making a 3% to 5% down payment might be plenty to put on the table when you're purchasing a home in a buyer's market. Your modest down payment – just like your small good faith deposit – is your way of kicking off negotiations for the house. In this case, you're negotiating strategy will be to try to get a house for less than the owner's asking price – perhaps as much as 10% or more.

### ■ Ask the Seller to Pay Some or All of Your Fees

In most real estate contracts, fees are entirely negotiable. Even if in your area some fees are typically split among the buyer and seller, in a buyer's market you can ask the seller to pay for all the fees. Among the fees you might get the seller to cover are: county or city transfer taxes, inspections, appraisals, or various mortgage fees imposed by your lender.

### ■ Request a Seller Credit

When you request a "credit" from a home seller, you're asking the homeowner to provide you with a cash amount that you'll get upon closing, or settlement. Seller credits are often given when repairs need to be made or when a home requires significant upgrading. Even if a house simply needs paint or carpet you can get a seller credit. Don't think that something has to be wrong with the house in order to squeeze a little money out of a seller. In a buyer's market you can also ask for a credit simply as a financial concession from the seller. Many banks allow you to receive a seller credit of as much as 6% of the purchase price of the home. So if you're interested in a $200,000 house and want to receive a 5% seller credit, you would essentially get a $10,000 price reduction at closing. That money can be used to help fund your down payment or closing costs – which will provide you with significant savings.

### ■ Request All Necessary Contingencies

In a buyer's market you have more flexibility to ask for, and receive, any number of contingencies when you make a purchase offer. Therefore, you should make your bid contingent upon mortgage approval, satisfactory inspections and appraisals, as well as any other reasonable contingency. Remember, some contingencies – like a home inspection – can help you save money on a house because you can ask a seller for a price reduction if the inspection turns up costly repairs or serious problems that need to be addressed.

### ■ Set an Expiration Date for Your Offer

When you bid on a home include an expiration date with your offer in order to get a fast response from a home seller – and to fend off competing offers that might come in later. If you want to be really aggressive, you can ask a seller to respond to your offer within 24 to 48 hours, but be careful. Make sure the offer gets conveyed promptly to the homeowner. If they're out of town or have some kind of personal emergency, 24 hours might not be a reasonable expiration date. Nevertheless, in many cases using a tight expiration date gets the negotiations started quickly and might get you a better price on a home if the seller has no other offers within that limited time frame.

### ■ Ask for a Home Warranty

No matter whether you're buying an older or a newer home, it can be a good idea to get a home warranty to cover system problems that might occur after the closing. The warranty can protect you against future financial loss if say, the furnace goes out or the electrical system goes haywire. In your purchase offer, ask the home seller to buy a home warranty or give you a credit at closing in order for you to purchase the warranty on your own.

### ■ Request Extras as Bargaining Chips

Did you notice fine china, nice appliances in the house, or furniture and fixtures of value? If so, you might make your purchase offer contingent upon the inclusion of those items in the sale. Even if you don't really want the items, this can be a good way to negotiate a lower price. For example, you can ask for a washer and dryer that are not included in the seller's asking price – even if the seller has specifically said those items aren't part of the sale. If the seller rejects your offer, you can counter by agreeing to forgo those items, and lowering your offer price.

## Knowing When to Walk Away

Sometimes, despite your best efforts to negotiate a good deal on a house, it just might not work out. Either the seller refuses to budge on the price of a home that's outside of your reach, or the terms of the sale are unacceptable to you. Whatever the case, you have to know your limits and be prepared to walk away from a home – even a home you love – if it's overpriced or you simply can not afford it. That can sometimes be a hard thing to do if your heart is completely set on that particular house. Despite your feelings of disappointment or frustration, realize that there really is another great house out there waiting for you. It's not smart to overbid on a home or agree on a price that's financially unrealistic for you to manage. You don't want to wind up in foreclosure a year or two later. If you crunch the numbers and know in your heart that you'd be very cash-strapped to pay for a given house – to the point where you'd have to struggle to pay the rest of your bills – it's better to tell a seller "thanks but no thanks," and keep looking for another, more reasonably priced home.

# CHAPTER

## 9

## Select the Right Mortgage and a Good Lender

When you apply for a mortgage, be prepared to answer a slew of questions about your financial circumstances and credit history. As you learned in the first few chapters of this book, you'll get the best rates and terms from a lender if you have high FICO scores and a solid track record as a saver. Credit and cash won't be the only questions you encounter from lenders. They might also ask you in what type of mortgage you're interested, whether or not you want to make interest-only payments, and how long you plan to occupy the house. Knowing the answers to these questions – as well as having a basic working knowledge of how mortgages work – can help you select the right mortgage and lender.

### The ABCs of How Mortgages Work

People often talk about "getting" a mortgage from a bank or lending institution. The truth of the matter is that you don't technically "get" a mortgage – you actually "give" or "pledge" a mortgage to a lender.

When you buy a home, you sign a ton of documents. Perhaps the two most important documents are the "note" and the "mortgage." The note is simply the "IOU" you sign, attesting to the fact that you owe a debt to the lender and that you are making a promise to repay that loan. A "note" is also sometimes called a "bond." The mortgage is the legal document that secures the note. Therefore, when a bank loans you money, you "give" or "pledge" to the bank that mortgage, and the bank "takes back" the mortgage (i.e. this signed legal document) as a legal claim in the event you default on the terms of the note or the mortgage. In some states, a deed of trust is used instead of a mortgage. Both a mortgage and a deed of trust are legal instruments that create a lien against the property. Once you sign a deed of trust, you receive title to a home, but convey that title to a third-party, a trustee, until your loan is paid in full. Regardless of whether your state uses mortgages or deeds of trust, both documents spell out how your loan should be repaid, and what happens if you don't pay as agreed. In a worst-case scenario, you could be foreclosed upon for failing to honor the terms of your note, mortgage, or deed of trust.

Home loans are typically "amortized" over a 30-year period. This means you have a set payment schedule to pay off a part of the principal amount of the loan as well as part of the interest on the loan. In the beginning, most of your payment pays off interest, but the longer you keep the loan, a greater portion of your payment starts to pay your principal balance. While most mortgages are offered at 30-year terms, some loans can be as short as 10 years, and others can run as long as 50 years.

Additionally, although most of us think about paying "down" a mortgage, there are some types of home loans that you can get where your balance actually increases over time. Can you imagine that? You buy a house for $400,000 and five years later you wind up owing $450,000 on the house. How is this possible? It can happen if you get a loan with "negative amortization." Unfortunately, 12% of all loans originated in 2006 featured negative amortization. I don't think these loans are good for any homeowners – least of all first-time homebuyers. Stay away from so-called "neg-am" loans.

What other kinds of loans spell trouble? To answer that question, you must first understand that a huge array of loan products currently exist in the mortgage arena. Some of them can get terribly complicated. Fortunately, despite all the hundreds of variations of home loans in today's marketplace, all mortgages really boil down to two types: fixed-rate mortgages and adjustable rate mortgages, also known as ARMs.

## Pros and Cons of Fixed-Rate Mortgages

Fixed-Rate mortgages are the "plain vanilla" loans of the home lending universe. In many regions of the country, under a variety of market conditions, and for the majority of homebuyers, fixed-rate loans are the most attractive, meaning safe and secure, loans you can get.

When you take out a fixed-rate mortgage, your loan has a set interest rate that doesn't change, so you know exactly what your payment will be month after month, year after year. The payment you make in year one of the loan will be the same dollar amount you make in year seven, 15, 23, or 30 of the loan – provided you keep the house and don't sell or refinance it. The big advantage, therefore, to having a fixed-rate loan is that you are permanently locked into a mortgage that is predictable – eliminating the risk of any financial surprises later on, even if interest rates go up.

On the flip side, if interest rates go down, then your fixed-rate mortgage might not look so attractive. Assume you are paying 7% on a mortgage and interest rates drop to 6%. All of a sudden, your 7% loan doesn't seem like such a great deal, right? To get a lower rate, you'd have to refinance your loan – a process that will involve additional fees and closing costs – because a "refi" entails paying off your existing loan and replacing it with a whole new loan.

## Adjustable Rate Mortgages: Are They Right for You?

Unlike their fixed-rate cousins, adjustable rate mortgages – as their name implies – feature variable interest rates that change or "reset" over time, resulting in a mortgage payment that also fluctuates. With a 30-year adjustable rate mortgage, the interest rate you pay on a home loan could increase or decrease every year, or even as often as every month, based on current interest rates. Lenders have gotten especially creative with ARMs in recent years. Banks know that many consumers favor fixed-rate mortgages for their predictability. Therefore, many popular ARM products try to mimic the stability afforded by fixed-rate mortgages. With these so-called "hybrid" ARMs, your payment could be fixed for two or three years, then move to an annually adjusted interest rate. This is the case with many 2/28 and 3/27 ARMS, which have become widespread in many markets. These loans have interest rates that are fixed for the first two or three years, then change annually for the rest of the 30-year loan term.

Consumers typically choose adjustable rate mortgages for two reasons: flexibility and affordability. Some ARMS feature "payment option" plans, which allow you to decide how much of the principal, if any, you pay on your mortgage each month. If your income is erratic, or if you find yourself in a financial pinch down the road, this can be an attractive feature. However, loans with payment option plans are also loans with negative amortization, so if you're not careful, you might not pay enough money on your home loan to reduce the principal sufficiently in order to build equity in the home.

The second (and primary) reason people choose ARMS is to be able to afford more house than they could get with a fixed-rate mortgage. Frequently with an adjustable rate mortgage you can get a lower-interest rate loan – initially at least – than you can get with a fixed-rate mortgage. Let's say your budget will allow you to have a mortgage with a maximum monthly payment of $2,400 a month. Assume you find a house that requires a $350,000 mortgage. If you take out a 7% fixed-rate loan over 30 years, your monthly payment (for principal and interest) would be $2,329. The only problem is that you're not completely in love with this particular house. Your dream home – the one you really want – is actually $100,000 more. With the traditional 30-year fixed rate mortgage, you couldn't afford it because with a $450,000 loan, your monthly mortgage would be $2,994 – nearly $600 above your financial comfort zone. However, if you could get a lower monthly payment simply by selecting a 5/1 ARM, an adjustable rate mortgage that features a low "teaser" rate of just 5.75% for the first five years and which converts, in the sixth year, to prevailing interest rates. Under this scenario, your initial mortgage payments (for the first five years) would be $2,628.

Many homebuyers facing this dilemma follow their hearts – not their wallets – and choose the higher priced house. Although it's $228 above their pre-set monthly limit, because the ARM features such a low initial interest rate, buyers allow themselves to "stretch" their budget and select a more expensive house. For those with steadily rising incomes, an ARM can be a reasonable option. However, it's risky to bet that "it will work out somehow," and take a mortgage loan without knowing precisely how you'll pay it. It's equally risky to get an ARM thinking "I can always refinance later" or "The house will definitely appreciate in value." Neither scenario is guaranteed. What happens if you lose your job or the real estate market suffers a downturn? Refinancing or selling won't be so easy. The typical home-owner with an ARM that resets to a higher interest rate experiences a $10,000 rise in payments over the course of one year, according to the Center for American Progress, a progressive Washington think tank.

**What Flavor is Your Mortgage: Plain Vanilla or Exotic?**

I've already told you that 30-year fixed rate home loans are the "plain vanilla" mortgages of the industry. These are classic loans – the one your grandparents likely had if they were homeowners. By contrast, adjustable rate mortgages come in many flavors, including many quite exotic ones. Here's a brief description of five commonly offered exotic mortgage products:

- **deferred interest or negative amortization loans**, which let you pay less than what you'd normally owe in principal and interest, potentially resulting in your loan balance increasing instead of decreasing

- **hybrid ARMs**, which feature a below-market fixed interest rate for a set period of time, after which your loan resets to a higher interest rate

- **balloon loans**, which feature low fixed payments for a set period of time, and then a lump sum payment due in the future to pay off the majority of the loan.

- **interest-only loans,** which offer very low monthly payments to start with because you only pay the interest due on the loan. After a grace period, your payments rise dramatically since you must also begin repaying the principal balance

- **option ARMs**, which let you pick a payment each month that's comfortable for you; the options typically are:
  - a "minimum payment" choice, which is less than the interest due on the loan, leading to negative amortization
  - an interest-only payment
  - a normal payment of principal and interest, which fully amortizes or pays off your loan in 30 years; and
  - a fully amortizing 15-year payment

Loan size also impacts how your mortgage is classified. Sometimes you might hear lenders talk about "conforming loans." They're referring to loans of $417,000 or less that can be purchased by the government-sponsored agencies Fannie Mae and Freddie Mac. So-called "non-conforming loans" are mortgages above the $417,000 loan limit, which can't be bought by Fannie and Freddie. If you get a mortgage for more than $417,000 it's called a "jumbo" loan. A mortgage above $750,000 is referred to as a "super jumbo." Even if you have great credit and superb loan qualifications, jumbos often carry slightly higher interest rates, simply because these non-conforming loans can't be sold off in the secondary market to mortgage investors like Fannie and Freddie.

**Interest-Only Loans: A Buyer's Dream or Nightmare?**

Between 2002 and 2006, adjustable rate mortgages became enormously popular in the U.S – particularly "interest-only" loans. It's not surprising that the explosion in ARMs during this five-year period coincided with the rapid increase in home prices across the country. In 2006, nearly one-third of all new mortgages were interest-only or "payment option" loans. Interest-only loans allow you to pay only the interest due on the mortgage for a period of time, usually 5 or 10 years. Later you also make principal payments so that your loan is fully amortized and paid off in 30 years.

When people select interest-only loans, it's usually because they want to have the smallest monthly payment possible.

You might think that it's a sweet deal to be able to qualify for a bigger loan and get a pricier house using an interest-only loan. Unfortunately, for many people, interest-only loans are mortgage products that turn out to be less of a dream loan and more of a nightmare. This normally occurs when someone anticipates having a higher income down the road, but those expectations don't pan out. At the end of the specified time period their payments jump because the principal balance must also be repaid. For cash-strapped borrowers who are unable to refinance or sell, an interest-only mortgage that has reset can become financially crippling.

In general, I don't recommend interest-only mortgages for first-time buyers. When new homebuyers use these loans, it's usually a dead giveaway that they're overextending themselves, trying to buy more than they can realistically afford. Interest-only mortgages do have a place in the market, though. Savvy real estate investors use them all the time. Indeed, they can also be useful to you later, if you buy investment property and you want to start with lower monthly payments which rental tenants will eventually cover. Additionally, if you trade up to a different or bigger house down the road, sometimes an interest-only loan makes sense while you have your first house on the market and are waiting to sell it. The purpose of an interest-only loan in this case is to reduce your out-of pocket costs in the event you have to temporarily carry two mortgages.

## Some Thoughts About Sub-Prime Mortgages

In 2007, you couldn't watch television, listen to the radio, or read the newspaper without hearing about the meltdown in the sub-prime mortgage market. After a steady stream of mortgage delinquencies and defaults by homeowners with sub-prime loans – many of them ARMs that had reset – the entire mortgage business experienced a major shakeout. Hundreds of thousands of homes went into foreclosure when borrowers experienced payment shock and could no longer afford their mortgages. Hundreds of lenders went out of business, resulting in scores of job losses in the mortgage, real estate, and home-building industry. Wall Street also took a beating because of the sub-prime mortgage market. The Federal Reserve Bank stepped in to calm the markets by cutting interest rates and making loans to ailing banks. As of this writing, the reverberations from the sub-prime mess are still being felt – among lenders, homeowners, would-be home buyers, and practically every one else tied to the real estate business.

What exactly happened and exactly what is a "sub-prime" loan? Sub-prime mortgage loans are made to people with less than perfect credit histories. As a result, they are more costly mortgages because lenders have to take into account a higher risk of default for customers with credit blemishes. In 2006, sub-prime loans represented 20% of the $10 trillion mortgage market. Yet in the first quarter of 2007, sub-prime loans accounted for 54% of all foreclosures. By the summer of 2007, the rising delinquency and foreclosure rate in the sub-prime market spread to the entire mortgage arena, causing lenders of all kinds to tighten their credit standards – even to customers with perfect credit.

Despite all the terrible press they've received, sub-prime loans are not inherently "bad" loans. In fact, the existence of responsible and fair sub-prime lending has given millions of people access to homeownership by expanding credit criteria and creating more flexible mortgage guidelines and products for buyers who don't have stellar credit records. The problems that occurred in the sub-prime market, however, resulted from a lethal combination of lenders offering too many "exotic" mortgages, falling home prices, higher interest rates, buyers stretching to purchase more house than they could truly afford and not understanding the types of mortgages they were getting, lax federal oversight of the mortgage business, and, finally, predatory tactics by some lenders.

Not all sub-prime mortgages are predatory loans – loans characterized by unreasonably high interest rates, abusive pre-payment penalties, or excessive loan fees including enormous commissions for mortgage brokers. Unfortunately, predatory lenders operating in the sub-prime arena have taken advantage of buyers in recent years – socking homebuyers with much higher interest rates and more punitive loan terms than warranted. The net result is that while sub-prime loans now account for about one out of every six mortgages, they result in more than two-thirds of all foreclosures.

For these reasons, I must caution you that if you do take out a sub-prime loan, it's imperative that you truly know what you're getting and also deal with a reputable lender who won't financially exploit the fact that you lack A-1 credit.

**Choosing the Optimal Loan for Your Situation**

You should be as careful about your selection of a mortgage as you are about choosing the home you will purchase. A mortgage is a major financial commitment, so it's incumbent upon you to take the necessary time and effort to pick the optimal loan for your situation. Your selection of the "right" mortgage must also be driven by future considerations. It's not enough to think about your financial picture and your circumstances today. Where do you plan to be five or 10 years from now? Is the home you're buying one that you plan to stay in for just a couple of years, or do you intend to occupy the home for many years to come? The answer to these questions can also help you choose the best loan product.

A key part of your decision-making should involve your financial temperament. Are you an economically conservative person – one who would sleep better at night knowing that your mortgage payment is fixed and that no matter how interest rates change you have an established house payment that won't fluctuate? If so, a 30-year fixed mortgage would obviously suit you best. On the other hand, if you are a more risk tolerant person – the type of individual who doesn't mind a bit of financial uncertainty regarding interest rates if that could result in possible savings down the road – an ARM is worth exploring.

Whatever type of loan you select, keep in mind that the typical borrower keeps a mortgage for about seven years before paying the loan off. More often than not, people refinance their loans or sell their properties and pay off the loans because they're moving elsewhere. Think about your own personal life, professional career, and future goals. Are you likely to stay put for a while, or could a move – due to job relocation, family, or other reasons – be in your future? In my opinion, if you are reasonably confident that you'll be in a home for at least seven years, then getting a fixed-rate mortgage is the best option. If, however, you're certain that you'll be in the house for fewer than seven years, perhaps because you'll marry or have a baby, you might consider an ARM that would only reset after you're likely to have sold the house and moved.

### Private Mortgage Insurance Vs. "Piggyback" Loans

With conventional mortgage loans, any time you put down less than a 20% down payment, you must also pay for something called "Private Mortgage Insurance." This insurance protects your lender against your defaulting on your mortgage loan. Many buyers hate the thought of paying for insurance that they feel benefits only the lender. In reality, Private Mortgage Insurance, commonly called PMI, does benefit borrowers. The existence of PMI has expanded homeownership in America because this insurance coverage makes lenders far more willing to issue low down payment loans – and even no-money-down loans – because lenders have a guarantee that PMI will help offset the lenders' losses if the borrower does not meet the mortgage obligations,. PMI also helps you get into a home faster, without having to save up 20% for a house down payment.

Over the past decade, many lenders pushed "piggyback" loans as a way for borrowers to avoid PMI. Here's how it worked. A homebuyer seeking a no-money-down loan could get 100% financing for a mortgage by taking out two separate loans. The first loan featured an 80% loan to value ratio. The second loan – the "piggyback" loan – would be 20% of the purchase price of the home. Since the primary loan fell within lender guidelines of having an 80% loan-to-value ratio, the borrower could bypass PMI. Let's say you had a 5% down payment. Lenders would suggest that you do what's called an 80-15-5 loan: the first mortgage for 80%, a 15% piggyback loan, along with your 5% down payment. With a 10% down payment, you'd do an 80-10-10 loan to avoid PMI. Needless to say, borrowers had to always do the math to see whether or not it was actually cheaper to take out a second loan, versus paying mortgage insurance. In many cases, making monthly payments on a second loan was less expensive than paying a monthly PMI premium, but in other cases it was not.

Nowadays, PMI is a lot more attractive as an alternative to piggyback loans. One big reason for the appeal of PMI is that it is now tax deductible, thanks to a new federal law passed by Congress, which went into effect in 2007. In previous years, borrowers didn't get a tax break for paying PMI, as they did for second mortgage loans. Since PMI and piggyback loans are on equal footing now in terms of tax deductibility, it's more important than ever that you compare your options and see which results in the best net financial result.

Under the new law, if your adjusted gross income is less than $100,000, you are entitled to deduct the full amount of your mortgage insurance premiums on your federal tax returns. Deductions are phased out in 10% increments if your adjusted gross income falls between $100,000 and $109,000.

Another reason PMI is attractive when compared to a piggyback loan is that PMI can be canceled after just two years if the value of your house has risen and you have at least 20% equity in the home. Additionally, mortgage insurance premiums are fixed payments, and remain unchanged regardless of what interest rates do. Many piggyback loans carry variable interest rates and fluctuate with changing interest rates.

Some of the largest PMI companies in the nation include Mortgage Guarantee Insurance Corp., General Electric Mortgage Insurance Co., and PMI Mortgage Insurance Company. Janet Parker, Senior Vice President of National Underwriting Operations for PMI Mortgage Insurance Co., says, "We have a tag line that we say: 'MI is simple, safe and smart.'"

"It's actually a very simple process to get mortgage insurance if you have less than a 20% down payment," Parker adds. "The MI can be folded into your loan or you can pay a separate monthly payment every month. It's cancelable. And most big servicers have a protocol by which they cancel PMI automatically once the loan to value ratio drops below 80%."

**Advice for Selecting a Reputable Lender**

When you approach a lender, you should already have in mind what type of mortgage you want: a fixed-rate or an adjustable rate loan. You should also know whether or not you'll need to pay PMI. Finding the right lender for a home loan can be challenging because there are three ways to get a loan: through brokers, mortgage bankers, and direct lenders. They are all regulated differently and each group of professionals makes different disclosures to you about the mortgages they offer.

The Federal Trade Commission suggests that you avoid any lender who:

- advises you to falsify information on your loan application,
- pressures you to take out a loan that is more money than you need or can afford,
- rushes you to sign paperwork you haven't read, telling you that the fine print isn't important,
- pulls a bait-and-switch on you, by promising you a favorable set of loan terms when you apply but then unfairly changing the terms at the last minute,
- requests that you sign blank forms, stating that they'll fill them in later, or
- refuses to give you copies of documents you've signed.

You should also stay away from lenders who do the following:

■ **Push single premium credit insurance**

Consumers Union and ACORN Housing Corporation, which helps low-to-moderate income first time buyers, have both called credit insurance "the nation's worst insurance ripoff," partly because this insurance is very over-priced compared to term life insurance. For example, a typical five-year credit life policy costs over $5,000 more than a comparable term life insurance policy of 10 years, according to ACORN. What is also especially onerous about single premium credit insurance is that when you take out this insurance in connection with a mortgage, the entire cost of the insurance policy is charged up front and added to your loan amount. The loan officer or broker gets as much as 40% of your premium, plus credit insurance doesn't even offer protection for the entire duration of your loan. Instead, the insurance typically only covers the first three to five years of a 30-year mortgage.

### ■ Ask information that violates the law

The Equal Credit Opportunity Act (ECOA) dictates what information a lender can request, and what information is none of their business. The law bans credit discrimination on the basis of your sex, race, religion, age, national origin, marital status, or receipt of public assistance income. Therefore, lenders can't ask you about these areas if they intend to discriminate against you. There are some exceptions to this rule. A lender can request your age to make sure you are legally of age to sign for a loan. A lender can inquire about your marital status to determine income or if you say you will have a co-signer on the loan. Even if you are married, if you choose to take out a mortgage exclusively in your own name the lender doesn't have the right to ask about your spouse's personal finances.

### Can You Benefit From Using a Mortgage Broker?

Mortgage brokers are essentially middlemen in the home loan business. When you use a broker, he or she will tap into his network of lenders and try to find a loan that suits your needs. In the best-case scenario, a broker will work to get you the best rates and loan terms for which you qualify. That's the ideal. In practice, however, it doesn't always work that way.

Critics say that abuses are more prevalent among brokers than others in the mortgage business. Observers contend fraud and abuse are more likely because of the looser regulations that brokers face. The Conference of State Bank Supervisors reports that 32 states don't require people to pass a test before obtaining a mortgage-broker license. Moreover, nine states don't require criminal background checks on license applicants. As a result, the Conference of State Bank Supervisors is creating a national database to let consumers and regulators verify whether brokers are licensed, or learn if they've had any regulatory enforcement actions. Senator Chuck Schumer of New York in 2007 introduced legislation that would establish a fiduciary duty for brokers and others who arrange home mortgage loans, mandating that they look after their customers' best interests.

Some people say that there needs to be better disclosures to consumers about how brokers are compensated. Since brokers find customers for lenders and handle the initial loan processing, brokers can be paid for their efforts by both the lender and the buyer. In many cases, brokers can get you better interest rates because they receive "wholesale" interest rates from direct lenders, such as Bank of America, Chase, or Washington Mutual. Let's say you went into a major bank for a home loan. They might quote you a rate of 7.5%. However, they might quote the broker – who is giving them multiple loans a month – a rate of 6.5%. The broker can then pass on that lower 6.5% rate to you. In most cases, however, brokers don't do that. Instead, they might quote you a rate of 7%, which is still better than what you could get on your own. If they can get you to accept that 7% rate, the lender will pay them a commission, which the broker also pockets as profit. This is called a YSP, or Yield Spread Premium, and it's one of the ways that mortgage brokers get paid in the industry. Banks and wholesale lenders typically pay brokers a YSP ranging from 1% to 4% of the value of a loan. You might say: "What do I care if the broker gets paid a commission by the lender? It's not coming out of my pocket." Well, actually it is – in the form of a higher interest rate, which translates into a bigger monthly payment. That's many thousands of dollars wasted – potentially tens of thousands of dollars over the life of a loan. Take the example I offered above. Assume you could get a 6.5% rate on a $300,000 loan with no YSP. Your monthly payment would be $1,896 a month, most of which would be interest. By the end of seven years, you would have paid a total of $129,058 in interest charges. Now compare that to a 7% loan, also for a $300,000 mortgage. Your monthly payment is $1,996, or $100 more. Here's the kicker: after seven years' worth of payments, you will have forked over $139,501 in interest – more than $10,000 in cash that could've been saved if you didn't get a loan with a YSP. For every half a percent your rate is marked up, your broker will usually earn a commission totaling 1% of the value of your loan. On a $300,000 loan with a half a percent mark-up, a bank is willing to pay a broker $3,000 because the lender will be making an extra $10,000 off you. Now that you understand that a bank pays a broker – or its own loan officer – a commission for providing you with a higher rate than which you qualify, I hope you're convinced that you should avoid loans with a YSP. Below I'll tell you how.

When you apply for a mortgage loan, by law a lender is required to give you a Good Faith Estimate (GFE) within three days of your application. In fact, many lenders will send you a GFE if you simply request it – before you submit a full, detailed application. The GFE is supposed to show you the Yield Spread Premium, or commission, that's going to a mortgage broker. The problem, however, is that until your loan is placed by a broker with a specific lender, it's impossible to know exactly what the YSP will be. Often, borrowers don't find out the YSP until the closing. Even then, many don't understand what it is.

If you work with a mortgage broker, the best strategy is to negotiate this issue at the outset. Tell a broker flat out that you want him or her to quote you rates and terms on a loan that has no YSP. To get the best rate, speak a broker's lingo and ask for a "Par Rate." That's the lowest rate you qualify for on a lender's wholesale rate sheet. Basically, it means you're getting a wholesale rate without a YSP mark-up. To confirm that you're getting the wholesale rate, ask a broker for his wholesale rate sheet. I can promise you this: they'll be shocked that you even know about it.

Another option is to use brokers who guarantee that they don't earn any Yield Spread Premium on your rate. You can find such a broker at http://www.applyclub.com, which is a mortgage warehouse club with a strict policy of passing along their wholesale rates to consumers. At ApplyClub.com, brokers don't charge any points and they earn a flat fee of just $995 per loan.

Lastly, you can take the tried-and-true advice of mortgage pro Rob Blake, who runs a consumer-friendly, information-packed website at http://www.themortgageinsider.net. Blake, a 15-year industry veteran based in Denver, Colorado, offers a free e-book called *Mortgage Secrets Exposed*. Even better, through his BUILD™ System, Blake teaches you how to pick a local broker and eliminate yield spread premium every time you get a mortgage.

Obviously, a broker should be compensated for his efforts. Don't think you can get away with using a broker's services free of charge, that's not fair or reasonable. I don't have a problem with a broker receiving as much as a 1% fee for his or her work. This is best paid at closing, in the form of a loan origination fee or a mortgage broker fee. However, you shouldn't sign off on a loan where a broker receives a Yield Spread Premium. That only benefits the lender and broker, and hurts you, by forcing you to pay a higher interest rate. Too often, brokers receive outrageous fees to originate mortgages – at the expense of naïve homeowners.

Even some brokers admit they've seen widespread fleecing of customers getting home loans. Mortgage broker Daniel Bedford says he's seen other brokers rip off customers by charging excessive points – often by slipping in a Yield Service Premium that most homebuyers were unaware that they were paying. "I knew a guy who made $50,000 one month [off excessive fees], and went out and bought a Mercedes," Bedford says.

"Minorities get taken advantage of a lot more than Caucasians," Bedford contends. Ironically, he notes, minority professionals are the ones more apt to take advantage of minority customers of the same race – a phenomenon known as "affinity fraud" – because consumers are often more trusting of someone with whom they share certain ties, such as race, religion, or membership in a common social organization.

"Unfortunately, I've seen the good and bad in this business – especially with foreigners who come here and get taken. If the broker and the homebuyer are the same nationality, it's worse," Bedford says, revealing "I once saw an Indian broker take an Indian customer for seven points on a loan." Needless to say, abuses in the mortgage world are hardly restricted to mortgage brokers, but I share Bedford's comments with you so that you know what to watch out for.

Despite the criticisms leveled at mortgage brokers, some people swear by them, especially in an environment in which banks are imposing tougher credit standards and other qualifications. Brokers are often better equipped to find a great deal on a mortgage simply because they work with so many lenders and keep abreast of the variety of loan products being offered in the marketplace. By contrast, if you deal with a mortgage banker or a direct lender, you are limited to the loan products – and rates and terms – offered by those specific institutions. Brokers are also more willing to negotiate their fees, whereas direct lenders often hold firm on their charges.

In the end, it's difficult to generalize about whether it's better to go with a broker, mortgage company, or direct lender. It really boils down to where you'll get the most attractive loan. Personally, I've obtained mortgages on different properties through all three types of lenders, and have been able secure favorable interest rates and terms from each.

## Advantages of Using Direct Lenders

There are several advantages to dealing with a direct lender. These are the "household names" of the home-loan industry, such as Bank of America, Countrywide, or Wells Fargo. First, if you choose a large institution or a well-established financial entity, you have the comfort of knowing that you're not dealing with a fly-by-night entity. Many borrowers pick big, direct lenders primarily to have the security of knowing that if you call, email, or write to that lender, you'll always be able to reach someone – without worrying whether that the company has gone out of business. Working with a direct lender might also mean a speedier closing, since you cut out the time and processing done by a broker-middleman. Another plus with direct lenders is that they're not known for using high-pressure sales techniques or lots of bait-and-switch schemes.

One major downside to dealing with a bank, and mortgage brokers too for that matter, is that while those entities make commissions off of you – just like mortgage brokers do – bankers don't have to reveal those commissions to the public. RESPA only requires mortgage brokers to reveal their Yield Spread Premium. Among banks, similar mark-ups occur, except that it is called a Service Release Premium, or SRP. Bankers are exempt from disclosing this profit to the public. Don't be fooled into thinking that banks don't make profits off your loan via commissions; they do. Unfortunately, consumers have no way of accurately knowing just how fat those profits are.

## Smart Questions You Must Ask About Your Mortgage

When you apply for a loan through a broker, mortgage banker, or direct lender, make sure you ask the following five questions:

### ■ What is the interest rate and the Annual Percentage Rate (APR) on this loan?

Many consumers make the mistake of shopping for a mortgage loan based solely on the interest rate. This is a big mistake for several reasons. First, it doesn't tell you about key terms that affect the loan – like whether or not it has a prepayment penalty. Also, when you look exclusively at the interest rate – and not the Annual Percentage Rate on a loan – it doesn't tell you the true borrowing costs you'll pay for a mortgage. The interest rate is a starting point but the APR will always be higher than the interest rate, because the APR factors in all the costs of the loan – like points, loan origination fees, and other charges. Expect to see a difference of .5% or less in the interest rate you're quoted and the APR. If the gap between the two is greater than .5%, it means the loan has high fees, so you may want to seek a better deal elsewhere.

Be aware that lenders can't accurately figure out an APR for an adjustable rate loan. If you apply for an ARM, make sure you know how frequently the interest rate can adjust. Is it every month, every six months, once a year, or at some other time interval? Ask also about the maximum amount of percentage points the rate can increase in any given year, as well as the overall "cap" on the loan, which is the absolute highest interest rate you could ever have to pay.

### ■ Are there Points charged on this loan?

A "point" is a fee that equals one percent of your loan amount. Lenders allow you to pay a point – sometimes called a discount point – in order to get a lower interest rate. While it might sound like a good idea to pay a one-time fee up front in order to "buy down" your interest rate, in reality, paying points is frequently a money-losing proposition. You should avoid paying points because, in most cases, for every point you are charged, your interest rate is only knocked down by $1/8^{th}$ of a percent, or maybe 1/4 of a percent. In my opinion, it's not worth it to pay points. A quick example will illustrate this concept. Assume you can get a $250,000 mortgage at 7% interest with no points. Then the lender offers to let you pay one point, or $2,500, to lower your interest rate by $1/8^{th}$ of a percent to 6.875%. The monthly payment on the no-point loan at 7% would be $1,458 a month. Meanwhile, the monthly payment on the loan with one point, at 6.875% would be $1,432, a difference of $26 a month. If you divide the $2,500 cost you pay for one point by $26, you'll get 96, which is the number of months required for you to "break even" on those points you paid. You would have to live in your house for 96 months (i.e. eight years) in order to recoup that one point. If you sold or refinanced before then, you would have lost money by paying that up front point. The one advantage to paying points is that they are tax deductible. Ideally, however, you shouldn't pay any discount points on a mortgage. Have the lender quote you a rate that's based on a loan with zero discount points. If you shop among multiple lenders, having everyone quote you a rate based on zero points will also make it easier for you to make an apples-to-apples comparison of the loans you're being offered.

### ■ What are all the costs for this mortgage?

The Good Faith Estimate you receive from a lender will outline all the costs you must pay in connection with your mortgage. Some fees are imposed by the lender. Others are charged by third parties, like attorneys, title insurance firms, or appraisal companies. Make sure you know all the fees you'll be expected to pay, so you don't have sticker shock at the closing when you see a laundry list of charges that might no have been previously disclosed. Ask your lender to guarantee the Good Faith Estimate – meaning that the lender won't increase the charges assessed. A lender doesn't have any control over what outside parties charge, but they can stand behind their estimates of what fees they assess.

### ■ Does this loan have a prepayment penalty?

Ideally, you want to hear the answer "No." In fact, some states, such as New Jersey, restrict lenders from imposing prepayment penalties, which allow lenders to charge you hefty fees any time you refinance your loan or pay it off early. Prepayment penalties can run as high as six months' worth of payments, so definitely avoid them if at all possible. Some people believe prepayment penalties can be useful to those who know they'll stay in the house for a long period of time since lenders will sometimes offer you a lower rate on a loan that includes a prepayment penalty. However, my thinking is why be saddled with a loan with potentially harmful terms if you can get an equivalent loan without those terms? The Truth in Lending statement that you receive from a lender will indicate whether or not your loan contains a prepayment penalty. Sometimes, the form will have unclear language, and will state something like, "This loan may have a prepayment penalty." That can be interpreted either way – that a prepayment penalty could be imposed, or might not be imposed. Should you encounter such language, tell your lender you want it to be explicitly stated that your loan "does not have a prepayment penalty." If necessary, write in such a statement yourself and initial it.

■ **How much, if anything, will it cost me to lock in my interest rate?**

Interest rates change every day. If you've got a good rate, and are worried about rates going up, you might want to lock in your rate to protect yourself against rising interest rates. Many lenders will allow you to lock in your rate free of charge for 30 days, or even 45 days. This might be plenty of time to close on your mortgage – especially if you've already been pre-approved. But if you think you'll need more than a month, you might have to pay a fee for a 60-day rate lock. The fee can be as much as one percent of your loan amount. If you do lock in your rate, always get it in writing. Don't rely on someone's word that your rate is guaranteed. It's not, until you have written proof of it.

### Recognizing "Junk" Loan Fees from Reasonable Ones

No matter which entity you choose for financing, getting a mortgage loan involves paying a whole host of fees beyond a down payment. Your closing costs will include a litany of charges ranging from one-time fees for things like credit checks to annual expenses that you prepay upfront, such as homeowner's insurance. Here are examples of the common fees you might see when you obtain a mortgage – along with estimated costs. Obviously, prices for different products and services can vary based on where you live and other factors. Nevertheless, the numbers presented below will give you an estimate – or in some cases a range – of what you can typically expect to pay for your mortgage.

■ **Typical Closing Costs on a New Mortgage:**

| Description of Fee | Cost |
| --- | --- |
| Application Fee | $150-$400 |
| Appraisal | $200-$400 |
| Closing Fee | $250-$350 |
| Credit Report | $15-$50 |
| Document Prep Fee | $150-$300 |
| Flood Certification | $10-30 |
| Legal Fees | $250-$750 |
| Loan Origination Fee | Usually 1% of the loan |
| Points | Each point is 1% of the loan |
| Recording Fee | $25-$50 |
| Survey | $150-$300 |
| Taxes | Varies (See more info below) |
| Termite Inspection | $50-$100 |
| Title Insurance | Varies (See more info below) |

Some loan costs – like interest on your loan and property taxes – must be escrowed, meaning that you pay for them for a few months, up to a year in advance. The same is true for homeowners' insurance, which covers the house in case of a fire or another disaster.

Other insurance you have to pay includes title insurance, which is an indemnity policy that provides protection against any loss that arises due to problems with the title (or ownership) of your property. Lenders require you to have title insurance because if the title is "faulty" – due to a tax lien, judgment or some kind of encumbrance on the title – then title insurance covers the lender. As is the case with mortgage insurance, you bear the costs of title insurance (in a single, up-front payment), but your lender receives the protection for this coverage.

Title insurance costs vary greatly nationwide, partly because the title insurance premium you pay often covers different services, depending on the company you use and where your home is located. For example, in some places your premium simply covers the lender for any title-related losses. In other places, though, the premium covers losses, as well as the cost of a title search, title examination, and closing services. Title insurance also varies based on the size of the mortgage.

Junk fees are those charges imposed solely to add to a lender's profit margins. In many cases, these fees have legitimate or official sounding names, like "document preparation fee." In truth, however, they're really just creative ways for lenders to pad their bottom line at your expense. Many lender charges that have the word "fee" slapped on the back of them are a dead giveaway that you're being charged for services that lenders are supposed to provide anyway. If you get charged for an "underwriting fee," a "loan review fee," a "warehousing fee," or other such nonsense, do not hesitate to ask the lender to waive those fees – or at least substantially reduce them. Even things like the "application fee" or the "loan processing fee" can be eliminated or cut, if you are savvy enough to ask.

**How to Decipher Your Good Faith Estimate**

When you obtain a mortgage, you will pay four sets of fees: Lender Fees, Title and Third Party Fees, Escrow and Interest Fees, and Government Fees. Each set of fees will be outlined in your Good Faith Estimate. Remember, however, that the GFE is not binding on a lender. In fact, it's likely to change at least once – right after your loan is approved. Later, when you go to the closing, take your Good Faith Estimate with you and compare it against the final bill you get at closing. That final bill is described as a HUD-1 Settlement Statement. For now, however, let's take an in-depth look at the fees you'll pay at closing as revealed in your initial Good Faith Estimate.

■ **Lender Fees**

Payments you make to a lender in order to obtain a mortgage can range from loan discount points to mortgage broker fees or underwriting costs. In general, lender charges include any fees that go directly to the financial institution providing your home loan.

### ■ Title and Third-Party Fees

Third-party fees for home borrowers include the costs for flood certification, appraisals, pest inspections, your title search, and title insurance. Third-party fees are paid to outside vendors or other companies, not your lender. In many cases, however, your lender might be affiliated with those third parties.

### ■ Escrow and Interest Fees

Lenders often require you to make advance payments into an escrow account to make sure you don't fall behind on your property taxes, homeowner's insurance, loan interest, or private mortgage insurance. Other escrow items include so-called "interim," interest, which is the daily mortgage interest cost you pay from closing through to the end of that month.

### ■ Government Fees

Most city, county, or state agencies require property transfer taxes or other levies for real estate purchases. Other government agencies charge for your mortgage deed to be recorded. These fees will all be detailed in your Good Faith Estimate. You can tell which fees are likely to be negotiable by carefully reviewing your Good Faith Estimate. On the GFE, you'll notice that fees are grouped into numerical categories that range from the 800s to the 1300s. Your lender's charges fall into the 800s category, and will include anything from application fees to loan origination charges or underwriting fees. These are the items that are most open to negotiation.

Anything classified as a "review," an "administrative" or a "document prep fee" should be questioned. Lenders will say that they charge for these items because loans have to be processed, underwritten, and reviewed. However, there's no justification in charging these junk fees to consumers for several reasons. First, lenders use automated underwriting systems, which spit out approval or denials in a matter of minutes. It's not as if some underwriter is spending weeks working on your mortgage application. Additionally, administrative and underwriting services are part of the normal course of a lender's business. Lastly, even if you should have to pay for these expenses – which you shouldn't – many lenders inflate these charges, saddling consumers with $500 "processing" or "administrative" fees – costs that far exceed the lender's actual incurred cost.

Fees that fall in the 900s category on the Good Faith Estimate represent items required by your lender to be paid in advance. Examples include pre-paid interest on your loan, mortgage insurance premium, or a hazard insurance premium. Likewise, fees in the 1000s category on your GFE are for reserves you must deposit with the lender, for expenses like property taxes or flood insurance. Generally speaking, you won't be able to negotiate away pre-paid costs that your lender mandates. However, you can save money on these items in other ways. For instance, you can schedule your closing toward the end of the month to reduce the number of days of prepaid interest you pay at closing. Also, you can shop around for the best rate on hazard insurance – the cost of which will be listed as item 903 on your Good Faith Estimate.

Most title charges and third-party fees will show up on the 1100s section of your Good Faith Estimate. Here you will the costs you must pay for title insurance or for title searches, notary fees, attorney fees, and perhaps other expenses, such as overnight courier service. Sometimes, third-party fees – like charges for an appraisal or the cost to run your credit – might appear in the 800s section instead of in the 1100s area of your Good Faith Estimate. These are legitimate third-party fees because your lender does incur these expenses. However, you have to watch out for lenders or brokers who try to pad these charges and impose a markup on them. To reduce the risk of this, let your lender know upfront (i.e. after you've been approved for your mortgage) that you want receipts for all third-party expenses you incur.

In states like Texas and Florida, title insurance premiums are set by the state. But in other places, you can save yourself money by shopping around for title insurance, a title exam, and attorney's fees. Many lenders will suggest that you use their title company or lawyers, but you don't have to – especially if you can find better deals on your own. A great place to find title insurance at competitive prices – and save money on all those junk fees often charged – is online at http://www.MyClosingSpace.com. Visit the website for an instant quote or call 888-TITLES-9.

Items listed in the 1200s category of your Good Faith Estimate are for government recording and transfer charges. Your lender imposes these fees because local municipalities charge for things like city and county stamps and documenting mortgages in city records.

The 1300s section of your Good Faith Estimate will detail any additional settlement charges in connection with your loan. These may include courier fees, the cost of a survey or expenses for pest inspections. When you get your GFE, make sure you don't see a laundry list of additional charges here or any unexplained "miscellaneous" charges.

**Protect Yourself from Excessive Loan Charges**

One way to protect yourself from excessive loan charges is to simply know what's loan services are customary – and what the going rates are for those services. The previous section in this chapter gave you those insights. Being familiar with the law can also help you avoid unfair or exorbitant loan fees. For instance, The Real Estate Settlement Procedures Act (RESPA) protects you by prohibiting "kickbacks" – including referral fees among settlement providers – which can make getting a house more expensive. Additionally, you can save money by shopping around, particularly by comparing interest rates and loan terms online. Lastly, you can get the help of outside professionals to tell you whether you're getting a suitable mortgage. That way you have a third-party's opinion about your loan – and you don't have to relay on loan officers who will almost invariably say, "Trust me. This is a great deal."

■  **Get price quotes from Internet auction sites**

On these sites, you'll fill out a questionnaire, answering a slew of questions about your personal finances, the property you intend to buy, and the type of loan you're seeking. After you fill out the required information, your request is sent to a handful of lenders, who will get back to you with mortgage offers. Just be aware that direct lenders, brokers, and mortgage banks can all supply "lowball" price quotes – just to entice you to call them and start the loan application. However, they're not bound to honor that initial rate quote and, indeed, few do.

Some Internet sites where you can get preliminary rates quotes are:

- Cityloans.com
- Eloan.com
- Lendingtree.com
- Loanweb.com
- Lowestmortgage.com
- Mortgageexpo.com

When you shop for a mortgage online you streamline the process, save time, and are more readily able to make an apples-to-apples comparison of the loans you're being offered. The advantage of getting online mortgage information is that you can receive multiple quotes on the same day, at the same time. By contrast, if you got on the phone and called five lenders, the process would be far more time-consuming and, between calls, rates could change.

Brokers in a group called the Upfront Mortgage Brokers guarantee their fees and disclose the wholesale costs of loans they offer. You can get a list of these brokers at http://www.mtgprofessor.com, a mortgage-advice website run by Jack Guttentag, a professor of finance emeritus at the University of Pennsylvania's Wharton School. Likewise, this site also lists a few "Upfront Mortgage Lenders," who also disclose and guarantee their fees when you apply for a loan – and not just at closing. Some of these lenders include Eloan.com and Amerisave.com.

### Get an Objective, Professional Evaluation of Your Loan

Getting an outside opinion of your mortgage offer is also a great way to independently check the suitability of that loan. Fortunately, this is now possible with the emergence of a handful of companies that will review your loan offer and give you feedback on it. One of those firms is Offer Angel (http://www.offerangel.com), an online mortgage advice site launched in May 2007.

"We are completely consumer driven," says Meghan Burns, co-founder of OfferAngel.com. "We're most concerned about educating the public and making sure they understand not just the rates and terms associated with their mortgages, but also the suitability of the loans they have."

According to Burns, far more people are being stuck with sub-prime, predatory loans than is necessary. "When you say 'sub-prime loans,' people immediately think those loans are going to uneducated or low-income people, but that's just wrong," Burns says. "There are doctors and lawyers making tons of money that have sub-prime credit." She adds that predatory lending isn't just being charged a high interest rate, or being assessed a pre-payment penalty. "Essentially it's somebody taking out a loan at a cost that's higher than what they qualified for," Burns says.

To fight that problem, and to educate you about your mortgage, OfferAngel.com will evaluate your loan free of charge, or for a nominal fee. Here's how it works. Offer Angel is an open access site, accessible to consumers and loan originators. Your loan officer fills out a form that contains information about your proposed mortgage. OfferAngel.com asks for details – what Burns calls the "nitty gritty of the loan being offered." The loan officer must indicate information such as whether or not the loan is fixed rate or adjustable, and whether it has a pre-payment penalty or not.

"We want factual data," says Burns, who is a former mortgage loan officer. "Our system is not easily manipulated. The answers are either yes or no." Based on the information your lender presents, Offer Angel gives you a free report that analyzes your mortgage. The company's complimentary side-by-side mortgage report lets you compare up to four loan officers. The free report also includes explanations about basic loan terms.

For $24.95, Offer Angel gives you more detailed analysis, in the form of a Personalized Mortgage Report. "We never say: this is the lender you should go with," notes Burns. However, the company does warn you about mortgages that might not meet your stated needs and goals. For instance, if you say you plan to live in the house for just three years, and the loan contains a five-year pre-payment penalty, OfferAngel.com will alert you to that fact. Or let's say you've indicated that you want a fixed interest rate, but the loan being offered is a 7/1 ARM. In such a case, OfferAngel.com would flag this and tell you that this loan's interest rate is likely to change. The Personalized Mortgage Report is designed to alert you to high costs in your loan or terms that might make your loan unfavorable right now – or down the road.

To use Offer Angel, simply submit your name, email, and the state in which you live. You don't have to disclose personal information, like your social security number, address, or phone number. Equally important, Offer Angel does not push one lender over another, sell or share your information, make mortgage loans, or act as a "lead generator" for others trying to sell you a mortgage. So if you're not sure whether you're getting a suitable mortgage, get help from a neutral, third-party source like OfferAngel.com.

Another great online tool for anyone in the market for a mortgage can be found at http://www.FreeRateSearch.com. This is a loan evaluation and information site developed by credit expert and consumer advocate Gerri Detweiler. What FreeRateSearch.com does is unique in that it reveals the best available "Par" rates in your area, based on the type of loan you want. Remember, the "Par" rate is equivalent to a wholesale rate, and is the best interest rate possible because it's not packed with any Yield Service Premium or commissions to brokers. To come up with this data, FreeRateSearch.com compiles up-to-date rate sheets every day from lenders, using software designed especially for mortgage brokers. If you send your contact information, and specifications about your credit and desired loan, FreeRateSearch.com forwards it to the local lender with the best rate with whom you can negotiate your mortgage loan.

**Common Mortgage and Home Buying Scams to Avoid**

Now I have to tell you about a pitfall you need to avoid while you're trying to land your dream home: scams perpetrated by home sellers, real estate agents, loan officers, and others. Each of these scams shares a common thread – a buyer who goes along with the con, either knowingly or unwittingly. Therefore, learn about these illegal schemes in order to avoid them, and keep yourself out of trouble financially and legally.

### ■ Pretending Someone Else's Money is Your Own

Some desperate would-be homebuyers will try to fake out a bank by "borrowing" someone else's bank account to get a mortgage. These consumers know that banks like to see cash reserves in an account. So the customer will ask a friend or family member to dump some money – just temporarily – into the homebuyer's checking or savings account to help the buyer qualify for a loan. This constitutes mortgage fraud, because you are knowingly supplying false information on your loan application.

### ■ Artificially Inflating the Sales Price of the Home

If anyone ever suggests that you take part in a real estate transaction in which the price of the home is faked for any reason, do yourself a favor and stay away from that person. In desperate times, or when market conditions are weak, people dream up all kinds of home frauds, most often in an effort to defraud a bank. A fake appraisal can be obtained. A buyer and seller might agree on a sales price that's higher than the current market value or above the seller's initial asking price, so that either the seller or buyer (or both) can get extra cash from a lender at closing. This deceptive practice is illegal and you should not engage in these kind of shenanigans for any reason.

### ■ Faking Documents of Any Kind

Watch out also for anyone who gives you fake documents, or encourages you to supply fake documents to someone else. The documents a seller might try to pass off as legitimate are false appraisals, forged deeds for properties they don't own, or fake inspection reports. This kind of fraud is rare, but it does occasionally happen. What is more common is that a real estate professional might encourage you, as a buyer, to falsify documents. They might ask you to fill out bogus information online just to get a pre-qualification letter or lie about your income, credit history, or the number of people who might be occupying your new home.

### ■ Using a "Straw Buyer" to Close a Deal

A "straw buyer" is a third party in a real estate transaction who is used to get a mortgage from a bank when the true buyer can't qualify for a loan. In a fraudulent real estate deal, the buyer and seller agree to let a third party, the straw buyer, act as a "stand in" of sorts to facilitate the purchase. The straw buyer's name might be used on a loan application, or perhaps his social security number, credit history, or assets – or a combination of all these items. Using a straw buyer to conceal the real identity of a prospective homebuyer amounts to real estate fraud and is a serious crime you should avoid at all costs.

Hopefully, you won't run into any mortgage scams in your effort to get a home loan. But if you do, being an educated consumer – which means having the ability and knowledge to recognize a scam – can be the best way to sidestep this pitfall. Even if a real estate agent, mortgage broker, or loan officer tells you to falsify information in order to get a home loan, don't do it. Bottom line: don't take part in any mortgage scams under any circumstances, for any reasons. It's wrong, and it's just not worth it considering the risks you face of getting hefty fines and maybe even jail time if you get busted. By the way, legitimate players in the mortgage industry actively are aggressive in trying to stamp out mortgage fraud, and they encourage you to join in that effort too.

For example, the Mortgage Banker's Association has set up a website at: http://www.stopmortgagefraud.com in an effort to combat fraud. You can report loan abuse by calling their toll-free number at 800-348-3931.

## 10

## Sail Through the Closing Process

All of a sudden closing day is here. It's the day you're finally going to sign on the dotted line for your mortgage and get the keys to your very first home. If you're like most buyers, you're filled with anticipation – and perhaps a bit apprehensive too about everything that's about to transpire. That's normal considering you're on the verge of making what is probably the biggest financial transaction of your life. It would be easy to go weak in the knees thinking about the big financial commitment at hand, but stand firm. Now is the time to be more confident and more informed than ever, knowing your journey to homeownership is the right thing for your overall well being. You can't afford to be a passive participant at this point. After all you've gone through – working hard to get approved for a loan, searching constantly and finally finding a home you love, negotiating with a seller, and more – you now need to be ready for the culmination of this entire process. Knowing what comes next – and preparing for the unexpected – is critical to closing the deal effectively and with a minimum amount of stress.

### What to Expect During the Process

One of the first questions you may have about your real estate closing is where it will take place. Out West, in places like California, your closing is apt to occur at a mortgage company or escrow firm. In various states in the Northeast, real estate closings are held in lawyers' offices. Meanwhile, in many other parts of the country, your closing will occur at the title agency's office. It really depends on local practices and customs.

No matter where the action takes place, when you first walk into the office for the closing, or "settlement" as it's called in some areas, you'll probably find a huge table with lots of people sitting around it – all of whom have an interest or a role to play in seeing your real estate purchase finalized.

## Knowing All the Players Involved in Your Closing

Let's start with the lawyers who are likely to be present. An attorney for the seller might be there and, if so, this person's job is to represent the seller's interests. The seller's lawyer might have also performed certain tasks, like creating the deed or calculating settlement figures that will be used during the closing. Your attorney as well as attorney representing your lender might also be in attendance at the closing. In fact, sometimes your attorney and your lender's will be the same person. This can sometimes save you a few hundred dollars, but many people feel more comfortable having their own lawyer represent their interest during a real estate closing.

Your attorney should intervene to help you if a last-minute problem arises with your lender. What could go wrong with your lender? Unfortunately, a whole host of issues: the lender might have increased the interest rate you were promised (accidentally or intentionally); your mortgage might contain terms that you explicitly wanted to avoid, such as a pre-payment penalty; or your lender could throw in a whole bunch of previously undisclosed junk fees, and hope that you'll just sign on the dotted line anyway. These are just examples of conflicts that could emerge. The lender's attorney will be tasked with collecting the settlement figures from the seller's attorney, putting together the slew of documents you must sign at closing, preparing the settlement statement, and generally making sure all paperwork – such as insurance policies or payoff statements – is in order.

Representatives from a title company might also be in attendance. They're present because sometime earlier in the process a review of the seller's title was done to make sure there were no impediments to that person's selling you the home. Additionally, that individual – or someone from his or her company – might have reviewed the title search, prepared a title insurance policy, or conducted other title-related services.

Lastly, any real estate agents involved in the deal will also attend your closing. Your agent's job is to make sure that no unexpected surprises end up short-changing you in this whole matter. Your agent will also negotiate on your behalf if any issues arise with the seller.

### Preparing for Problems That Could Occur at Settlement

Home sellers have been known to renege on certain terms at the last minute, or event to try to back out of a deal altogether. So if the seller says something like, "I know we agreed to throw in the washer and dryer with the house, but now we actually want to keep those appliances," or even worse, if the seller says, "I've changed my mind. I don't want to sell," your agent and attorney will definitely step in – likely before you start screaming bloody murder – and will remind the seller, and his or her agent, that you have a legally binding contract and that they'd better stick to the agreement or face serious legal repercussions. A seller flat-out refusing to turn over the keys doesn't happen often. Nevertheless, I'm giving you a worse-case scenario so that you know the extent of what can go wrong. Please don't let these kinds of possibilities keep you up at night as you wait for your closing. If you've done the right thing by having a real estate pro in your corner, and hiring an attorney, whatever issues that arise at your closing – whether financial, legal, or something else – should get resolved favorably and quickly.

### Typical Closing Costs

I've encouraged you throughout this book to make smart choices concerning homeownership and that same philosophy holds true at your settlement. Therefore, if you get to the settlement table and find that your closing costs are far greater than you anticipated, do the smart thing and voice your concerns immediately. So many people going through a closing make the mistake of just signing whatever documents are pushed before them – even when they know they're being taken. What happens all too often is that the closing costs borrowers were promised wind up being nothing like what comes out of those borrowers' pockets. In fact, by some estimates 50% of borrowers wind up paying far more in final closing costs than they anticipated.

Some of you might be wondering how your closing costs stack up against what other people pay. For starters, you should know that closing costs generally add up to roughly 3% of your loan amount. In some cases, closing costs can be as much as 5% of your mortgage loan.

According to Bankrate.com's most recent annual closing costs comparison survey, New York is the state with the highest mortgage-related fees in the country. Closing costs in New York for lender, title, and settlement fees totaled $3,830 on a $200,000 loan in 2007, versus a national average of $2,736 in closing costs, according to Bankrate.com. These closing expenses exclude county recording fees and recurring charges, like homeowner association dues, property taxes, or homeowner's insurance. Following New York was Texas, Florida, Pennsylvania, and Ohio. The state with the cheapest closing costs (just $2,339) was Indiana, followed by Wyoming, Illinois, Nevada, and North Carolina.

■  **States With the Most Expensive Closing Costs**

| New York | $3,830 |
|---|---|
| Texas | $3,413 |
| Florida | $3,175 |
| Pennsylvania | $3,169 |
| Ohio | $3,047 |

**Source**: Bankrate.com 2007 Closing Costs Study

■ **States With the Least Expensive Closing Costs**

| Indiana | $2,339 |
|---|---|
| Wyoming | $2,390 |
| Illinois | $2,401 |
| Nevada | $2,467 |
| North Carolina | $2,487 |

**Source**: Bankrate.com 2007 Closing Costs Study

### How to Know for What You're Paying

At your closing, the best way to know what you're paying is to adopt a three-part strategy that limits a lender's ability to sock you with unexpected or higher-cost fees.

■ **Take your Good Faith Estimate to your closing**

With your Good Faith Estimate in hand, you'll be able to immediately compare the costs your lender said you would incur against what you're now actually being charged at the settlement table. Some discrepancies are inevitable – particularly with third-party charges. Lenders have no control over those. However, a lender who claims to charge $250 for an application fee and then raises that fee to $500 at the closing is being dishonest. Watch out for these kinds of tactics that can cost you money if they go unchecked.

■ **Scrutinize Your HUD-1 Settlement Statement**

The HUD-1 form is the document that lists all of your final closing costs in detail. Based on the information in the HUD-1, the closing agent will tally up all the expenses you've already paid – for things like appraisals and inspections – and will generate an itemized list of all remaining payments to be made. The HUD-1 is the main document at the closing table that all parties will refer to in order to make sure that all the numbers add up – for both the seller and the buyer in the real estate transaction. Double-check the math on this form. Make sure that your payments are shown as credits, not debits. Otherwise, you could wind up paying for something twice. Also, make sure that any price concessions or seller credits you negotiated are accounted for on the HUD-1 form. If you spot an error later on the HUD-1, it will probably be too late to do anything about it. The time to raise any objections is at the closing table. In fact, you can even get your HUD-1 statement before settlement. Under RESPA rules, you are entitled to receive your HUD-1 a day *prior* to closing. To be an especially vigilant home buyer, take advantage of your rights under RESPA and tell your loan officer you want the HUD-1 form 24-hours ahead of settlement. This is a great way to minimize any surprises and make sure you're not under pressure to sign on the spot for a loan that has any terms or fees to which you haven't agreed. On the last mortgage my husband and I obtained, we requested and received our HUD-1 statement prior to settlement. I caught numerous errors on the HUD-1 form and disputed many charges. By the time closing occurred a few days later, the mistakes were fixed and a host of fees were eliminated or reduced. In the end, scrutinizing that HUD-1 before settlement saved us more than $8,000.

### ■ Ask for receipts for third-party fees

Remember when I told you earlier to let your lender know that you wanted receipts for third party services? Now is the time to ask for those receipts. This is a power play move – one done by bold borrowers. Trust me, however, it's a way to keep lenders in check and make sure that they aren't making extra, unjust profit off of you by inflating the fees they charge, even if those fees are indirect, and ultimately passed onto third-party vendors.

### Dealing With Buyer's Remorse

Plan to be at your settlement for at least one hour, although it's possible the process could be speedier. Be sure to bring a photo ID with you and, of course, the funds you'll need to close in the form of a cashier's check or certified check. Your real estate agent or lender can tell you which is preferred.

Once you make it through the closing, many of you will no doubt want to shout from the rooftop, "I did it! I bought my first home!" If you're in such an elated state of mind, congratulations on making it through the tough part of finding and financing the home of your dreams. You deserve to feel like a winner – and indeed you are!

Others home buyers, however, might unexpectedly feel emotionally drained or let down. In fact, some home buyers report a sense of regret or disappointment at the closing table. This range of emotions is normal. Whatever you are feeling, don't let a last minute case of cold feet derail your efforts. Get through your closing and go take a look at your new house. Just seeing the new property you own, walking through it, and realizing the incredible accomplishment you've made will help ease your mind.

Some of you who experience buyer's remorse – particularly during settlement – might be apprehensive because you feel like you "missed something." Indeed, that is quite possible if you elected to forego a very important step that precedes your closing, the final walk-through. The final walk-through is your last chance to re-inspect the house you're going to buy just before closing. Arrange this walk-through after the seller has moved out so that you can view the home, make sure everything is in order, and be 100% confident in your purchase. At the final walk-through you'll want to check for any repairs that were supposed to have been made. You'll also be able to more closely examine walls and floors that might have been covered by pictures, paintings, or furniture. The point of a walk-through is to eliminate any surprises so that the next time you walk through that house – as it's owner – you absolutely feel like you made the right decision.

No home is perfect, so don't use the walk-through as an opportunity to nitpick over small things. However, you should certainly make sure the home is in as good a condition – if not better – than when you previously saw it and made your purchase offer. If you take the time to do a walk-through, and all buyers should, this will give you peace of mind and help you avoid, or at least minimize, a bad case of buyer's remorse.

**You've Got the Keys, Now What?**

So now that you've successfully closed on your home, it's time to celebrate. And why not? You've joined the ranks of this nation's homeowners, those who have realized a big part of the American dream. Your celebration doesn't have to be anything over-the-top or expensive. It can be as simple and low-key as you and a supportive friend toasting your success over pizza and soda – in your new house, of course.

With the keys to your new home, you can start planning all kinds of things – which bedrooms you'll paint, where you'll hang your nice art work, or perhaps which section of the backyard you'll plant with some colorful chrysanthemums. A word of caution to the wise: don't make the mistake that so many first-time homebuyers make by taking out unnecessary loans or using credit cards to finance furniture and other purchases once you get into a house. Hopefully, you set aside the funds I recommended (roughly 2% of your loan amount) to have cash on hand for furniture, moving expenses, or home improvements and repairs. All these items add to the true cost of homeownership.

Whatever you do, please allow yourself the luxury of some quiet time, no matter how brief. When it's all said and done, you should take a moment to just reflect on the process, consider what homeownership means to you, and appreciate the long, hard-fought battle you've just won. Only you know the personal and financial sacrifices you had to make to get into that home. Only you know the struggles you endured and the worries you faced. Only you know the obstacles encountered along the way and the naysayers who tried to dissuade you in your efforts. If you are a person of faith, give thanks for your house. Even if you don't believe in God, now is still the time to have a moment of gratitude for the enormous blessing you currently have: your very own home.

# Part III: The Future Part: Determining Your Own Destiny

# C H A P T E R

## 11

## Manage and Preserve Your Biggest Asset

As a property owner, you now have the privilege of coming home each day to a place that is bound to become more than just a roof over your head. Your very own house is the residence where you can raise your children, create family memories, or simply take pleasure in enjoying all by yourself – in your own unique ways. Soon enough, though, you'll find that the home you have come to love so much isn't merely a place of emotional comfort and joy. It's also an asset – one that can help you build wealth and financial security if you manage that asset properly and care for it in the right way.

Your home will give you enormous tax benefits. It can help you pay for major expenses, like a child's college education or that business you've been dying to start. Your house can also provide you with investment opportunities – perhaps to buy more real estate. It's unlikely that you'll stay in this first home until you retire, although that depends on your personal goals, as well as your present age. It's not inconceivable that the first home you buy – at age 25, 35, 45, or whatever age you happen to be – can even help you provide for a comfortable retirement with some adequate financial planning. The good news is that it doesn't take a Ph.D. to reap all these benefits and more. Just get up to speed on some real estate basics, and then proceed to make a few smart financial moves.

## The Seven Critical Goals of Responsible Homeowners

As a homeowner, you should have several goals in order to successfully manage and preserve your biggest asset:

- always pay your mortgage on time
- keep up with all required property taxes
- make sure your home is consistently and adequately insured
- maintain your home in the best possible condition
- properly manage the equity in your house
- increase the rate of appreciation on your property
- take advantage of the financial planning and tax strategies that are available only to homeowners

In this chapter of *Your First Home*, I'll focus on the last goal, as well as the overall financial implications of being a responsible and wise homeowner. In the next chapter, I'll give you practical advice on how to achieve each of the other goals listed above.

## Your Home as an Asset

When you think about the assets you own, does your house immediately spring to mind? It should, if you made any down payment on the house. That down payment – whether it was from funds out of your own pocket or money secured elsewhere – represents equity in your house. Your equity in a home is defined as the market value of the property minus any mortgages or liens on the home. If you just bought a house worth $350,000, and you had a 10% down payment, your current mortgage balance is $315,000, which means you have $35,000 in equity in your house. Knowing how to skillfully manage that equity – and properly maintain both your home and your finances so that you avoid financial loss or foreclosure – is the focus of the final section of this book.

First, let's take a look at why you should consider your home an asset –

because not everyone views your primary residence as an asset. Some people say a home that you occupy isn't really an asset because a home is constantly taking money out of your pocket with mortgage payments, insurance, taxes, and so forth. For this reason, you might hear various assertions that a home is not really as asset, but a liability.

I agree with the obvious conclusion that owning a home entails ongoing out-of-pocket expenses. However, I don't concur with the notion that just because something costs money, it doesn't qualify as an asset. Using that line of thinking, one could argue that the $250 sitting in your checking account isn't an asset since having a low balance means your bank is going to charge you $10 a month for that account, or nickel-and-dime-you to death with service charges. Although we know that getting nickel-and-dimed happens all too often, the part about your hard-earned cashed being deemed a "liability" instead of an "asset" could be true simply because your checking account actually costs you money each month.

Your home is, indeed, an asset for several reasons. First of all, you can sell the house whenever you choose and put cash in your pocket at closing. Those are real dollars, not phantom profits. The fact you'll likely pay a real estate commission on the sale doesn't diminish your home's status as an asset, just like paying a commission to a stockbroker when you sell a mutual fund doesn't negate that fund's standing as an asset. By the same token, it might take you one month to sell your house, whereas unloading the furniture in your house could be done in one day, at a garage sale. In both cases, a sale is a sale and you're still making money off the assets that buyers agree to purchase.

You can also borrow against the value of your home – via home equity loans or lines of credit, attesting to the fact that all bankers consider your home an asset and will allow you to use it as collateral. Moreover, the home you've just bought – or are about to purchase – will likely appreciate in value over time, holding out the potential for a good return on your investment. Clearly, real estate markets don't go up every year. However, homes have historically risen at a rate of 6.6% annually, according to the National Association of Realtors. This growth has represented a significant form of wealth for countless homeowners nationwide. Meanwhile, stocks have experienced annual appreciation rates averaging 10% when you look at 10-year investment cycles for every decade going back to the 1920s.

When you think about your assets, you should now definitely count your home among them, just like the value of any car you own, the cash value of your life insurance policy, or any retirement money you've squirreled away in stocks, bonds, or mutual funds.

As with all assets, you don't want all your wealth tied up in your home. You've no doubt heard the investing advice that you shouldn't pour all your money into a single stock. Whether you're talking about a house or stocks, "putting all your eggs in one basket" is neither safe nor prudent in terms of diversifying your assets. That's one reason why it might be wise to utilize the equity in your home – after careful consideration and planning – for other investment purposes. I'm not suggesting that you tap into your equity to go play the stock market, but I am pointing out that for any asset you have – home equity included – you must always think about "opportunity costs," or what you might be sacrificing by tying up your money in one investment when another, higher-paying alternative might be available.

## What Makes a Home a Unique Investment?

In many ways, owning a house is a very unique investment. A home is not instantly liquid, or able to be readily sold, like stocks or mutual funds. A home is a tangible, hard asset. You can see it, touch it, and change it. By contrast, stocks bonds, and mutual funds are paper assets. The large transaction costs associated with buying a home – typically 3% to 5% of the mortgage – can only be recouped over time, another factor that makes a real estate purchase unique. Right now, the equity in your home offers you a stored source of wealth. Unlike other investments, you don't have to sell your home in order to access that wealth/equity. You can refinance your home and take cash out, obtain a home equity line of credit, or get a home equity loan. Perhaps what is most important and unique about owning property is that you get the advantage of significant leverage. In one of my previous books, *The Money Coach's Guide to Your First Million*, I described leverage as "the language of millionaires." I made this comment because in the course of re-searching that book I found that most millionaires in this country shared one similar trait: they were property owners. These people had all learned the value of using leverage to make strategic – and financially prudent – real estate purchases. Lever-age, simply put, is investing a minimal amount of resources – whether time, money, or effort – to achieve maximum results. Leverage operates in full force when you buy a house. You get the rare opportunity to put a relatively small amount of dollars on the table (on a percentage basis) in order to control a very pricey asset. This is the ultimate case of the "minimum investment, maximum results" philosophy of leverage. Try going to a Wall Street broker to make your first purchase of stock, and saying: "I want to buy $250,000 worth of stocks, but I only want to pay $12,500, or 5% of the value of those assets." The broker would likely laugh you out of his office.

## Turning Your Net Worth and Property Into a Legacy

Lots of people would love the chance to pass along some amount of wealth to their family members. Harvard University's Joint Center for Housing Studies reports that home equity constitutes roughly 20% of total household net wealth. While roughly two-thirds of Americans own a house, only about 50% of them own stocks or mu-tual funds that hold stocks. Also, six in 10 homeowners have more equity in their homes than they do stock equity. You should consider that when you think about assets you'd like to pass along to your heirs or others.

If you pay off your mortgage, or even significantly reduce the principal balance, you'll be able to leave a home to whomever you choose and help that person get a great financial start. Pause for a moment to think about your own situation. How much better off would you be right now if you'd had someone in your life – a family member or another person – who had the foresight and financial wherewithal to have left you a home free and clear? All those years you spent wasting your money on rent could've been avoided freeing up that cash for other purposes. If you manage your finances correctly, maybe you'll be the person who can be a blessing to someone else by leaving that person a house – or at least considerable equity in a home. The home in which my husband and I live is a perfect example of such a blessing. He inherited the home after his Great Aunt Helena passed away. I'm always appreciative when I think of her, and of the legacy she passed on, which now benefits our entire family.

Even if you don't have anyone in mind to whom you would like to leave a home, does the idea of living in your house free and clear appeal to you? If so, think of how you'd really enjoy the benefit of homeownership without a monthly payment. To be able to live rent free in a residence is a scenario that economists call "imputed rent," meaning that with a paid-for home, you don't have a monthly housing cost. Even absent a mortgage, however, you would still have property taxes to pay, and likely homeowner's insurance too. For now, take heart in knowing that the more you pay down your mortgage, the more your personal wealth grows because mortgage payments represent forced savings. Every additional payment translates into bigger savings and additional wealth accumulated by knocking down your principal loan balance.

During the early years of your mortgage, most of the monthly payments you make are applied toward interest. For instance, after 10 years of paying on a 30-year mortgage, you're likely to have knocked off just 13% to 17% of your principal balance. Once you get into the 18th or 19th year of your mortgage, that's when you start really making headway on your loan. It's at that point when you'll discover that more than half of your payment gets credited toward reducing your principal outstanding.

## Five Tax Benefits for Homebuyers

As a homeowner, you are entitled to a remarkable number of tax and financial benefits that don't exist for renters. To take advantage of these economic perks, you must first know that they exist. Here's a quick summary of the benefits Uncle Sam offers to homeowners just like you.

### ■ Mortgage interest deduction

If you're married, you get to deduct all the interest you pay up to $1 million on your mortgage for a first or second home. The deduction is $500,000 for single people or married taxpayers filing separately.

### ■ Mortgage points

Any points you paid in connection with your home loan are tax-deductible. Remember: a point is 1% of the value of your mortgage. This can be a big tax savings worth thousands.

### ■ Property taxes

Any city or county property taxes you pay can be deducted from your income taxes, with the exception of tax money set aside in an escrow account. That can only be deducted when it's paid.

### ■ Moving costs

If you moved due to a job relocation, you could be entitled to write off some of your moving costs. Certain requirements must be met: For instance, your move must have occurred within one year of starting your new job. Also, your new job must be at least 50 miles farther from your old residence than your old job was.

### ■ Mortgage tax credit

Low income, first-time homebuyers can qualify for this home buying tax credit and get a mortgage interest tax credit up to 20% of the mortgage interest payments made on a house. You get to keep using this credit each year that you live in a home purchase with a tax credit certificate.

## Estate Planning Tips for Homeowners

A handful of more general financial planning and estate planning strategies can also put you in good stead as a homeowner. Use the techniques recommended below to keep your finances in tip top shape, and save yourself on taxes too.

### ■ Create a Will

If you die without a will, it's called dying "intestate." This leads to a very bad situation that could cause your family members to fight over your home or other assets. Take the time to create a simple last will and testament, which is the basic foundation for a solid estate plan. Your will can spell out to whom you would like to leave various assets, as well as who should be responsible for any minor children you have. Get a lawyer who specializes in wills and trusts to draw up a will for you. If you can't afford a lawyer, use an online service, such as Buildawill.com or Legalzoom.com. After you create a will online, just make sure you get it properly notarized and signed by at least two witnesses.

### ■ Buy a Good Life Insurance Policy

In the event of your death, life insurance will cushion the economic blow to your spouse, children, or anyone else who relies on you financially. Term life insurance is very affordable – on the order of $30 to $50 a month for a $500,000 policy for most non-smokers. Buying life insurance will give you peace of mind that if something happens to you, your heirs will be able to use the proceeds from your life insurance policy to pay off your mortgage and keep the house.

### ■ Establish a Basic Estate Plan

It may seem premature right now, but if the value of your house really grows, you purchase a lot of life insurance, or you build up considerable wealth outside of your home, you'll be doing yourself a favor to consult with a financial planner or tax adviser about smart ways to reduce the impact of estate taxes on your home. Currently, through 2008, you can transfer up to $2 million to your heirs, tax free. Federal estate taxes are slated to expire in 2010 and then be reinstated in 2011, so a qualified professional can help you stay abreast of the law and take the proper financial steps. One of them might involve setting up something called a "House Trust." In IRS lingo, it's known as a Qualified Personal Residence Trust, or QPRT. This is typically done when your most valuable asset is your home. You set up a trust that allows you to pass along your home – or even a vacation property – on a tax-free basis to your children. The goal is to substantially reduce estate taxes, which now can claim as much as 47% of your assets. Setting up such a trust is complicated and must be done in accordance with IRS laws. This isn't something you'll do on your own. When properly handled, though, a QPRT can save your heirs literally hundreds of thousands of dollars in estate taxes.

For more general information as well as general tax guidance, get IRS Publication 530, Tax Information for First-Time Homeowners (http://www.irs.gov).

# CHAPTER

## 12

## Follow the Path to Sustainable Homeownership

Nobody buys a home thinking they'll wind up in foreclosure at some point down the road. Unfortunately, the wave of foreclosures spreading throughout the country indicates how widespread this problem has become. In 2007 alone, there were more than two million foreclosure filings in the U.S., according to RealtyTrac Inc. During the peak of the housing boom in 2005 and 2006, many borrowers took on adjustable rate mortgages with low "teaser" rates that rise after two or three years. As a result, the Mortgage Bankers Associations predicts that foreclosures will peak in 2008 as those ARMs continue to reset and more homeowners fall behind on their payments that will rise by hundreds of dollars. By some estimates, up to five million individuals and families could lose their homes to foreclosure between 2007 and 2010.

The rise of sub-prime lending – which peaked in the five year period before the mortgage crisis of 2007 – has contributed greatly to a growing number of homeowners stuck with high-rate mortgages they can no longer afford. I don't excuse predatory loan tactics or banks that used incredibly bad judgment in making loans that should never have been approved. Clearly, however, lenders are not solely to blame for the country's foreclosure mess. Homeowners bear a degree of responsibility as well. In this chapter, I want to talk about your rights and responsibilities as a homeowner. The choices you make as a property owner directly impact your ability to have sustainable homeownership.

### The Seven Commandments of Successful Homeownership

In the previous chapter, I walked you through some of the financial planning and tax strategies you could use to effectively bolster your status as a homeowner. As you might recall, proper financial planning represented just one goal for which all homeowners should strive. There are seven goals in total. Think of these objectives as the "Seven Commandments of Successful Homeownership":

- always pay your mortgage on time
- keep up with all required property taxes
- make sure your home is consistently and adequately insured
- maintain your home in the best possible condition
- properly manage the equity in your house
- increase the rate of appreciation on your property
- take advantage of the financial planning and tax strategies that are available only to homeowners

We've already addressed the last issue. Now let's talk about the other ways for you to successfully preserve homeownership, avoiding foreclosure and other pitfalls property owners face. I don't want you to become a statistic in the unfolding foreclosure crisis, and I know you don't either. By adhering to the "Seven Commandments" listed above you can have peace of mind and be assured of keeping your home for as long as you want it.

### Always Pay Your Mortgage on Time

It sounds like a simple enough rule: always pay your mortgage on time. Unfortunately, that's often easier said than done. Some people pay their mortgages late – that is, after the due date – but before the grace period on their mortgage expires. This could be due to carelessness or a simple oversight on their part. The good news is that banks often give home borrowers a 10 or 15-day grace period on mortgages before a late charge is imposed.

### ■ Set up Automatic Mortgage Payments

Avoid the mistake of accidentally getting your payment in the mail, or forgetting to make a payment by setting up your mortgage on an automatic payment system. Have the money come right out of your checking or savings account each month to bypass the hassle of getting stamps and writing a check for your mortgage. Instead, let the payment get electronically deducted. This way, if you are traveling, your spouse neglects to pay the mortgage, or for some reason you're not around to mail a check, your house payment will still get made.

### ■ Prioritize Your Bills

We all have a laundry list of financial obligations – from house payments to utility bills to food and clothing expenses. Throw in transportation, various kinds of insurance, and the cost of raising kids and you can easily see how all those bills can really add up. No matter what debts you have, always think of your mortgage as top priority in terms of items to be repaid. If push comes to shove, you can work out a deal with your cell phone carrier and pay that large, unexpected cell phone bill you received over a few months, but you never want to get behind on your mortgage. Pay your house note first, next put other debts such as credit cards, auto loans, or student loans in order of importance. If you're delinquent on any of these debts it can hurt your credit – a fate you definitely want to avoid.

### ■ Establish a Cash Reserve

You'll recall that in an earlier chapter of *Your First Home* I explained why having a cash cushion was vital for homeowners. Once you get into a house, having extra cash on hand to deal with emergencies or unanticipated events can mean the difference between making your house payment on schedule and being delinquent on your mortgage. If something happens that impacts your finances – like you lose your job or suffer an illness that leads to big medical bills – you'll be counting your lucky stars that you had the foresight to stash away some money for a rainy day.

## Keep up With All Required Property Taxes

Missing mortgage payments isn't the only way you can lose your home. Falling behind on your property taxes also puts you at risk of foreclosure. In fact, tax lien foreclosures take place every day in America. When you don't pay property taxes you owe, your city or county has the legal right to put a high-priority tax lien on your property in the amount of the past due taxes, plus interest and penalties. After a set period of time – typically anywhere from six months to two years, depending on where you live – if your taxes are still unpaid the taxing authority's tax lien gives them the right to foreclose on your property. Your home then gets sold at an auction to anyone willing to pay off the back taxes due. Lots of investors buy "tax lien certificates" in the hopes of getting a home in tax foreclosure. For these investors, it's a way for them to purchase a home at a fraction of its value – without even having to pay off the mortgage due on the house.

The number one reason people become delinquent on their property taxes is because these taxes can run into the thousands, driving up the cost of homeownership considerably. Some lenders want you to add your property taxes into the monthly mortgage payment you make – to be sure those payments get paid on time. So if the principal and interest on your mortgage totals $2,000 per month and your annual property tax bill is $2,400, that's an additional $200 a month tacked onto your payment.

Check out the taxes paid in the following 10 states, which have the highest property taxes in the country. You'll notice that the top five states with the biggest tax bills are all located in the Northeast. However, even Midwest states, such as Illinois, and Western states, like California, make the list.

| State | Median Property Tax |
|---|---|
| 1. New Jersey | $5,352 |
| 2. New Hampshire | $3,920 |
| 3. Connecticut | $3,865 |
| 4. New York | $3,076 |
| 6. Massachusetts | $2,974 |
| 7. Illinois | $2,904 |
| 8. Vermont | $2,835 |
| 9. Wisconsin | $2,777 |
| 10. California | $2,278 |

**Source**: Census Bureau, Tax Foundation

Even if you live in a community with high property taxes, there are some smart ways to go about lessening your tax burden – and subsequently keeping your home.

### Proven Strategies to Slash Your Property Tax Bill

Almost everyone hates to pay taxes, and it doesn't matter whether they're federal income taxes, state taxes, or local taxes on the house you own. Americans dread property taxes more than any other tax, according to the Tax Foundation, a Washington, D.C.-based research group. Not to worry. If you tax bill is particularly onerous – or out of line with what others are paying for similar homes – you can often make a case for why your taxes should be reduced. To slash your property tax bill, try these tried and true techniques.

### ■ Analyze Your Property Tax Card

As a homeowner, you're entitled to visit your local tax assessor's office and request a copy of your property tax card. This tax card contains detailed data about your house, such as the lot size, the number of bedrooms and bathrooms in your home, as well as information about improvements or upgrades to the house. If you find mistakes in this card, point it out to your tax assessor and request a reevaluation. That reevaluation could lead to your annual tax bill being lowered.

### ■ Know the Tax Implications of Home Additions

Many homeowners want to improve or beautify their houses – or simply make their residences much more livable. Before you satisfy your hankering for a new pool, an extra bathroom, or even a new storage shed in the backyard, find out how such an addition or structural change would impact your property taxes. Any permanent structures you build – such as a deck or additional bedroom – will wind up adding to your tax bill.

### ■ Compare Neighboring Properties to Your Home

Not only can you get tax information about your home, you can also research your neighbors' homes. This can be invaluable if you approach a tax assessor's office to ask for a property tax reduction. Let's say you notice that the taxes on your three-bedroom, two-bathroom home are higher than all other three-bedroom, two-bath homes in your area. This gives you a factual basis upon which you can make a claim that your taxes are too high.

### ■ Deal Honestly With Your Tax Assessor

If you ask for your property bill to be lowered, expect your local municipality to try to schedule an appointment with you for a tax assessor to come inspect your home. Some people try to dodge the tax inspector, afraid that this person might see nice things in the home or quality amenities, and raise the property taxes. If you've done your homework, and you're dealing in a forthright manner with the tax man, don't worry too much about a tax increase. On the other hand, some cities automatically impose the highest tax rate possible on a home if a property owner refuses to grant the tax assessor access. So when the tax assessor comes to your house, whether the visit is scheduled or not, graciously welcome the person inside. Be sure to walk through the home with him or her – pointing out the good and the bad in your house.

The tax assessor might note your nice hardwood floors or the granite countertop in your kitchen, but miss the fact that your house doesn't have new replacement windows or updated appliances. It's your job to candidly point out these flaws – without going overboard. Just be matter-of-fact in mentioning your home's high points, as well as all of its drawbacks.

### ■ Keep up With Current Market Values

One big reason that property taxes exploded during the past decade is because home prices escalated so dramatically. Since skyrocketing home values led to reassessments on the upside, in theory, declining home values can also lead to lower assessments. Therefore, keep abreast of local market values. If you live in a community or a state where prices have stagnated or fallen substantially, you might be due for a reduction of your property taxes. Just realize that reassessments, (excluding those done when a home is sold), typically lag behind local market conditions.

## Make Sure Your Home is Consistently and Adequately Insured

When you obtained your mortgage, your lender undoubtedly required you to have property insurance. Homeowner's insurance covers your house in the event of a fire or some other catastrophe. In some states – such as earth-quake prone California, or hurricane-prone Florida, you must purchase supplement insurance coverage to guard against these disasters, which homeowner's insurance typically doesn't cover. All told, insurance premiums can run in the thousands of dollars each year. Despite the cost, you always want to make sure your home is adequately protected. It can be disastrous if you let your insurance coverage lapse and then suffer a calamity like an accidental house fire. Expect basic insurance coverage to cost you at least $500 to $1,000 per year. To get proper insurance coverage at the best rates possible, follow these five suggestions.

### ■ Increase Your Deductible

The rule of thumb with insurance of any kind is that the higher your deductible, the lower your premiums. By increasing your deductible from $250 to $500, or from

$500 to $1,000, you can typically shave 10% off your homeowner's insurance premiums. A higher deductible means that you won't be able to make smaller claims with your insurer – say if a window gets broken or a pipe leak causes a modest amount of damage. The upside, though, is that you'll keep your rates low with a squeaky-clean claims record.

### ■ Buy Smoke Alarms

Purchasing a smoke alarm isn't just a smart thing to do to keep your family safe. It's also a low-cost way to save money on your insurance. Smoke alarms are cheap, just $10 or $20, but these life-saving devices can slash another 10% from your annual insurance costs.

### ■ Install a Security System

By putting in a burglar alarm in your house – especially one that's linked to your local police station – you can cut your insurance costs by roughly 5% to 10%. To get this discount, send a copy of the bill for your burglar alarm or proof of your security system contract to your insurer.

### ■ Ask for a Multiple Policy Discount

If you have auto insurance or health insurance with one particular insurer, it might pay to place all your insurance coverage with that company. Ask your insurer about a multiple policy discount, which is given to consumers who give all their insurance needs with one insurer. The upshot is that you might also get a multiple policy discount on your auto and health insurance too – saving valuable dollars on that coverage as well.

### ■ Comparison Shop Annually

Experts recommend that you review your homeowners insurance regularly in order to make sure your current coverage adequately meets your needs. Mark a date on your calendar to do a once-a-year policy review. When you do your annual insurance check up, make sure you comparison shop to see if you can get better rates elsewhere. Insurers eager to win over new business may offer good deals to new customers. It's fast and easy to compare insurance rates online at sites like http://www.insurance.com or http://www.insure.com. Whatever company you choose, protect yourself by only buying a policy that offers "Guaranteed Replacement Value" insurance. This means that if disaster strikes and your home gets completely destroyed, the insurance company will pay you the full current market value for your home – not just what you paid for your house.

## Maintain Your Home in the Best Possible Condition

Have you ever driven through an older, established community and seen homes in disrepair? You know what I'm talking about: those nice big, but shabby-looking homes you can find in practically any working-class or middle-class community in America. Maybe the porch has gotten dilapidated or the 40-year-old roof needs replacing. Perhaps a home is in desperate need of a paint job or even just a decent trim of those overgrown hedges and a good mowing of the front yard, which now resembles a mini forest.

Viewing the outside of some of these residences, you can just imagine how they must have looked in their prime. They were probably elegant and stately, with well-manicured lawns and eye-catching exteriors. Unfortunately, these homes are now anything but eye-catching. In fact the words "eye sore" are far more appropriate.

What happened? In some cases, homes were passed along from one generation to the next and the recipients of the houses were unable to afford proper upkeep. At other times, properties fell into disarray after their owners experienced a host of personal problems, ranging from job loss to divorce to medical illness. In certain instances, property owners simply neglected their homes, allowing them to look more like caves than castles.

If you want your home to truly be your castle, you must treat it with the tender loving care it deserves. The payoffs for doing so are enormous. Not only will you enjoy living in the home, but you'll help maintain or increase the value of the house, as well as give yourself more financial options if you ever need to sell or tap into the equity in your home.

Believe it or not, many of the people caught up in the foreclosure wave right now have shot themselves in the foot simply because they haven't properly maintained their homes. Some unsuspecting homeowners, when faced with financial difficulties, mistakenly thought they would be able to sell or refinance their homes. However, when appraisers and inspectors visit a home all sorts of problems – such as a leaky roof, broken windows, or electrical problems – can derail a deal in no time flat.

You can avoid a lot of headaches and financial problems simply by regularly tending to your property and giving it routine care. Think "pick up, clean up, and repair." Start by getting into the habit of walking around the perimeter of your property at least once a week. We all have a tendency to enter or exit our homes the same way. Sometime we leave via the front door. However, many people, especially those who own single-family detached homes, frequently leave their houses via their cars, exiting from a garage. By doing so, you can miss issues large and small. Is there a rusty soda bottle that the wind blew onto your side lawn? Did the neighbor's garbage or recycling somehow spill over onto your property? It might be someone else's trash, but now it's your problem. Minimize unwanted junk and other miscellaneous objects outside your house simply by picking up things outdoors on a regular basis. I'm not asking you to go overboard. No need to turn into the town trash collector. However, at the very least you should do your part to keep the outside of your house looking decent and in order. If you happen to walk by a neighbor's property and they have something lying on the ground that shouldn't be there, it wouldn't hurt you to pick that up either. You'll be beautifying the community and, who knows, your neighbor might one day return the favor.

As you survey your property, remember that outside issues can trickle indoors if problems aren't addressed. Keep your gutters clear of leaves, so you don't have interior leak problems. Also, small nuisance issues left unattended can turn into big, costly headaches. For example, that toilet leak which goes drip-drip-drip everyday can ultimately cause your bathroom floor to buckle or wind up creating mold or rust problems. Take care of "minor" defects as soon as you notice them. Think of your home as you would your automobile. Every moving part needs some kind of attention at some point or another. If your doors squeak, lubricate them. If your window screens are tattered or ripped, replace them.

Power washing is a great way to beautify any patio, walkway, entrance, front door, or exterior. If you house is vinyl sided or brick-faced, chances are you can power wash. You can rent a power washer from a local home improvement store or hire an expert to do it for you for just a few hundred dollars.

## Properly Manage the Equity in Your House

I've already explained how the equity in your house represents a source of personal wealth. It's an asset you don't want to squander for any reasons. To avoid that misstep, it's vital to understand how to properly manage your home equity and make sure it continues to grow.

There are three primary ways that the equity in your house builds: by paying down the principal owed on your mortgage, through natural market appreciation, and by making property improvements that increase the value of your house. As a homeowner, you have no control over whether or not the real estate market goes up or down but you can bolster home equity by reducing your mortgage balance and making smart choices about home improvements.

Let's start with the strategy over which you have the most control: the rate at which you pay down your mortgage. Under normal circumstances, you make a monthly payment to your lender and little by little your outstanding principal balance begins to dwindle. I say "little by little" because during the early years of your mortgage most of the monthly payments you make are applied towards interest. For instance, after 10 years of paying on a 30-year mortgage, you're likely to have knocked off just 13% to 17% of your principal balance. Once you get into the 18th or 19th year of your mortgage, that's when you start really making headway on your loan. It's at that point when you'll discover that more than half of your payment gets credited toward reducing your outstanding principal. This is typical for a loan that amortizes over 30 years.

What if you wanted to accelerate your loan payoff? You could do so in any number of ways. You can send your lender additional money each month – in any amount of your choosing – and write a letter to your bank specifying that you want those funds applied to your principal balance. You can also remit one extra full payment on your mortgage each year to hasten your mortgage payoff. Both are powerful strategies that rapidly reduce your mortgage debt and save you tens of thousands of dollars in interest charges. Assume you took out a $400,000, 30-year loan for a home at an interest rate of 7%. Your monthly payment for principal and interest would be $2,661. By adding an extra $300 a month to your payment, you can pay off your mortgage in just 22 years and four months. You'd also save an incredible $168,392 in finance charges. Similarly, by making one extra payment of $2,661 each year, you would be mortgage-free after 23 years and 10 months, and would save $134,177 in interest. Equally important, both scenarios allow you to dramatically increase the equity in your home.

As a homeowner – especially one who has a good deal of equity in your home – you need to be prepared for the onslaught of offers you're apt to get from lenders of all stripes. All kinds of banks and financial institutions will flood your mailbox with loan offers, each of which will encourage you to tap into the equity in your house. You'll find these offers particularly plentiful when home prices are rising. Some lenders will want you to refinance your house. Others will suggest you take out a home equity loan or home equity line of credit. If you agree to any of these offers, realize that those loans are secured by the value of your home. Thus, any additional mortgage debt you acquire diminishes the value of your home equity. I don't mean to suggest that you should never refinance your house or take a loan against it. One the contrary, both refinancing and home-equity loans can be prudent strategies – when done carefully and for the right reasons.

Home equity loans appeal to property owners for several reasons. First, they're fairly easy to come by, since your house is collateral for the loan. Additionally, the interest on home equity loans is generally tax deductible up to $100,000. Moreover, the interest rates you pay on home equity loans and lines of credit are typically lower than other consumer loans. Lastly, you could use the money for any purpose you want, such as making home improvements or paying high-rate credit card debt.

Despite all of these attractive features, you must take care in both applying for and using a home equity line of credit. For starters, you don't want to use your home as a piggy bank, tapping your equity for the wrong reasons, like to pay for vacations, cars, holiday spending, and the like. Resist the temptation to borrow more than you can afford or more than you really need. If you've ever been seduced into spending money on a credit card with a high credit card limit, think of how you will deal with the temptation of having a big home equity loan or line of credit at your disposal.

## What Nobody Tells You About Home Equity Loans

Speaking of credit cards, did you know that a home equity line of credit operates very much like a credit card? Both of them have a pre-set limit and each allows you to access your credit by simply drawing down on your credit line. With a home equity line of credit, you access your available funds by writing a check or using a card that your lender provides. You only make payments each month based on the amount of credit you've utilized.

A home equity loan works differently. You receive a lump sum amount of cash to spend on what you'd like. Since you receive the money upfront, you start repaying the entire loan balance back immediately. Therefore, you could have a $100,000 home equity line of credit, spend just $15,000 from that credit line, and make principal and interest repayments based on those $15,000 worth of charges. With a $100,000 home equity loan, all the funds are immediately disbursed to you and your repayment is based on the full amount of your loan.

Most bankers will tout the tremendous benefits of home equity lines – and indeed, it can be advantageous to be able to pull cash out of the value of your house. Relatively few lenders, however, will seriously warn you about the pitfalls of home equity loans, or the dangers of unnecessarily or unwisely draining your home's equity. What are the downsides to these loans?

For starters, they're not like unsecured credit cards where, if you don't pay, creditors have fairly limited recourse against you. With a home loan, your house is on the line, so if you don't repay an equity loan or line of credit, you could lose your biggest asset.

Home equity lines of credit also frequently carry variable interest rates. This means what starts out as a manageable payment could quickly rise if you're not careful.

Additionally, home equity loans aren't always the best way to borrow. In certain instances it might make better sense to use other forms of financing. For example, if you're thinking about using a home equity loan to pay for college expenses, you should first explore traditional student loans. They might have lower rates, and the interest on many college loans is tax-deductible as well. Moreover, when you or your child secure federal student loans – like a Stafford Loan or a Perkins Loan – these are often subsidized, meaning the government pays the interest on the loans while the student attends school.

Another point of note: while the government uses tax benefits to stimulate homeownership, Uncle Sam's generosity for property owners only goes so far. That equity loan or line of credit you take out will only be tax deductible up to a maximum of $100,000.

Lastly, home equity loans can sometimes give you a false sense of security, making you feel a bit "richer" than you are and leading you to make unwise spending choices or even extravagant purchases. Lenders know that many consumers use their home equity as a ready source of cash. As a result, some unscrupulous lenders might try to take advantage of you by charging ridiculously high interest rates or excessive points and fees in connection with a home equity loan. For these reasons, think long and hard before you open an equity line of credit or taken out a loan secured by your home.

The good news is that federal laws do offer some protection to prevent homeowners from being abused when they take out home equity loans. First, the Home Owners Equity Protection Act prevents fraud and predatory lending by banning the following on home equity loans for owner-occupied properties:

■ An Annual Percentage Rate (APR) that is more than 10 percentage points higher than the yield on Treasury securities with similar maturities (i.e. the APR on a 15-year or 30-year home equity loan gets compared with the yield on a 15-year or 30-year Treasury bond, respectively)

- Total fees and points in excess of 8% of the loan amount

- Prepayment penalties after the first five years of the loan

- Balloon payments of less than five years with negative amortization

- Any terms that make it impossible for homeowners to cure a loan default

The HOEP Act applies only to home equity loans, not equity lines of credit because the latter are not considered "closed-end" loans. Additionally, if you ever take out a home equity loan, and you soon have a change of heart, you can terminate the deal. The Truth in Lending Act gives you a three day "right of rescission," allowing you to cancel a home equity loan for any reason within 72 hours (excluding Sundays) after you sign a loan agreement. If you cancel a home equity loan during this three-day period, your lender must refund any closing costs you've paid and remove any liens placed on your property within 20 days.

I'm often asked if it makes sense to use a home equity loan to pay off high-rate credit card debt. My answer is yes, if two specific conditions are met. First, you have to identify how it is that you got into a mess with credit card bills. If you racked up credit card bills because you fell victim to one of the Dreaded D's – Divorce, Downsizing, a Death in the family, Disability, or Disease – then you should consider using a home equity loan to pay off those credit card bills. If, on the other hand, you simply have a shopping addiction, or lack proper money management skills, I wouldn't recommend taking out a home equity loan to payoff credit cards. In such instances, people usually wind up with far more mortgage debt – and go out and run up the credit cards all over again. The second condition for using home equity to reduce credit card debt is: has the problem that caused your debt been fixed? Even if you got into debt through no fault of your own – because of a downsizing or you and your spouse split up – the fact remains that it's a bad idea to put your home at risk if those issues haven't been resolved. If you've got a new job, have financially rebounded from a divorce, or have beat a disease or disability that left you previously unable to pay your bills, that is a different story. In these instances, by all means, get caught up on your debts by paying off those credit card bills with low-rate, tax-deductible mortgage debt.

### Do's and Don'ts When Refinancing Your Home

After owning your home for some time, you might start to consider whether or not you should refinance your mortgage. If interest rates have dropped considerably, or if your credit has improved dramatically, it's possible you might be able to get a much better deal on a new mortgage than your original loan. Before you commit to refinancing, however, make sure you realize the implications of doing so.

To begin with, refinancing can eat away at your home's equity because refinancing is not free. A refinancing entails paying off your old loan and replacing it with a new one, and banks aren't in the business of making loans free of charge. Even if you hear lenders talk about a so-called "no cost" refinancing, don't believe it. A lender might not have an application fee, or charge you points to refinance, but those costs and others associated with refinancing are essentially priced into a loan with a higher interest rate. As you've heard many times before, "There's no such thing as a free lunch."

You probably remember that points you pay to obtain a mortgage are tax deductible. When you refinance, however, any points you pay must be amortized over the life of the loan. In other words, you can't take the full deduction for the points in one year, as you can do when you buy a house.

As with a home equity loan, you should never refinance into a larger loan than is necessary. Unfortunately, scores of homeowners do this all the time when they sign on the dotted line for a "cash out" refinance, which allows you to not only get a better rate or more favorable loan terms, but which also allows you to get some dollars back in the deal as well. A cash out refinancing saps equity from your home, so you should only take that money if you plan to use the proceeds wisely. Guard against frequent refinancing, too. If rates drop a half point or even a full percentage point, do the math to figure out if any monthly savings you can generate will really outweigh the closing costs and other fees associated with a refinance. I can't help but wonder if many consumers are really just cheating themselves out of the opportunity to build wealth due to excessive refinancing.

Consider these facts: Nearly nine out of 10 consumers who refinance their home loans take cash out in the transaction. In 2006 alone, Americans cashed out $352 billion worth of home equity – more than a 10-fold increase in the amount cashed in the year 2000. Moreover, when the Joint Center for Housing Studies (JCHS) at Harvard released its annual survey of housing, called the "State of the Nation's Housing 2007," the results were especially sobering. The JCHS report indicated that 13% of individuals and families who bought homes in recent years (in 2003 and 2004, to be exact), already have "negative equity" in their homes. This means their outstanding mortgage debt exceeds the market value of the houses in question. Unfortunately, the news is even worse for more recent buyers. A November 2007 survey by Zillow found that nearly 16% of homebuyers who purchased houses in 2006 had negative equity, as did 17.5% of those who bought in 2005. The number of homeowners facing negative equity will no doubt rise considerably if real estate prices remain soft in 2008 and 2009, as many experts predict will occur.

As with all financial products, you should shop around for the best loan terms you can get in the event you decide to refinance your mortgage. Don't just accept the first offer that comes your way. In considering a refinancing, follow the same vigilant standards you used to evaluate lenders and their offerings when you bought your house. This means you should know the annual percentage rate on your new loan, all fees charged, as well as key payment terms, such as whether a prepayment penalty exists.

Don't ever sign any loan documents that you don't understand and don't' agree if any loan officer or mortgage broker asks you to put your signature on a blank document with the promise that he or she will fill it in later. You don't know what they could insert into those loan documents. Also, make sure you get copies of everything in connection with a new mortgage, including a Good Faith Estimate, a Truth in Lending form, as well as the mortgage, note, and/or promissory document you must sign.

## Increase the Rate of Appreciation on Your Property

As a homeowner, it can be either terribly frustrating or wildly exhilarating to sit on the sidelines and watch the value of your property change. Obviously, if you're living through a down market, where real estate prices are dropping, that's probably the time you'll be frustrated or at the very least mildly disappointed that your home's value is declining. On the other hand, in boom real estate cycles, you can pretty much just ride the wave and watch your home appreciate in value due to natural market forces. This typically occurs when the economy is strong, housing demand outstrips supply, interest rates are attractive, and borrowers can readily obtain mortgages from lenders. While you can't single-handedly influence any of these factors, that doesn't mean you can't push up the value of your home, increasing your equity in the property.

One major factor within your control as a homeowner is the extent to which you renovate or improve your house, boosting its market value and making your house far more valuable than you might imagine. Not all home improvements are created equally. You need to be strategic about your efforts if you want to make home improvements that will truly add value to your house – as opposed to simply making it more cosmetically appealing.

## Home Improvements That Pay Off

The key question to ask is whether this improvement will significantly increase your home's resale value. If the answer is yes, chances are it's an item worth considering. Remodeling a kitchen, upgrading or adding a bath, or constructing a new bedroom all rank as high-return investments in your home. Lower-return improvements include finishing a basement or adding structures, such as a shed, swimming pool, or extra garage.

If you take out a loan for home improvements, you can deduct the interest on the loan if the work is considered a "capital improvement." The IRS says capital improvements are anything that prolongs the life of your house, increases its value, or makes it suitable for new uses, such as adding a porch or driveway or installing new, built-in appliances. Always keep good records of your home improvements. You can't immediately get a tax write-off for these upgrades but when you sell your house those improvements will increase your basis, or tax cost, in the property, which could lower any taxes you might have to pay.

Whether you decide to add a room, put in storm windows and doors, pay for professional landscaping, or install an air conditioning system, fireplace, or fence around your property, each of these actions can increase the tax basis in your home. What's more, if an appraiser, home inspector, or real estate agent came out to evaluate your house, these upgrades would also undoubtedly immediately boost your home's value. Some people do massive upgrades right before they plan to put their homes on the market, but resist the urge to over-improve your house. You don't want to buy into a neighborhood of 2,000-square-foot, 3-bedroom homes and convert your house into a 4,000-square foot, 5-bedroom McMansion in the hopes that you'll double the value of your property. That won't happen. Besides, as a homeowner, any improvements you make shouldn't be driven exclusively by financial considerations and possible resale value. You should also personally enjoy the home improvements you make. After all, the ability to change or upgrade your house – and still be able to afford and sustain it – is both a right and responsibility of successful home ownership.

# CHAPTER

$$\boxed{13}$$

## Avoid Foreclosure and Other Pitfalls

Once you live in a home for any amount of time – whether it's a year or a decade – you naturally start to develop some emotional attachments to your house. You can probably recall family celebrations there, major life changes that occurred while you lived in the home, or even just things you did to personalize the house and make it your own. For all these reasons and more, it can be devastating to come to terms with losing the house you love and worked so hard to obtain. Nevertheless, sometimes a big mortgage payment, in combination with all the rest of the bills and curve balls that life throws at you, can simply become too much to bear financially.

When you miss multiple mortgage payments, you become subject to foreclosure proceedings. There are two primary forms of foreclosure in America: judicial foreclosure and non-judicial foreclosure. Judicial foreclosure – which is normally used in states where a mortgage is used as the security instrument on a home – is a lengthy process, involving a court lawsuit. Non-judicial foreclosures typically occur in states that use a deed of trust as the security instrument. Non-judicial foreclosure allows a trust to initiate foreclosure without having to go to court. Other types of foreclosure methods exist, but they are far less common. For instance, strict foreclosure allows a lender to foreclose on a house simply by declaring that a borrower has defaulted. Strict foreclosure is legally permitted in only a few states, including Connecticut, New Hampshire, and Vermont.

The foreclosure process can vary widely from state to state, but the following is a synopsis of what usually occurs in a judicial foreclosure, where a lender sues you in order to get a judgment to seize your home and auction it off. After you fall anywhere from three to six months behind on your mortgage, your lender will file a court complaint and also a "Notice of Lis Pendens" with your county recorder's office. (Some lenders are more aggressive and want to file official notices as soon as legally permissible in order to cut their losses. Others will first try to do everything possible to avoid commencing foreclosure.) The Lis Pendens is your official notice that you face foreclosure and that the clock is now ticking in order for you to bring your past-due payments current. The lender will seek an entry of judgment or summary judgment from the court. The judgment spells out the entire amount due and establishes a sale date for the property. If your defaulted mortgage isn't brought current, usually another three months will pass before most lenders send you a "Notice of Sale," indicating that a foreclosure date has been set. This notice will be posted on your property and also recorded at the County Recorder's Office. Depending on your lender and the state in which you live, foreclosure proceedings can vary – especially with regard to the speed with which your bank acts. Since a Notice of Sale also gets published in a newspaper, you might feel like it's open season on you as investors, questionable foreclosure-prevention firms, and others contact you, claiming they can help you save your home. Later in this chapter, I'll tell you who to trust – and what to look out for in order to avoid con artists and other predators. For now, let's talk about what you can do to prevent foreclosure from happening in the first place.

### What to Do If You Face Financial Difficulties

In the midst of trying personal circumstances or severe economic difficulties, the very last person you probably want to talk to is your lender but, believe it or not, that's the very first thing you should do. The single-most important thing you can do when you face financial trouble is to pick up the phone and let your lender know what is going on. If you experience one of the five "Dreaded D's" – Downsizing, Divorce, Death in the family, Disability, or Disease – it is especially important to act as quickly as possible. The best time to get help and to work out something with your lender is *before* you've missed a payment – not after.

Unfortunately, precisely the opposite phenomenon occurs during most fore-closures. All too often, homeowners flat out refuse to communicate with their lend-ers, which only exacerbates the problem. In fact, roughly 50% of all homeowners who wind up in foreclosure and lose their homes never talk to their lenders even once, according to NeighborWorks. Taia Lockhart, Vice President of Housing Ad-vocacy at PMI Group, says she understands why homeowners are reluctant to discuss their situations. "They're embarrassed, disappointed, and confused," says Lockhart. "They don't know how to handle it," she adds. As a result, many people make the mistake of refusing to directly address the issue.

The problem, however, is that your silence can be painfully costly, causing you to lose the very home you're trying to protect. So instead of sticking your head in the sand, or ignoring a lender's repeated calls and letters, if you get behind on your mortgage, please muster up the strength and courage to make contact with your mortgage company. Chances are you'll be glad that you did.

**Foreclosure Myths and Realities**

One of the advantages of reaching out to your lender as early as possible is to rid your mind of a number of foreclosure myths and to open your eyes to the range of options that might exist for you. Here are some of the myths that people often believe about their homes as it relates to foreclosure. By buying into these miscon-ceptions, you put yourself at risk of losing your home due to inaction or ignorance.

■ **The Bank Wants to Take My Home**

There is perhaps no bigger or more dangerous myth in the mind of the homeowner in crisis than the misconception that some big, bad bank wants to snatch your house from underneath you. This widespread, unfounded belief is simply not true. For starters, banks loathe having defaults and foreclosures because federal regulators frown on financial institutions with too many bad loans on their books. Also, banks are not in the business of owning property. They are in the lending business. They sell mortgages and earn a profit (i.e. interest) on those loans. More important, fore-closures are extremely costly for lenders. The non-profit group ACORN, the Association of Community Organizations for Reform, estimates that banks suffer an average loss of $58,000 for every foreclosed property. This is due to the lost interest, legal fees, eviction expense, and other costs a bank incurs during foreclosure – such as repairing a home, marketing it for resale and paying an agent's sales commission. Therefore, responsible lenders know that it is definitely not financially prudent to return a home to its inventory. Consequently, banks will often bend over backwards to help you avoid foreclosure.

### ■ There's Nothing I Can Do to Fix My Situation

Yes you can. You can make financial sacrifices that might enable you to pay your mortgage. You can get credit counseling or learn to budget better. You can take on a second job if it means helping you to pay your house note. You can possibly sell your house or refinance your loan. If you talk to your lender you will find that lenders have an array of alternatives they can recommend. Many times, the assistance or financial options they suggest are made on a case-by-case basis, to best aid you in resolving your particular problem. Believe it or not, some lenders have even hired employment specialists to find new jobs for homeowners that have received pink slips. So even if you have a problem that you think is hopeless, don't let that dissuade you from at least trying to see if a helpful solution can be found. Even reputable third-party sources can help – but only if you reach out to talk to someone, sooner rather than later.

### ■ I Can File for Bankruptcy and Keep My Home

While it's true that bankruptcy can fend off certain creditors and help you stay in a home, oftentimes bankruptcy merely buys you some time and then a foreclosure might still be unavoidable. That's why if you're contemplating bankruptcy solely as a means to save your home, be 100% sure that better alternatives don't exist. You might be counting on money to come in from some source – planned for or unexpected – in order bring your mortgage payments current. If that money doesn't materialize, you've severely damaged your credit with the bankruptcy filing and you will likely still lose the house anyway. Bankruptcy is a very, very serious step that should never be done without careful consideration for the short and long-term consequences involved. Since a bankruptcy stays on your credit record for 10 years, you should only pursue bankruptcy as a last-ditch option if everything else has failed and the bankruptcy will ultimately help you keep the house.

## Strategies and Alternatives to Ward off Foreclosure

I've already explained a bit of the process in terms of how foreclosure can legally proceed. Even if you've missed several payments, there are still several strategies and alternatives available to help you ward off foreclosure. To take advantage of any of these options, you'll have to contact your lender and work out a deal. If you're too nervous about dealing with your lender directly, there are reputable homeownership preservation groups that will work on your behalf. Here are some of the options that a lender might agree to in order to help you remain in the home of your dreams. For any of these foreclosure prevention strategies, get your agreement in writing. Also, to get the most desired results, make sure you talk to the right people. This means calling the "loss mitigation" department or the "workout" division of your lender. Don't try to arrange a deal with the credit and collections staff. They'll just try to get you to pay as soon as possible. The loss mitigation specialists, however, are trained in dealing with cases like yours, and they have the power and flexibility to work out a deal.

### ■ Repayment Plans

Some of you might not have missed any payments yet, but maybe you're experiencing a cash crunch and your mortgage is making you feel financially squeezed. In this instance, you can ask your lender for a repayment plan that would allow you to make most – but not all – of your normal monthly payment. The amount of money you don't pay can be tacked on to the end of your mortgage. Alternatively, if you are facing a short-term financial issue which will soon pass, you can ask your lender to let you pay off the past due amount little by little, tacking extra payments onto future regular payments.

### ■ Reinstatements

For those of you who've missed one or two payments, and now have the money (or will soon have the cash) to bring your account current, a reinstatement may do the trick. With a reinstatement, your lender will let you pay off what you owe over an agreed-upon time frame. You might have to pay late fees and penalties, or your lender might waive those charges.

### ■ Forbearance

Lenders often use forbearance as a method of helping delinquent borrowers who are behind on their mortgages. Forbearance allows you to pay your arrears, or past due amount, at a later point in time. Whatever is overdue can be paid off in a variety of ways, over a period of many months or perhaps at the end of your mortgage term, when you sell or refinance your home loan. Sometimes, forbearance agreements even allow you to skip payments altogether or reduce the payment you must make for a set number of months.

### ■ Loan Modifications

If you have an adjustable-rate mortgage that has reset and you can no longer make the higher monthly payment, consider asking for a loan modification. Two solutions might be for your lender to convert your ARM to a fixed-rate loan, or for your loan interest rate to revert back to its previous level. Even if you don't have an ARM, lenders have discretion to modify loans in any way they choose. For example if you are five years into repaying a 30-year fixed-rate loan, the lender can convert the remaining loan balance into a new 30-year term or even extend the loan from a 30-year loan to a 40-year loan. Each of these alternatives would obviously cost you more in finance charges in the long run but might prove helpful if you need to lower your payments and stay in your house. Loan modifications are typically granted to those who've maintained a good payment track record. Unfortunately, a recent

survey from Moody's found that loan modifications occur on only 1% of all financially troubled mortgages.

While loan modifications clearly happen far too rarely, lenders have been
known to go on the offensive in trying to work out deals with borrowers. Such was
the case with Countrywide, when in October 2007 the company announced that it
was offering loan modifications to some 82,000 customers who collectively owed
about $16 billion on their mortgages. Two of the options for borrowers included
refinancing into prime loans and refinancing into government-insured, FHA loans.
The unprecedented step by Countrywide came amid the mortgage meltdown, as
scores of the bank's customers faced ARMs that were resetting to higher interest
rates by the end of 2008. Upon announcing the massive loan modification program,
David Sambol, Countrywide's president and Chief Operating Officer said, "Unprecedented times call for unprecedented remedies. We are determined to assist
borrowers who have the willingness and the wherewithal to remain in their homes,
but need a little help to do it."

**Beware of These Foreclosure Scams**

Being on the verge of foreclosure is nerve-wracking enough. What's worse, however, is that there is no shortage of scammers out there who will try to prey on you
at your most vulnerable point. Their goal: to cheat you financially out of considerable
dollars, sap the equity out of your house – or maybe even steal your home altogether
with underhanded tactics. To fight off foreclosure scams, you must be able to recognize them. Here is a summary of some of the most prevalent tricks that swindlers
might try in their never-ending efforts to pull the wool over your eyes.

■ **Foreclosure Rescue Scams**

As foreclosure rates rise, one unfortunate byproduct of this crisis is the emergence
of con artists out to bamboozle vulnerable homeowners. Make sure you don't fall
for a foreclosure rescue scam, also known as a mortgage rescue scam. In these
types of fraud, a bogus or ill-intentioned company will promise to "fix your mortgage

problem." They'll tell you that they can intervene on your behalf with a lender, which is a legitimate tactic used by reputable companies that truly want to help you. With the con artists, however, they simply take your money and run. They convince you to pay a fee, frequently $1,000 or more, and then they claim to "negotiate" with your lender to resolve your loan default. The problem, though, is that these fraudsters usually just pocket your hard-earned money and then go on to the next victim.

Unfortunately, the more foreclosures an area has, the more scams abound. For example, many parts of Ohio have been wracked by foreclosure, and the Ohio Attorney General has filed numerous lawsuits against foreclosure rescue companies. These firms stand accused of taking people's money, promising to work out deals with lenders, and then doing absolutely nothing. While these criminals typically prey on low-income homeowners, minorities, or the elderly, anyone can fall victim to a conman's shenanigans. Don't write a big check or give anyone a lump sum cash payment to supposedly help you get back on track with a past due mortgage. There are far too many legitimate foreclosure assistance agencies, including non-profit charities and others, that will help you free of charge, or for a nominal fee at most.

### ■ Equity Stripping Schemes

Another common foreclosure scam involves fleecing you out of the equity in your home. This is often done in conjunction with a rental or lease-back scheme. In this scam, the con artist tells you that they'll save your house by having you put the title in their name. They're supposed to then rent it to you, letting you stay in the home. Because you still have possession of your house, you might feel like everything is legit. However, the scammer might really be stripping away your home equity by failing to make mortgage payments, charging you excessive fees or doing bogus renovations. In some cases, once a con artist has title or the deed to your home, they even sell it to another unsuspecting buyer, leaving you and that person to deal with the mess. It's risky at best to ever sign over your title or deed to some stranger who approaches you out of the blue and offers that as a solution to your foreclosure worries. Just don't do it.

### ■ Fake Counseling Agencies

If you fall into foreclosure due to financial mismanagement or a lack of financial skills, it's not a bad idea to get credit counseling or advice about budgeting. However, some hucksters offer bogus financial counseling – and add insult to injury by charging you lots of money for bad advice. Sometimes, they might actually work out a deal on your behalf, but at a steep price. Be wary of anyone who says "don't talk to your lender" because they might be trying to drive a wedge between you and the lender who can offer legitimate help. Also, say "thanks, but no thanks" to any counselor who wants to charge you hefty, upfront fees for their "assistance."

### ■ Loan Scams

A loan scam occurs whenever an outside lender comes in and offers to let you refinance your mortgage into a new, exotic loan. A common ploy would be to get you to sign off on a loan with a balloon payment. Typically, in the beginning of this new mortgage your payments might be considerably lower, giving you some short-term relief. What most people don't realize is that this is usually because the lender has given you an interest-only loan. In short order, you will find that at the end of a set term – like maybe six or 12 months – a big balloon payment will be due that you probably can't afford. If you can't make this required lump sum payment, you could lose your home to this new lender – the very fate you were trying to avoid.

## Reputable Homeownership Preservation Groups to Know

Hopefully, I didn't scare you with the previous section about foreclosure scams. That information was meant to protect you against unscrupulous characters found all around the country who prey on financially troubled homeowners. Fortunately, there are a number of reputable, trustworthy homeownership preservation groups in the U.S. that offer assistance to homeowners nationwide. Below is a list of some of them. This list is not meant to be comprehensive but it does represent some of the better-known agencies and groups that are active in trying to help American homeowners facing foreclosure.

### ■ ACORN (http://www.acorn.org)

ACORN, the Association of Community Organizations for Reform Now, in October 2007 estimated that as the foreclosure crisis widens it could cost banks, lenders, governments, and homeowners as much as $25 billion in losses. Less than a month later, as bank after bank began to publicly report mortgage-related losses, estimates about extent of the mortgage meltdown grew exponentially. In mid-November 2007, Goldman Sachs chief economist Jan Hatzius said mortgage defaults will cause losses of as much as $400 billion for lenders. To battle the problem, ACORN has a homeownership preservation initiative that involves approximately three dozen mortgage companies, including Citibank, HSBC, J.P. Morgan Chase, and Wells Fargo, among others. Participating lenders are flexible in offering workout solutions to homeowners behind on their mortgages. ACORN also has foreclosure avoidance classes, financial counseling, and other services.

### ■ NACA (http://www.naca.com)

NACA, the Neighborhood Assistance Corporation of America, is a national non-profit agency that promotes sustainable homeownership and affordable housing. The group is vigilant in its efforts to stop predatory lending, mortgage fraud, and foreclosure scams. In 2007, NACA struck a historic agreement with Countrywide to help homeowners facing foreclosure refinance into loans with interest rates as low as 5%. NACA's foreclosure prevention initiative, called the Home Save Program, focuses on consumer education and financial counseling. The group's philosophy is that more homeowners can be helped in the long run if consumers are adequately educated about mortgages, personal finances, and proper money management techniques.

### ■ HOME Ownership Preservation Fund (http://www.995HOPE.org)

This group's financial counselors have helped well over 100,000 consumers in the past five years, telling them their options to prevent foreclosure and assisting them in dealing with lenders. The fund operates what is perhaps the country's best-known foreclosure hotline (800-995-HOPE) for NeighborWorks, which also is active in foreclosure prevention. To show you the extent of the growing foreclosure problem, consider these statistics. In 2006, the hotline fielded approximately 75 calls a day nationwide. By June, 2007, the number skyrocketed to 750 calls daily. In September 2007, the group's counselors were taking an average of 1,300 calls a day. By December 2007, after President Bush announced a plan to help homeowners facing foreclosure, the hotline was receiving a record 5,800 calls per day.

### ■ National Foundation for Credit Counseling

The NFCC has a Homeowner Crisis Resource Center helpful for any homeowner at risk of foreclosure. You can talk to a certified housing counselor and take the groups "Mortgage Reality Check" quiz to assess your risk of foreclosure and explore various financial options. Additionally, the organization's website contains useful information and tools to help you make the best decisions possible. To take advantage of these tools, visit the NFCC's website at http://www.housinghelpnow.org.

### ■ NeighborWorks (http://www.nw.org)

NeighborWorks' motto is "strengthening communities and transforming lives." Indeed, the group helps to do just that by keeping scores of homeowners from losing their homes every year. NeighborWorks is a national non-profit organization that employs a team of mediators to act as go-betweens for lenders and borrowers. NeighborWorks counselors often work out deals for homeowners. In some cases, however, they encourage borrowers who are comfortable talking to the lender to discuss the borrower's situation directly, as early as possible. As mentioned, one of NeighborWork's most successful efforts is its toll-free foreclosure prevention line: 888-995-HOPE.

The non-profit sector and consumers groups around America are really stepping up to the plate to deliver needed intervention for homeownership preservation. For instance, in 2007 NeighborWorks added some 1,800 staffers to its ranks, according to a group spokesman. Other entities, such as the PMI Foundation, have also donated considerable sums of money to many non-profits to help boost local home preservation efforts.

■ **Hope Now**

In addition to the non-profit arena, the mortgage community itself is also banding together to prevent foreclosures. Hope Now is an industry coalition of 11 major lenders whose companies originate 60% of all mortgages in the United States. Mortgage counseling agencies, investors, and industry trade groups such as the Financial Services Roundtable and The Housing Policy Council also belong to Hope Now. Together, these participants are using their collective muscle to beat back the nation's mounting rate of home loan defaults, especially by helping homeowners get out of adjustable rate mortgages that will reset to higher interest rates. Hope Now launched in October 2007 with the backing of U.S. Treasury Secretary Henry Paulson. The alliance's goal is to use coordinated efforts that maximize outreach to distressed homeowners, providing mass-based solutions to as many troubled homeowners as possible. By March 2008, 1 million homeowners avoided foreclosure with Hope Now.

**State and Federal Efforts to Prevent Foreclosure**

Foreclosures can wipe out entire neighborhoods. Whenever a foreclosed upon home becomes vacant, that hurts property values for the homeowners left behind. A 2007 study by the Woodstock Institute, a nonprofit community development research group, indicated that just one single foreclosure negatively impacts a neighborhood. The report said that when one home is foreclosed upon, homes within an eighth of a mile of that foreclosure immediately lose 1% or more of their value. As a result, many states in the country are trying to aid homeowners in saving their properties, which in turn, helps keep local communities strong.

At least six states – including Maryland, Massachusetts, New Jersey, New York, Ohio, and Pennsylvania – are spending more than $500 million to help borrowers with sub-prime adjustable rate loans refinance into more manageable fixed rate loans. The goal is to stem the rising tide of foreclosures impacting numerous low-to-moderate income neighborhoods in those states.

Additionally, state legislatures in various territories – particularly in the Northeast – are holding hearings and scrutinizing lenders. Some efforts are afoot to clamp down on sub-prime and predatory lending practices, which critics say have helped contribute to the nation's growing foreclosure dilemma.

A growing recognition that foreclosures hit both low and moderate income neighborhoods – and more well-to-do communities too – is also spurring federal assistance. One of the ways the federal government is trying to help is by allowing the Federal Housing Administration to make 40-year FHA-insured loans that would ease the monthly payment burden for cash-strapped homeowners. As of this writing, Congress is still considering that legislation.

Separately, the federal government also provides HUD-approved credit counselors that provide education and guidance to homeowners in the throes of foreclosure. You can call the HUD Housing Counseling and Referral Line at 800-569-4287 to find the nearest HUD-approved counseling agency in your area.

### Unexpected Sources That Will Pay Your Past-Due Mortgage

If you face the threat of foreclosure, a handful of entities you may not have considered might be able to come to your rescue – by providing you with immediate cash to pay off overdue mortgage payments. These sources include the government, the company to whom you're paying private mortgage insurance, and your employer.

#### ■ The Government – Namely FHA or the VA

If you have an FHA loan or a VA-backed mortgage, one way to prevent foreclosure, is to turn to these agencies for help. You can receive a one-time payout from the FHA's insurance fund, sometimes called a "partial claim payment," in order to satisfy any mortgage balance that is currently in arrears. You can qualify for this FHA payment if you are at least four months delinquent, but no more than 12 months behind on your mortgage, and if you have the financial capacity to begin making full mortgage payments on your own. The process works like this. Your lender files a partial claim. HUD then pays your lender the money required to bring your mortgage current. You then sign a Promissory Note, and a lien gets placed on your home that stays in place until the Promissory Note is paid in full. The Promissory Note is free of any interest charges, and you pay it off when you refinance or sell your home.

With VA loans, a series of VA Regional Loan Centers provide financial counseling and guidance to help you prevent foreclosure. You can call the Department of Veteran Affairs at 800-827-1000 to get a referral to a VA loan service representative in your region.

## ■ Your Private Mortgage Insurance Company

You may recall that I earlier explained how Private Mortgage Insurance, or PMI, benefits consumers by making home loans more plentiful and allowing lenders to offer mortgages to those who lack a 20% down payment. Here's another way that your PMI company earns brownie points. It can actually help you repay your delinquent mortgage.

According to Taia Lockhart of PMI Group, the company asks credit counselors to contact any borrower who suffers an "early payment default," which is a delinquency within the first 12 months of a mortgage. "We are proactive" in working with homeowners in trouble, says Lockhart. "We also work with lenders and the GSEs (Government Sponsored Entities)" like Fannie Mae and Freddie Mae to preserve homeownership.

PMI Group's servicing and claims department have developed a way to evaluate a borrower's potential success at managing a mortgage. When the chances of repayment are high, and when a customer appears to have merely suffered a short-term setback, "We offer unsecured loans to help people get back on their feet," Lockhart says. Therefore, if you run into financial trouble, it can't hurt to ask your Private Mortgage Insurance company for help. The cash assistance that the PMI Group provides is complimented with an array of education tools for consumers, including a web-based training guide that explains the entire home buying process, a tutorial on loan products, and budget worksheets. Additionally, PMI Group offers a self-study, computer-based learning program for people who are thinking about becoming homeowners.

### ■ Your Employer

No employer wants their employees thrown out on the street due to foreclosure. When employees have financial stress and money worries, it leads to higher absentee rates and decreased productivity on the job. Many companies already offer employer assisted housing in the form of down payment assistance or educational resources to help workers become homeowners. It's possible too that your employer might aid in your effort to keep your home during times of crisis. Therefore, if you encountered an unexpected blow to your finances, or a one-time event that drained your cash resources, consider the prospect of seeking aid from your job. You might request a loan or an immediate lump sum bonus to deal with a mortgage that's overdue. Some employers might be willing to provide you with money in exchange for overtime work, your taking on additional duties, or your simply agreeing to pay back the money over time via paycheck deductions. Even if your company has never provided such home assistance loans or direct cash payments to troubled homeowners in the past, it can't hurt to ask.

### Last-Ditch Efforts if Foreclosure is Inevitable

Maybe you've tried everything and have come to the conclusion that your situation is particularly dire. If you've exhausted all possible workout options with your lender, no source of outside financial assistance is available, and refinancing is also out of the question, you still want to do everything you can to avoid a foreclosure.

The strategy here is to prevent severe financial damage to your credit rating, which can hurt you for years. A foreclosure can jeopardize your ability to buy a new home in the future, and even impact your chances for renting a decent apartment. If foreclosure is inevitable and imminent, then consider these two strategies. In each instance, you lose the home, but at least you preserve your credit standing.

### ■ Deed in Lieu of Foreclosure

When you execute a deed in lieu of foreclosure, you sign your deed back over to the lender, and walk away from the home with no further obligation. It's a painful choice to make, but in especially troubled circumstances, it might be your best alternative to prevent an official foreclosure notice from scarring your credit report.

### ■ Short Sale

With a short sale, you bring in a third-party to buy your house for an amount less than what is due on the mortgage. These days, with a glut of homes on the market, and falling housing prices, more and more lenders are accepting short sales, even if the third party pays significantly less than the mortgage balance. A short sale works for lenders who want to avoid the time, expense, and aggravation involved in a full-blown foreclosure proceeding. One company, called HouseBuyerNetwork.com, arranges short-sales for homeowners and provides foreclosure prevention advice too. Sales can often be done in 10 days or less.

### How to Bounce Back if Foreclosure Does Occur

A wise man – my husband, Earl Cox – once remarked that many people desperately trying to save their homes should instead pour their energies into saving themselves and their families. He compared a homeowner facing foreclosure to a captain of a ship whose vessel has unexpectedly hit an iceberg. "The goal is to save the passengers, not the ship," Earl noted. His point was that when a crisis strikes, the ultimate measure of success is whether the participants survive the disaster. In the worst possible plight, the passengers are of utmost importance to a captain, not his multi-ton ship. Likewise, you and your family – the people you love – are what are most valuable; worth far more than your property.

So despite your very best efforts to save your house, the sad truth is that sometimes it simply isn't possible. This might be the case when your credit score has suffered, making a refinance unrealistic, if your home's value has declined in value, making sale or accessing equity impossible, or if for some reason your income is no longer enough to support a mortgage that is likely many months past due. It might also be the case that time has simply run out and a sheriff's sale can no longer be prevented.

If you do find yourself in the unfortunate situation of giving up possession of your beloved home, take heart. As crushing as the situation is, it truly is only a temporary setback. There's no question that foreclosure can be devastating – financially and emotionally. However, you can bounce back from this unfortunate circumstance, and probably quicker than you might imagine.

To recover as quickly as possible from the blow of losing your home, start by taking an honest look at what went wrong. I realize that in the overwhelming majority of home foreclosures personal tragedy has played a role. You might have gone through a divorce or lost your job. Or maybe you got behind on your payments due to medical illness. You must also analyze other realities that led to your troubles and how they might have been prevented. Did you fail to have a cash cushion or wait too long to try to get help? Did you take out a mortgage that, in retrospect, you never should have accepted? Perhaps your finances took a nosedive due to fiscal mismanagement or overspending. Whatever the case, don't beat yourself up emotionally. It is, however, important to acknowledge what actions contributed to your predicament so that you won't repeat those mistakes in the future.

You should also know that you are not alone in your misfortune. According to various estimates, as many as one million or more homeowners will wind up in foreclosure this year alone. Promise yourself now that the foreclosure you experienced will not have been in vain. Learn from it. Get stronger from it. Resolve to be a smarter consumer in the future and a better steward of your finances. Read books like this one – and reread it for future reference – as a way to constantly remind yourself about the joys, rights, and responsibilities of homeownership.

Yes, it's great to own a home, but it's only great when you do it the smart way. I hope *Your First Home* has given you the confidence and knowledge to make the best possible decisions when preparing for, finding, and financing the home of your dreams – and keeping it too.

# E P I L O G U E

## Enjoy the Ride –
## And Strategize to Buy
## Your Second Home

Homeownership is a thrilling adventure, and you should do your very best to enjoy the ride. Sometimes everything will be smooth sailing. Other times, you'll encounter bumps along the way. Overall, the journey is well worth the effort.

As your Money Coach, I've given you all the strategies and insights you need to prepare for, find, and finance a home wisely. Moreover, I've taught you how to avoid foreclosure, preserve your house, and turn it into a wealth-building tool in order to get the best possible return on the largest investment of your life. Once you make real estate a cornerstone of your asset base, you might find that you love it so much that one home simply isn't enough. That's why I'd like to now whet your appetite for your *next* real estate deal.

It might seem premature, but you might want to start thinking about your *second* piece of property. I'm not suggesting you rush out and buy another home. On the contrary, you'd be smart to ease into the transition you've just undergone. Once you've been a homeowner for two years or more, if you find that you are readily managing the rights and responsibilities of homeownership, I believe at that time you should consider the prospects of buying additional real estate. If this concept seems far-fetched to you at this point, trust me when I say that it's never too early to begin strategizing about building a solid financial future.

Why purchase a second piece of property? Four reasons spring to mind: finances, fun, family, and the future. A rental property can boost your finances, giving you cash flow each month. A vacation home can be loads of fun, serving as a nice getaway spot for you and your loved ones. Many people buy property for family members too, including investment buildings that are rented out and later sold when their heirs come of age. Lastly, you can buy a second home for your Golden Years, locking in your future retirement home at today's prices. As you can see, getting your first home was just the beginning. Best wishes to you in all your future endeavors – personally, professionally, and financially!

– Lynnette Khalfani-Cox,
The Money Coach (http://www.TheMoneyCoach.net)

# APPENDIX A:

## The True Cost of Homeownership

Don't make the mistake of thinking that your principal, interest, taxes, and insurance (PITI) are the only costs associated with owning your home. Below is a list of hidden expenses that all contribute to the true cost of homeownership.

| It's a Pity It's Not Just PITI |
| --- |
| |
| Appliances |
| Carpets, Flooring ,and Rugs |
| Chimney Servicing |
| Furniture |
| Gardening Supplies |
| Home Improvements (Additions, Renovations, and Upgrades) |
| Lawn Care |
| Lighting Fixtures |
| Maintenance |
| Moving Costs |
| Repairs |
| Supplemental Insurance (Earthquake, Flood, Hurricane, or Tornado Coverage) |
| Utilities |
| Window Treatments |

**Tip:** Set aside money in a Home Expense Fund each year. Stash away at least 2% of your home's value in order to pay for the items above without going into debt.

# APPENDIX B:

## State Websites for First-Time Homeowner Programs

Contact your State Housing Finance or Development Agency to find free money or low-cost loans to be used for a home down payment or closing costs:

| |
|---|
| Alabama Housing Finance Authority<br>http://www.ahfa.com |
| Alaska Housing Finance Corporation<br>http://www.ahfc.state.ak.us |
| Arizona Department of Housing/Arizona Housing Finance Authority<br>http://www.housingaz.com |
| Arkansas Development Finance Authority<br>http://www.state.ar.us/adfa |
| California Housing Finance Agency<br>http://www.calhfa.ca.gov |
| California Tax Credit Allocation Committee<br>http://www.treasurer.ca.gov/ctcac |
| Colorado Housing and Finance Authority<br>http://www.colohfa.org |
| Connecticut Housing Finance Authority<br>http://www.chfa.org |
| Delaware State Housing Authority<br>http://www.destatehousing.com |
| District of Columbia Department of Housing and Community Development<br>http://www.dhcd.dc.gov |

District of Columbia Housing Finance Agency
http://www.dchfa.org

Florida Housing Finance Corporation
http://www.floridahousing.org

Georgia Department of Community Affairs/
Georgia Housing and Finance Authority
http://www.dca.state.ga.us

Hawaii Housing Finance and Development Corporation
http://www.hawaii.gov/dbedt/hhfdc

Idaho Housing and Finance Association
http://www.ihfa.org

Illinois Housing Development Authority
http://www.ihda.org

Indiana Housing and Community Development Authority
http://www.in.gov/ihfa

Iowa Finance Authority
http://www.ifahome.com

Kansas Housing Resources Corporation
http://www.kshousingcorp.org

Kentucky Housing Corporation
http://www.kyhousing.org

Louisiana Housing Finance Agency
http://www.lhfa.state.la.us

Maine Housing
http://www.mainehousing.org

Maryland Department of Housing and Community Development
http://www.dhcd.state.md.us

Massachusetts Department of Housing & Community Development
http://www.state.ma.us/dhcd

| |
|---|
| Mass Housing<br>http://www.masshousing.com |
| Michigan State Housing Development Authority<br>http://www.michigan.gov/mshda |
| Minnesota Housing<br>http://www.mhfa.state.mn.us |
| Mississippi Home Corporation<br>http://www.mshomecorp.com |
| Missouri Housing Development Commission<br>http://www.mhdc.com |
| Montana Board of Housing/Housing Division<br>http://www.housing.mt.gov |
| Nebraska Investment Finance Authority<br>http://www.nifa.org |
| Nevada Housing Division<br>http://www.nvhousing.state.nv.us |
| New Hampshire Housing Finance Authority<br>http://www.nhhfa.org |
| New Jersey Housing and Mortgage Finance Agency<br>http://www.nj-hmfa.com |
| New Mexico Mortgage Finance Authority<br>http://www.housingnm.org |
| New York City Housing Development Corporation<br>http://www.nychdc.com |
| New York State Housing Finance Agency/<br>State of New York Mortgage Agency<br>http://www.nyhomes.org |
| North Carolina Housing Finance Agency<br>http://www.nchfa.com |

| |
|---|
| North Dakota Housing Finance Agency<br>http://www.ndhfa.org |
| Ohio Housing Finance Agency<br>http://www.ohiohome.org |
| Oklahoma Housing Finance Agency<br>http://www.ohfa.org |
| Oregon Housing and Community Services<br>http://www.ohcs.oregon.gov |
| Pennsylvania Housing Finance Agency<br>http://www.phfa.org |
| Puerto Rico Housing Finance Authority<br>http://www.gdp-pur.com |
| Rhode Island Housing<br>http://www.rihousing.com |
| South Carolina State Housing Finance and Development Authority<br>http://www.schousing.com |
| South Dakota Housing Development Authority<br>http://www.sdhda.org |
| Tennessee Housing Development Agency<br>http://www.tennessee.gov/thda |
| Texas Department of Housing and Community Affairs<br>http://www.tdhca.state.tx.us |
| Utah Housing Corporation<br>http://www.utahhousingcorp.org |
| Vermont Housing Finance Agency<br>http://www.vhfa.org |
| Virgin Islands Housing Finance Authority<br>http://www.vihfa.gov |

| |
|---|
| Virginia Housing Development Authority<br>http://www.vhda.com |
| Washington State Housing Finance Commission<br>http://www.wshfc.org |
| West Virginia Housing Development Fund<br>http://www.wvhdf.com |
| Wisconsin Housing and Economic Development Authority<br>http://www.wheda.com |
| Wyoming Community Development Authority<br>http://www.wyomingcda.com |

# APPENDIX C:

## Mortgage Pre-Approval Checklist

Before contacting any lender for a pre-approval, make sure you have the following required information and documents handy:

- Your Social Security number

- Your Driver's License or other official form of identification

- Your two most recent paycheck stubs (self-employed people must have two years' tax returns, a CPA letter, and/or a business license)

- Three months' bank statements

- List of assets you own. Write down the current amount in each of the following accounts, then add up the total and write that down also:

    o 401(k), 403(b), IRA or other retirement accounts
    o Savings accounts
    o Checking accounts
    o Mutual funds/brokerage accounts
    o Stocks or Bonds
    o Certificates of Deposit

- Itemized debts you owe. Write down the required minimum monthly payments for each bill listed below:

    o Total minimum monthly payments on all credit card debts

- o   Student loans (indicate if they're in repayment or deferment)
- o   Automobile loans
- o   Personal loans
- o   Alimony or child support
- o   Other obligations which require more than 10 months repayment

**NOTE:** If a co-applicant is applying for the mortgage with you, then that person's information will be required as well. Ease the process by gathering all documents before seeking a loan pre-approval.

# APPENDIX D:

## Lender Comparison Chart and 10 Questions to Ask

Whether you call financial institutions or go online to obtain initial loan offers, try to get three Good Faith Estimates from different lenders or mortgage brokers. You don't have to fill out detailed loan applications or provide your social security number but be prepared to tell the loan officer your FICO credit scores. Use the data from the Good Faith Estimates to fill in the information below. For any information you don't have, call the lender or broker to get what's missing.

| 10 Questions to Ask: | Lender #1 | Lender #2 | Lender #3 |
|---|---|---|---|
| Interest Rate: | | | |
| Annual Percentage Rate: | | | |
| Points Charged: | | | |
| Yield Spread Premium: | | | |
| Total of All Fees: | | | |
| Do you guarantee your fees? | | | |
| Rate lock available? Cost? | | | |
| Loan type: Fixed or ARM? | | | |
| For ARMs, what is the cap? | | | |
| Pre-payment Penalty? | | | |

# APPENDIX E:

## Recommended Reading for Renters and Owners

### Recommended Books:

*All About Mortgages* (By Julie Garton-Good)

*Mortgages 101* (By David Reed)

*Mortgage Confidential* (By David Reed)

*Mortgage Rip-Offs and Money Savers* (By Carolyn Warren)

*Nolo's Essential Guide to Buying Your First Home* (By Ilona Bray, Alayna Schroeder, and Marcia Stewart)

*The National Association of Realtors Guide to Home Buying* (With Blanche Evans)

### Recommended Magazines:

*Better Homes & Gardens* – chock-full of creative solutions and tips for your home life, whether you're looking to decorate, plan a party, remodel, or cook

*Country Home* – offers step-by-step advice for turning your house into a beautiful country home

*Dwell* – a hip, design-oriented publication that features the latest information on modern houses and the people who live in them

*First Time Homebuyer* – consumer-focused magazine that keeps you abreast of all aspects of homeownership, from house-hunting tips to mortgage advice

*Home* – devoted to building, remodeling, and home makeover ideas, especially those that save money and conserve energy

*Metropolitan Home* – targeting readers who enjoy fine living, this publication covers a range of subjects including home design, wine, entertaining, and home electronics; also highlights solutions for small spaces and eco-friendly living

*Smart Homeowner* – offers information to help you make better decisions about home projects and renovations; also provides tips on working with contractors

# APPENDIX F:

## Homebuyer Resources Available Online

### Credit Bureaus and Credit Information:

http://www.annualcreditreport.com

http://www.equifax.com

http://www.experian.com

http://www.myfico.com

http://www.transunion.com

### Home Price/Estimating Websites:

http://www.cyberhomes.com

http://www.Eppraisal.com

http://www.homegain.com

http://www.propertyshark.com

http://www.realestateabc.com

http://www.reply.com

http://www.zillow.com

### Mortgage Advice and Rate Information:

http://www.applyclub.com

http://www.freeratesearch.com

http://www.mortgage-helper.com

http://www.mtgprofessor.com

http://www.offerangel.com

http://www.themortgageinsider.net

### Foreclosure Prevention Groups

http://www.acorn.org or call 866-67-ACORN

http://www.995Hope.org or call 888-995-HOPE

http://www.naca.com or call 888-302-NACA

http://www.nnwa.us or call 888-995-HOPE

# About the Author

Lynnette Khalfani-Cox, The Money Coach, is a personal finance expert, speaker, and *New York Times* bestselling author.

Besides *Your First Home*, Lynnette's books include *The Money Coach's Guide to Your First Million* (McGraw Hill), *Investing Success: How To Conquer 30 Costly Mistakes & Multiply Your Wealth*, the *New York Times'* bestseller *Zero Debt* (Advantage World Press), and its sequel *Zero Debt for College Grads: From Student Loans to Financial Freedom* (Kaplan). Lynnette also recently co-authored with Susan Beacham *The Millionaire Kids Club*, a series of five personal finance books for children between the ages of five and 12.

As an award-winning financial news journalist, Lynnette worked for nearly a decade as a Dow Jones Newswires reporter and a *Wall Street Journal* reporter for CNBC. At CNBC, Lynnette filed weekly television segments on personal finances, investing, and small business, and conducted online chat sessions.

Lynnette has interviewed thousands of financial experts, and personally paid off more than $100,000 in credit card debt before turning her financial life around. Now she shares the secrets to wealth with audiences nationwide, using insights based not just on her professional knowledge, but also on first-hand experience.

A popular keynote speaker, Lynnette also conducts workshops about credit and debt, money management, real estate, investing, and entrepreneurship. Lynnette has been featured in *The Washington Post*, *New York Times*, *USA Today*, *BusinessWeek*, *Redbook*, *Essence*, and *Black Enterprise Magazine*, among other publications. She is a frequent guest on national TV and radio, and has been seen on *Good Morning America*, *The Oprah Winfrey Show*, *Dr. Phil*, *The Tyra Banks Show*, *Rachael Ray*, and numerous other talk shows and news programs.

She presently serves as a Money Coach for AOL, host of the "Ask The Money Coach" advice section on BlackAmericaWeb.com, and a columnist for *Health Magazine*, where she dispenses her unique brand of personal finance wisdom.

Lynnette earned a Master of Arts degree in Journalism from the University of Southern California, and a Bachelor of Arts degree in English from the University of California, Irvine. She is a board member of WorldofMoney.org, a non-profit devoted to financial literacy for teenagers. When she's not chasing after her own three young kids, Lynnette can be found taking a much-needed break in the Caribbean.

To learn about Lynnette's "Financial Boot Camp" or speaking services or to sign up for her free personal finance newsletter, please visit Lynnette's website at http://www.TheMoneyCoach.net.

# Notes

# Index